Captured!

Captured!

By

Ferdinand Huszti Horvath

Kismet Publishing
2018

Captured! by Ferdinand Huszti Horvath. First published in 1930.

Published by Kismet, 2018.

First Printing: 2018.

ISBN: 978-1-387-71652-4.

Contents

Chapter I

The Innsbruck Kaiserjaegers were trained for the Russian front. A soldier was standing on the narrow board atop of the cow-catcher of the locomotive and with chalk, wrote on the front of the boiler the words: "On to Moscow!" For five days we rattled, but we did not get quite so far as Moscow. In Lemberg we got out, with rather stiff joints. Moscow was still eight hundred miles farther. We were still a little enthusiastic, but not much. Lemberg had just been evacuated with feverish haste. Long trains with wounded stood at the station and the faces behind the windows looked dirty, worn and haggard.

Some of the wounded took Russian bullets out of their pockets and we looked at them. We had never seen a Russian bullet before. They were pointed; ours were blunt, cone-shaped. Large Red Cross marks were painted on the sides of the boxcars. Wounded men stood in the open doors. Some had bloody and torn blouses. There was contempt in their eyes, looking down on us, green troops from the hinterland. After our baptism with fire, of course, it would be a different thing; but now we were not much more in their eyes than mere civilians.

"Look out, you snot-noses," said a dragoon from a car window; "look out for the machine-guns. They'll hide in hollowed out haystacks and let you walk up close. 'Ra-ta-ta-ta' and your company is going to hell."

"Get all the spades you can in Lemberg," said another swarthy fellow, "and learn to dig. You'll feel more than you'll ever see of them."

Other Red Cross trains rolled in, and still others; there seemed to be no end to them.

We marched out of Lemberg towards the east. As soon as we had left the suburbs, we held our rifle muzzles high and loaded. A strange feeling that was, to load for the first time with the intent to kill.

It was noon. When it grew dark, we were still marching. We had to keep to one side of the road to leave passage for retreating troops. They came in an endless stream: infantry, train, artillery.

Now and then the shrill horn of an automobile howled, and we had to crowd into the ditches. Generals and staff officers whizzed by and were gone. Then we got back to the road and marched on.

More wagon trains came and still more troops from the opposite direction. There was no moon, just the stars, but the road was smooth; we could march without lights. Sometimes, at a crossroads we were halted, to let another column pass. We were tired, but those troops coming from the opposite direction seemed to be still more so. A thick candle was burning in a dusty lantern hanging from the rear axle of a train wagon. Very faintly it lit up the legs of the soldiers, standing close together. You could see steel-lined rifle butts and sagging knees. The shoes were white with dust and the feet in them were smarting. Then our column moved again and we marched on. After midnight we swerved from the road and halted in a stubble field.

Outposts spread out in all directions, like oil dropped on water. We stacked our rifles in long rows of pyramids. Food came and we ate hastily, in order not to lose any sleep. When the dawn came, we marched on. So we marched for nine days. It seemed to us that we were led around and around in an endless circle. Most of the time we marched in columns; then one of our battalions branched off here, another there, and for long hours we lay in a ditch, crowded close to one another, expecting something finally to happen.

So far not a shot had been fired, and we were very tired and disillusioned. We really felt inferior to those battered troops, retreating, that we were always meeting. Here we were on the march for over a week and we had not yet seen one of those plate-shaped Russian caps! Newspapers used to print stories about thundering cannons—we wondered what became of them. And this marching was very tiring. Many of the men had blistered feet and there were always more and more stragglers. Then, on a pitch dark night, a furious shooting began. Well—here were the Russians at last! When the fire stopped, finally, we found out that it was just a mistake. We had been attacked by one of our own battalions. There were polite apologies on both sides and the little incident was settled—eight dead, six wounded, and three men shot blind. Of course this did not count as a regular baptism of fire.

At day we sweltered in a terrible heat on those wide plains, and at night thin ice formed over the pools and icy crystals jingled in the canteens. We froze miserably. One day we advanced twenty miles; next day we retreated just as much. It seemed as if we were getting nowhere. Long columns of fugitives clogged the roads. Their household goods and furniture were piled on wagons. The poor ones had to do with push-carts—even baby carriages.

Little children trotted along weeping, holding on desperately to their mother's skirts. Women carried babes on their backs, sucklings on their bosoms. They were unkempt and unwashed, muddy and dusty, with a wild look in their eyes. They begged us for bread and we gave it to them. We gave it to ladies, too; they were just as hungry but were ashamed to beg.

Sometimes, when a woman was close to a breakdown, my men would take the child from her arms and carry it themselves. One would give his rifle to his neighbor in the file and carry the child for a while, then pass it on to his neighbor so that he might smoke. One could not smoke while carrying the child, dropping fiery ashes over its little head. Sometimes the baby would fumble around and grasp one of those drooping mustaches, worn proudly upturned in the garrisons. Then the man would smile and think of his own baby left at home.

One day the fugitives were driven from the highways which were needed for the troops.

At night we marched through Grodek. It was ablaze; the heat was unbearable. From the trees that lined the road corpses dangled, miserable Ruthenians, hanged for treason, with popped out eyes and thick blue tongues.

They dangled until the ropes burned. Now we could hear the rumblings of the guns.

We marched to a great open field and camped there. The rain came down in torrents. We put up small tents, each just large enough to hold two men. Those rhomboidal tent sheets could be buttoned together to construct larger tents, more comfortable, which would accommodate six men; but they were too complicated to make; we never got the sides right.

In those small tents, supported by a rifle with its bayonet fixed, two men could crowd in, but the feet, from the knees down, had to remain outside. We lay down and fell asleep immediately. We were drenched when we pitched the tents; the rain pattered on the tents and also on our shoes and pantaloons; water was streaming in on all sides, but we slept soundly and did not care.

In the morning we were allowed to rest longer than usual. The sun shone bright and warm and we hung our clothes to dry.

In the afternoon, all the officers had to report to the Battalion Commander—a major. We stood in a circle around him and had our maps out. He said we would attack in the evening on both sides of the railroad tracks that led to Lemberg. If anybody started to dig in without his special orders, he would shoot the man with his own hands. The retreat ended right here and now; from now on we would advance again "Thank God!" He said "Thank God," and it was no empty phrase with him.

In less than twelve hours he was shot to a bloody pulp—without ever seeing a Russian. At that time field officers were not in safe dugouts somewhere in the rear. Assembly was sounded and we pushed forward. There was some excitement as we approached the front and the cannonade grew stronger. Now we could hear the crackling of the infantry, but we were still advancing in columns.

Now and then we stopped for a long while, then marched on. The sun began to sink. Transports of wounded drifted back, borne on stretchers.

Those who could march, came afoot. Some were limping in evident pain, using their rifles as crutches. Ambulance wagons drove past.

We spread out into extended order. It takes some time for a battalion to do it. We advanced again. Suddenly the Russian batteries opened up and shells began to slam among us. They howled above our heads. We ducked nervously whenever we heard a howl. Everybody grew very pale; some were trembling. I was trembling with nervousness and fear. I thought my heart would leap out of my breast, but it kept there, just hammering furiously.

Flames burst out of the ground where the shells hit, spreading black clouds, and dark geysers rushed toward heaven. White, fleecy clouds massed at our backs—shrapnel. It was deafening.

We started to run, panting, and reached a shallow trench. There we lay down for a while and calmed down a little, seeing that we had not suffered any losses yet.

Shrill whistles blew and we advanced again. The ground was littered, with all kinds of material, as if sprayed with junk—coiled Russian mantles, bandoliers, rifles, bayonets, our own furry knapsacks, camp kettles, shoes, boots, bloody rags, tin cans and caps. Ammunition boxes and machine-gun belts were lying around, like so many dead snakes; mounds of empty yellow shells were heaped close.

We passed the first dead—Russians, in soft high boots, Austrians in long baggy pantaloons, clasped tight at the ankles, Hungarians in close-fitting trousers. There they lay, rigid and silent, all mixed up. Some clenched their fists; grass protruded among their dead fingers. Others had grown stiff with fingers clawing, like talons of some huge bird. All were pale and waxen, even more so than we.

Some of my men shuddered; others grew sick. I, too, felt nauseated.

A Russian was lying on his back, his legs and the lower part of his body torn away. With one foot entangled in the Russian's entrails, an Austrian lay on his face—dead. Before he fell he had dragged this ghastly lasso for five or six yards. It was pulled taut like a string, this horrible, parched human rope. Farther on lay other dead; one with his legs broken and bent backward, his soles under his armpits, like some contortionist. Then bodies without heads, torn limbs, large black pools of blood. We jumped into another trench. This was deeper. Dead lay here, too. In some of them rifles were stuck, the bayonets pinning them to earth, like so many strange beetles.

On the bottom of the trench was a thick layer of empty cartridges. It was like a well-kept garden path, paved with pebbles. We sank to the ankles in them. Infantry bullets whizzed over our heads like so many invisible wasps. This was far more hideous than the artillery fire.

Another shrill whistle sounded. We climbed out of the trench and started to run. Bullets hissed. Some, we could nearly feel. We ducked and jerked our heads. Some of the men fell, groaning and screaming. We came into a little grove and passed it quickly. Bullets smacked and crackled with a hideous sound among the stems, it rained small twigs. When we emerged from that grove, we opened fire.

"Fire, five hundred!" I yelled. According to regulations, I should have specified where to fire, but I could not see anything. The distance might have been well over five hundred meters or much less than that.

Now our rifles cracked briskly. We had no targets to shoot at; they were so completely hidden by the camouflaged deep trench that we did not see a thing. We just shot at random in the direction from which the bullets came.

We officers, commanding platoons, were not supposed to lie down, but to kneel and observe with our field glasses the effect of our fire. I did it for a while, but bullets came so thick that I lay down. Suddenly, the Major was standing right behind me, kicking frantically at my soles.

"Get up, Cadet!" he yelled and was gone again. I knelt upright. As soon as he was gone, I flattened out again—there was nothing to be observed here. None of those infernal marksmen showed as much as the top of a cap.

Slowly it grew dark. We did not advance any farther.

The fire kept up furiously. Gradually it became so dark that we could not see what was happening ten yards away.

An order came to fall back slowly, man by man. Slowly we got out of the range of the bullets. In the dark we stumbled over dead and all kinds of littered, rattling equipment. There was a wild mix-up among the units. Somehow we reached the railroad. By now all order was gone; we streamed back for a few miles, all muddled up. We were halted and order was made, the companies and platoons were straightened out and checked up. The Battalion had not lost more than twenty men, among them five officers. A rather mild baptism—nothing to brag about. We had heard of battalions which lost as much as a third of their men in the very first encounter.

We got some food and then it was midnight again. We were ordered to lie down, fully equipped, and to rest until further orders should come.

For an hour I slept soundly; then an orderly roused me and told me to report immediately to my captain. My platoon was to wait for me right here, ready to march, whenever the order came.

The captain explained to me that I was to go immediately with my platoon and take ammunition to a regiment in a very exposed position. They were right where the railroad viaduct was marked on the map—I would have no difficulty in finding them, even in the dark.

We were to transport as much ammunition as we were able to carry. That meant twenty-seven cases, counting two men for each. We were to start immediately, deliver the cases, ask for a receipt and then report back to him without delay.

We got the cases and started to feel our way in the dark. At first we walked beside the tracks on the embankment, but it was too badly torn by shells. My men stumbled into craters and slipped on the coarse ballast.

The going was very bad with those heavy cases. Besides, bullets came thick, like hail. So we went down and proceeded along the bottom of the embankment where it was easier going. There was no road here, but soft muck, and to our left there stretched a large swamp.

Frogs croaked, and in the dark pools, which showed here and there among the vegetation, the stars danced on the surface—as on a black mirror. Here we were not much molested by bullets, so I stopped now and then to give my men a rest.

There was a lively fire at the front all the time. It sounded like some vast rattle, going at full speed. Again, wounded were transported back. They hobbled and crept painfully with a grim determination to get as far back as possible before it dawned. We could not see much of them, just their white bandages. There was a man with his entire head bandaged, with small holes left open for his eyes and nose. As he felt his way in the dark, he looked like some walking ghost with an immense skull. From the swamp came horrid yells—soldiers sinking in the dark slime, gurgling with glassy eyes until the foul-smelling black mire oozed down their throats. The frogs kept on croaking just the same, splashing into the scarcely ruffled surface, maybe splashing mud into the eyes of those poor dying men.

This was an altogether different war from what we had expected to find! We thought the hostile armies would march upon some vast plain—possibly smooth as the drill grounds, to facilitate movements. When they came into sight of each other, the infantry would start to shoot, carefully aiming, like rifle practice, in order not to squander the ammunition, which we were told cost a lot of money. The artillery would be a little farther back, because guns were expensive. Furthermore, they had a longer range. Then, there was the cavalry, which always used to look down upon us very haughtily from their high saddles. This would be kept in reserve somewhere, after they had reported the enemy—kept for an emergency, so that they could charge and scatter the enemy, after we had shot enough of them.

As we figured, the whole thing shouldn't last much longer than two weeks—by no means longer than a month. The Kaiser himself had said that we would be home when the leaves began to fall.

We did not know there could be so much marching in a war. Here we had been marching for more than ten days—and we had not seen a Russian yet, except those captured, wounded or dead.

And we got so little sleep—that was the worst part of it. We had thought that—as it used to be before—armies fought bravely until it grew too dark to shoot, and then went to rest for the night—just like calling it a day at five-thirty. And here things really just started as it grew dark.

Then those dying heroes, we had had in our minds!

All buttoned up tightly in snug uniforms, with such slim waistlines, re-clining on a rock. A little blood trickled between their fingers, placed gracefully over their breast, and they died smiling, always looking at some picture of a fair lady in their last minutes. Those were heroes!

But these torn, folded, twisted, ragged corpses that lay around here— headless bodies, the heads grinning somewhere else, others with bloody stumps, where arms and legs used to grow, others with practically no bellies to speak of—why, there was nothing romantic about these.

We felt cheated even out of a romantic death. What romance was there about spitting in a bog of greenish-black slime, until you could spit no more, but had to gulp down the rest?

It took us about an hour to get to the viaduct. Wounded were crowded under the stone arch, lying thick like some bloody mosaic. There was the stench of putrid blood and other excreta.

We delivered the ammunition, got the receipt and started back. On our way back—again that ghastly gurgling, again those desperate yells—maybe a little fainter now.

When I got back to report, the battalion stood ready to march. The cap-tain told me to report immediately to the Major.

In company with that regiment to which I had delivered the ammuni-tion, we were to storm the Russians. It would be at daybreak—that would be around three o'clock. As I knew exactly where the regimental commander was located, for I had just returned from the place, I would have to be a spe-cial guide to the Major and lead him there. After I had led him there, I was to return to my platoon and take over command again.

So I reported to the Major and we started out immediately. He did not mention that little incident of ours, the evening before, when he had kicked my soles to make me kneel up.

The companies marched at the bottom of the fill, but he personally pre-ferred to walk on the top, beside the tracks. I led, he followed; farther back marched four orderlies—one of each company—to be at hand to dispatch orders.

Occasionally I turned and called to the Major to look out for some deep hole, torn by a shell, or some twisted rail that lay across our way. He never replied but just walked on silently.

Down below, to our left, marched the battalion. A little farther off was the bog. One could still hear them crying for help that never would come— but I did not hear any more of that hideous, gasping gurgle. A whole battalion, no matter how noiselessly it tries to march, always makes enough rattle to drown such noises. We were about halfway when there was suddenly a burst of fire. Bullets hissed and prattled amidst the steel rails and gravel. The Major kept on going, just as before, as if nothing had happened. After a while, I turned and said: "Sir, down there, where the battalion marches, we would be covered."

"I don't bother about a few lousy bullets," he said with profound contempt. We went on.

"What are you in civilian life?" he asked.

"Nothing yet, sir. I had just finished school."

We marched on. More bullets whizzed by.

He asked: "Losses there in front?"

I replied: "Very heavy, sir."

"These are great times," he said after a while. "History is being made now."

"Yes sir, quite so."

Then after a pause he said: "Everybody should be proud to be permitted to participate in this great fight."

I felt deadly tired and very sleepy, not proud at all, so I just replied: "Yes, sir."

By this time we had reached the viaduct and I led the Major to the Colonel with whose regiment we were to storm in half an hour. I returned to my platoon and then we lay in a shallow trench, very crowded.

We were to attack at three o'clock. We waited for our artillery to open up and do its stuff. Regulations said that, before infantry went to storm, the artillery would annihilate the enemy positions, kill and demoralize the defenders.

In front, the fire died down a little. It was five minutes to three now and dawn was coming. Everything looked ashen gray at that lurid pale hour. Our artillery was silent. There was no artillery behind us to give its support. We were just a plain, unimportant reserve battalion that would have to get along somehow, without artillery. And if the Major said that we would storm at three in the morning, that did not mean three five or three fifteen, but three o'clock sharp—artillery or no artillery.

Bayonets snapped on the muzzles. We unwound the golden tassels from our sword hilts and slipped them over our wrists, so as not to lose the swords. The swords were razor sharp.

There—the high pitched blare of the battalion bugler, "Attack!" A medley of deeper horns repeats the call—all bugles of all companies. "Attack!" Dozens of shrill whistles blow and shriek, "Attack!" "Forward!"

A dense gray mass tumbles out of the trench, with thundering feet, clattering equipment. The rifles are aslant.

"Hurrah! Hurrah!"

Swords are up in the air, but you don't see them long. It is breathtaking to rush forward with an arm uplifted, the pack cutting into the shoulder.

There is a murderous fire now. Any of those Russians that might have been dozing are thoroughly roused now by this bedlam of bugles and human voices. We are running in thick droves; there is no place to spread out. One man runs behind the other. And we don't see anything of the foe. Everything is so gray and misty. They might be six hundred yards away. Ordinarily such an objective should not be farther than a hundred yards, especially if it is to be taken by surprise.

We throw ourselves to the ground, to catch our breath. The ground is flat and hard here. You could run well if it were not for the heavy pack. If you throw yourself to the ground, it feels as if someone jumped on your back to press you down.

Now we run again. Somewhere in the grayness the bugles are still blaring but the sound of shooting drowns everything. Men fall—one here—one there—over there, two. Now my orderly is shot, right beside me. He tumbles and shrieks, but I have to run on; I am commanding the platoon.

"Down!"

Again we are on the ground, panting. You can hear your heart thump. Whistles quaver.

"Forward!"

Now they are shooting with machine-guns. I can distinguish two guns—no, three guns. Now I don't know how many are shooting, but they are right in front of us. Men fall by the dozens. There is a constant whizz and buzz, like a strong wind.

Again we are down; now we even press our faces against the ground, but it's too hard to press them in. I feel as if I had no lungs anymore. Up again! Now I see small flames, like fiery tongues, quite near to the ground. The rifles lick their lips. Quite short flashes—many of them. There is a steady, quivering flash over there; that's a machine-gun.

I am quite dazed, but I am still running. I have to tear my collar open, it would choke me otherwise. Now somebody got it in the belly; he howls like an animal. God! —only not in the belly; they say it's terrible—rather in the head or heart!

Men are running, crouching with bent knees, to offer smaller targets, like humped animals. Those who have spades cover their faces with them. I can still hear one of the bugles. It's far back now; now it's cut short; the bugler must have been shot. Five men fall to my right, plunging to the ground. The one nearest to me wasn't more than a yard away.

I am down again. I am up again. I want to turn and run back in that spitting, gray, deadly mist. This is too much. I think my nerves will snap any minute now.

Over there to the left a bunch of men are still running. I am all alone here; I'll join them. Now we are running together—forward of course. Again a man drops—another one. I have to take a breath. I can't go on.

Once more I'll try. Now the scabbard gets between my knees and down I go, headlong, sprawling. Something hit my shoulder. No, it's nothing; something just brushed it. It's good to be once more down, to press the face against the cool dirt. That accursed sword still dangles from my wrist. I'll run immediately; it would be terrible if the Major caught me here, lying on the ground, without his permission—just a few gasps more.

I contract my elbows to jump—then I get my eyes all spattered with dirt. Not farther away than three yards the machine-gun bullets rip the ground and spit a steady stream of dirt into my face. The groove gets deeper, as if clawed by some invisible hand.

If that muzzle is lifted now, by only a hair's breadth, I'll be shot to frazzles. Quite automatically I set my palms on the ground and try to push myself back. My head is down. Why can't I push my head into the ground? Everything is fading out—it's getting so dark—When I came to again, the sun stood high and I was bathed in sweat. There was no life around me; dead lay scattered, wherever I looked. The wounded lay very still; they had to keep quiet, for the Russians shot at everything that moved. The fire was still undiminished.

About twenty yards from where I lay, I saw the earth fly; there was a low mound, behind which a dozen men were digging with great haste. They had thrown their equipment off, to work unhindered, and they stood about waist deep already. Not everyone had a spade; some worked with their bare hands. A few leaned against the parapet and were shooting.

When they saw me move, they beckoned and shouted to me to join them. I had to be very careful, for bullets came prattling dangerously near. Between me and the trench lay two dead. I tried to get behind the first one.

Lying quite flat, I slowly put both arms close to my sides and then down to my legs. Throwing my weight on my right shoulder, I pushed myself forward with my left palm and helped with the toes. In this way I could advance two or three inches at a time, with a perfectly rigid body and with the least appearance of movement.

But even so I had to pause often. When I finally got behind the first dead I rested for a while. It was very hot now, the sun was burning. Shielded by the corpse, I unbuckled my canteen and drank its entire contents. Then I proceeded to the next dead man. It was a laborious and very slow affair, and I must have been creeping for more than an hour. The men were digging as fast as they could. Those with spades loosened the dirt and the others threw it out with their hands and mess kits.

Already they stood much deeper.

I continued to creep very carefully, but the Russians must have noticed my movements, for they were shooting at me now. I was not farther from the protecting trench than four or five yards. Bullets spattered around and I rose to my knees and started to crawl as fast as I could. Suddenly I felt a sharp pain in my right foot.

With a last desperate effort I reached the trench, and the men pulled me in head first.

I threw off my equipment. The scabbard which made me stumble was bent and crooked. One of the men straightened it on his knee in order to sheath the sword.

The upper part of my right shoe was cut away by the bullet, and my sock was bled through. I examined the wound. It was not bad—it could have been much worse.

There was no skin on a place as big as a thumbprint, but the wound was not deep. One of those ricocheting bullets, probably. I cauterized and bandaged it. Somebody gave me his pair of reserve shoes, large comfortable things, with canvas tops—excellent for sore feet. It did not bother me much—it scarcely hurt now.

To the left of our own, there was a longer trench in construction. There were about thirty men digging there. Now we were working towards each other to link the trenches. Scattered here and there were still other trenches, with a few men in each.

Late in the afternoon we got very hungry. It was strictly forbidden to touch our reserve rations; nevertheless we opened some cans of beef hash and heated their contents over candles. The bottoms grew hot, the tops remained cold and everything became smoky. However, they tasted all right. But nobody had a drop of water and we needed it badly. It occurred to one of the men that we might dig for some. Not deeper than three yards we struck underground water. It was muddy, but after a while, when it had settled down, we could drink it, ladling it carefully, not to stir it up. It was a tremendously long day, but finally darkness came. None of us knew what was going to happen; we had no contact with other troops in either direction. I had the intention to gather all the men around me, when it grew dark enough, pick up all the wounded we could carry and then go back to the viaduct. I told them my plan.

There was a man who formerly had been a regular officer, an ensign. For some offense he had been degraded and reduced to the ranks, where he now did service as a private. He advised me not to retreat without special orders, for they could court-martial and shoot me summarily for that. This gave me something to think about. Finally I decided that we would wait until dawn—but not longer.

It grew quite dark and the fire died down. Midnight came. Here and there we heard the moans of the wounded, crying for water and for help. Those we could find, we brought into our trench. Some crept in alone. All wanted to drink, and that water trickled so slowly. It was still far from daybreak; each minute seemed like an eternity. Then—at one o'clock—an orderly came with orders to retreat.

Again we walked beside the railroad embankment. No word was spoken. There came no sounds out of the swamp except from the frogs and the birds. We marched for hours. Now we were marching with other troops. There was a complete mix-up and great disorder in the gloomy darkness. Nobody knew where we were going; we were just marching back to somewhere. The shooting was growing always fainter.

At dawn we came to a great brickyard; it was in ruins. Some officers were there, trying to create some sort of order. The numbers of regiments and of battalions were called out and repeated often. Finally I heard the number of our battalion and I took the men in that direction. A lieutenant stood there, with some men from the battalion, and we joined them. We shook hands and proceeded together.

"The captain is waiting over at that smokestack," said the lieutenant. "He has about forty men with him. How many have you?"

"I didn't have a chance to count them," I said, "but I don't think they'll be more than fifty. That surely was Hell itself yesterday."

"The Major is dead," said the lieutenant. "I saw him fall; he was way front. They made a regular hash out of him. I got his things, after we pulled him into the trench. Look at his watch!"

There were two bullet holes in his watch alone; it was all dented.

"See his signet ring," he continued. "It came off easy enough from the stub that remained of his finger. I think a machine-gun must have got him; he was just riddled with bullets."

I thought of what the poor devil had said, that he did not bother about a few lousy bullets.

"That fat Prass," went on the lieutenant, "got nine bullets—all through his fat. They didn't do him much harm; he came back on his own feet. He looked as if he'd been fed through a sewing machine."

We got to the smokestack. It must have been a huge one once, but now just a short stub of it was standing. Brick was scattered everywhere.

The captain was sitting on a pile of bricks, looking very tired and dejected. In the garrison he used to be always such a nice gay fellow. Now he was unshaven, tousled and dirty. He rose and came to meet us, trying to smile a little. He got hold of our hands and shook them heartily.

"I'm so glad," he said, "that at least you two are here. We seem to be all that's left after yesterday."

We were ordered to remove our equipment and rest for a while. From one of the field kitchens we got coffee. The captain wanted to wait for a few hours, in the hope that other survivors of the battalion would join us—but nobody came. We were assembled and counted and the lieutenant reported to the captain: "Sir, I beg to report two officers and a hundred and fifty-three men."

The captain saluted and put it down in his notebook, while he muttered something.

Yesterday, we had well over nine hundred men. This had been a better baptism than the one we had had the day before. It seemed to me that his infernal Majesty, Lucifer, had taken care of this affair himself. But now we were full-fledged combatants.

Chapter II

To escape the deadly grip of that immense mass of advancing Russians, the remainders of the Austro-Hungarian army were ordered back, two hundred and fifty kilometers. Here the army was to be reorganized and the gaps filled up somehow by hurriedly dispatched reserves.

This was to be the largest, the most cruelly trying retreat ever staged in the history of a modern army. The once precisely functioning vast organization, the Imperial and Royal Army, dragged its tired bones over the endless plains of Galicia. Its task was accomplished—with a fatal result.

Never was such a hopeless task demanded from any army in modern warfare. With only three-fifths of our forces—for two-fifths were against Serbia—we had been sent to attack the Czarist army, to divert its crushing march against Eastern Prussia, which lay practically open, to engage all the forces that Russia had to offer, and it offered four times our number. This was the logical outcome, it would have been a miracle if it had turned out otherwise.

In the rear roared the guns and rattled the rifles of the victoriously advancing, rushing and crushing Russians. They too were badly shaken, but they still had plenty of fresh troops, coming up in hurried marches. This was the result of driving cavalry brigades against solid walls of barbed wire entanglements, of ruthlessly ordering regiments to storm whole rows of invisible machine-guns in disastrous frontal attacks. This was the natural result of the spirit that flamed in the pudgy hearts of senile, half-witted generals, who now raced to security in their powerful cars, to have their pompous shakos exchanged for silk hats.

Little did they see of those starved, wobbly skeletons, dying of fatigue, with watery blood of dysentery dripping from their entrails, straggling in dust clouds and in bottomless muck, under dreary gray skies, until they sank into miserable heaps...

For days we marched in dust. It was suffocating. Your lungs felt muddy, you could not recognize anybody. Lazy dust clouds puffed up behind those dragging feet; tired hoofs kicked up dust and rolling wheels whirled it up. Dust on the fields, dust on the miserable villages, the whole country boiled with dust—fine, gray, penetrating everywhere.

Humped and bent Jews stood before desolate hovels, in dirty long caftans. Horror was in their bleary eyes; their unkempt beards looked like moss. It was their country we were giving up—it did not mean much to us. Frail, overworked Jewesses stood around, wailing, with greenish little infants in their arms.

One village after the other. Some were burning still, fired and plundered by marauders. The streets were littered with torn cloth, broken dishes and furniture. And everywhere those miserable Jews—whimpering prayers, with snarling lips, in guttural tones.

Some tried to sell bread, demanding atrocious prices.

"Get it from the Russians," said the soldiers, while they tore the bread out of their hands and knocked them over their heads.

One mile after the other. At some well an officer would stand with drawn revolver—the water was polluted. Men growled and stormed the next well, overpowering the military police, fighting like savages for a drink.

When night came, we camped near a potato field, so that we would not starve. After a few hours of sleep, we continued our march, at daybreak.

For days we did not see field kitchens. I never knew how painful hunger could be while you burned up all your remaining energy in forced marches. It's not just appetite—it hurts.

Once I traded a cigar for a piece of bread from one of those unbelievably filthy Ruthenian peasant drivers. He pulled it out of his trouser pocket; it was moldy and so foul you wouldn't let your dog touch it. I just devoured it.

We were passing through a fair-sized village. There were no Jews here, but Poles only. On the porch of the parsonage stood a kind-faced old curate, hugging a huge loaf of bread with one arm and cutting slices with his free hand. His long black robe was white with flour.

There was a crowd of soldiers milling around him, with outstretched hands, reaching eagerly for the bread. He cut a slice and handed it out to any soldier that stood within his reach. They nearly swept him off his feet, but he just kept on slicing the loaf good-naturedly. Some kissed the hand in which he held the knife when he handed over the bread. They made his kind hand all dirty and smudgy with their dusty faces. He protested mildly: "Don't kiss my hands, boys. God bless you all! How shall I cut bread for you?"

On the rare occasions when we succeeded in finding field kitchens, everybody gorged himself ready to burst.

In most cases we got only soup—a very thick soup. There was plenty of beef in it and still more groats, over-boiled into a thick mass. But it stilled the hunger. We had no bread, however; the field bakeries seemed to have broken down completely. And what we missed most was sleep. On we went, always on. Painfully devouring one mile after the other in a gruesome grind. Often we marched at night. On such occasions forced halts were not uncommon. For those few minutes, while we stood waiting, some of the men sat down and fell asleep immediately.

When the column moved forward, they had to be tugged to their feet forcibly. Many fell in a half slumber, while they kept on marching quite mechanically, and would awaken only when they bumped against a knapsack in front of them.

Everybody was teeming with lice, the greatest scourge in any war. There is no way to get rid of them. Out of those few hours of rest, when we could have slept, they made hours of torture. They made one crazy. One can get used to fire, one can get used to almost any kind of hardship, but one can never get used to these tormenting pests.

Our captain didn't have to walk. He had a horse which carried him, a skinny, poor nag, now all bones, with a loose dusty hide and broken tired eyes. These poor animals have to suffer just as men.

Now and then the captain would bend from his saddle and say a good word to his men. Men marched holding their shoulder straps, trying to lift for a while the heavy knapsacks which cut into the aching shoulders. When the captain saw that a man was about to break down, he would take his knapsack and hang it over his saddle.

One afternoon we got to a village before it grew quite dark. It looked as if we would have some hours of rest. The men went to dig for potatoes and turnips. Small cooking fires were lit all around.

Somehow the captain got hold of two ducks, very lean ducks—but ducks nevertheless. He invited two of us officers to a duck supper. He told us to turn in for a couple of hours. While we slept he would pick the ducks and roast them, for he did not feel so tired as we. So we lay down for a while. When we awoke, the field kitchens were just arriving—we did not see them again for days—but we did not care for beef today, as long as there were ducks for supper.

We went to the captain's fire. A good-sized fire it was.

Over it hung limply a gleaming wire with two charred longish clumps on it. They might have been our ducks an hour ago. The captain was snoring, right at the fire.

I shook him for a while before he came to.

"Damn it," he said, "I must have been sleeping."

"Are those the ducks, Captain?" I asked, pointing to the charred remnants on the sagging wire.

"That's what they were, when I put them on," he said. We simply had to laugh. It was the first good laugh we had had in weeks and it made us feel better.

After that, we went to the snubbed field kitchen for some beef, of course.

Sometimes my wound hurts. If I have no chance to take off the shoe for a long while, the bandage sticks to the wound and then it burns. A surgeon gave me some Vaseline, but only a little is left. In a few days, there will be none and I don't know how I shall be able to march if it gets worse.

It has been raining for two days. The dust is gone. The men who have tent sheets, keep them over their heads while they march. At least it keeps part of their bodies dry. Their overcoat tips are hooked back and tucked away, they look like crude cutaways.

It is impossible to roll these coarse overcoats if they get wet; they are heavy as lead. Even while they are worn under the tent sheets, they get soaked and become heavier all the time.

I have no tent sheet, and my frogskin was lost when my orderly fell on that fateful morning. Of course, I could order a man to give me his tent sheet, but there is good comradeship here. After all, there is really no difference between his hide and mine. So I have no tent sheet and I am all drenched to the marrow. It's raining through my cap, and water trickles through my hair and runs down my face.

The hot body evaporates the water; you do not feel cold while you keep on marching. But whenever we stop and I lift my arm, I can see a faint steam rise from my drenched sleeve. My neck is steaming, too. However, if you stand too long, you feel the chill and you start to shiver. The chances are good to get pneumonia or anything else. Then we march on and the steaming starts again. The strap of my wristwatch looks like boiled tripe. The matches in my inner pocket are drenched and fit to be thrown away, for the wet heads have crumbled. My pants are like wet rags; they cling to my legs. I can hear the water squash in my shoes with each step, and I am sure the bandage is not sticking now. Pieces of rags are stuffed into the rifle muzzles, to prevent them from rusting inside. Large puddles of muddy water form on the road. For a while we go around them, but there are too many, so we just wade through. What difference does it make to the soaked feet anyhow?

Every day we join other troops, retreating from different parts of the broken front. They tell the same stories, the same carnage everywhere, regiments reduced to a few weak companies.

And now these night marches have become more frequent. Every day we are crowded off more and more by endless columns of artillery, wagon train and even cavalry.

The cavalry isn't proud anymore. Mounted soldiers are sleeping on the necks of their horses, with arms dangling down on both sides. And how we envy those gunners, sleeping on their guns!

Some of the men, who have broken down completely, are permitted to spend a few hours on the train wagons; others, by special permission of the surgeon, are allowed to load their packs on the carts.

Every day more of the horsemen have to dismount. The backs of some of the horses are broken by the heavy saddles; many of the horses are going into harness, to replace those lost by the artillery and supply train. If a horse breaks down, and can't be made to move, it is shot on the spot and dragged aside. Each time a horse drops, it stops the long row of rattling conveyances. And the roads are getting worse every day, they are a maze of soaked, deep ruts. Tens of thousands of wagon wheels have cut them into obliteration. They are simply ground away by the milling, heavy wheels. On the way back, always more depots have to be moved; every one increases the congestion.

Now the troops are not to use the highway at all; it is to be reserved for the vehicles. Things are bad enough, as they are. Men drop, weakened by dysentery and exposure. How will it be if the going gets still worse?

Mud—everywhere mud—nothing but mud. Mud below and above our feet, up to the knees. Now we are trying to march on side paths, amidst plow-land, across country.

Nobody who did not wear a pack on his shoulder, and try to lift smarting, leaden feet weighed down with sticky clay, will ever understand, for you sink well to the middle of the shinbone. You go down slowly as the thick, glutinous mud opens sluggishly under your sole and when you reach the bottom you have shrunk two spans.

Then you try to lift the foot behind out of the hole, but it holds you fast.

You must place the full weight of your body on the foot in front, otherwise you cannot move. After a while, you hear a squashing sound, as your foot—like some clay piston—is dragged out of its clay cylinder. When you hear the water gurgle back into the empty hole, you can be pretty sure your foot is out.

You don't feel your feet after a while. Now and then, when you reach the point where you won't have the strength to lift your foot with the next step, you have to halt, to take your bayonet and whittle off the mud—starting at the knees. When the last thick slice is cut off from under your sole, and drops with a wet thud, you feel your feet again, so light that you don't believe they belong to you. But after a very short time you will have to scrape again.

Men hold their bayonets in their hands all day long, as if going to some wholesale murder, just to have them ready to scrape when necessary. We were proceeding at a snail's pace. The units opened and dragged out into great depth. There was no way to keep the men closed up.

Sometimes you would step on the edge of some hidden stone, deeply embedded in the mud, and, your ankle giving way, you slipped into the mud. Your arms got muddy to the elbows and you had to press the mud out of your sleeve.

We passed fallen horses, already half sunk into the deep mire; they looked like clay statues. One could not sit down to rest; nobody could carry his weight with his mantle plastered into a solid mass of clay.

There were limits to this gruesome grind. When we reached some huts and were ordered to rest for the day, we could still see the wooden steeple of the church from which we started out in the morning. Not more than six miles—it took us a day.

Next day nobody could move and we got a day's rest. The rain stopped and the wind made the mud crusty. These Ruthenian hovels are dreadful. We never go into one, unless we have to. You enter the hut through a small opening and you have to double up to get in. There is an acrid smoke inside that makes you cough and causes the tears to flow. The huts are round, made of mud-plastered wicker, and there are no windows. There is no chimney and no fireplace. A fire burns on the stamped clay floor and the smoke rises to the top of the low hut, where it finds its way out slowly through the reed of which the roof is made.

Besides the whole family, a hog, a cow and any other animals they happen to have are kept all in the same place. There is an incredible stench. Chickens and ducks are housed here. Men and women reek with filth. Their long black hair is glossy with thickly spread grease; they are clad in dirty rags. Black clouds of flies buzz in thick whirls and the miserable place is alive with vermin.

If it is not pouring, we prefer to sleep in tents, or we just huddle up close together, wrapped in our blankets. Our feet are in terrible condition, swollen to brownish, spongy pulps. Our foot rags are worn to shreds and we cannot get any others. We tear up our dirty shirts to make foot rags out of them. The trouble is our tallow is all used up.

Those unripe plums, raw turnips and polluted water will do as much damage as any good battle. Many of the men have dysentery already. Some break down on the road in deadly exhaustion; they are left there to die or fall into the hands of the Russians. It is impossible to overload the wagons with sick anymore. Wagons break down every day.

Sometimes at the morning roll call men are missing, sick men who during the night have crept to some hiding place, unable to stand anymore—to await the oncoming Russians.

We were marching again, but the road was fairly good. If only it would not rain, I might be fairly dry in two or three days. There were large gaps between the marching ranks. A major—the temporary commander of the battalion to which we now belonged—was furious and raised hell. As he rode past me, I saluted.

"Where is the visor of your cap, Cadet?" snapped the Major, reining in.

"Sir," I replied, "it shriveled and burned when I dried my cap at the campfire. I had to cut it off."

"So! Did you?" the Major said. "Well, this is no cavalry,[1] but infantry, and I don't want to see you tomorrow without a visor. Did you get me?"

"Yes, sir!" He rode off, fuming.

Where in the dickens should I get a visor? It seemed to me like a tragic joke that, after ten days of such hardships—hungry and drenched, wounded, dragging along somehow on hurting feet—a major should have nothing else to worry about than to find fault with a visorless cap.

Later on, the captain rode up to me and we talked for a while. You never felt the tiredness so much when your mind was occupied with something else.

"Look here," said the captain good-naturedly, "try to keep the men together. I know it's hard for those poor devils; they're all in; I can see that. It's no wonder—but we can't march with such gaps. We're taking up the space of a division." He turned to the men: "Come on, boys, close up, close up! We'll rest very soon!"

There was an effort to close the gaps between the ranks, but it was not very successful.

For a while he rode without a word, then he said quietly so that only I could hear him: "Yesterday—one of the stragglers was shot. A lieutenant-colonel shot him. I saw the poor fellow—he did his best to get along—he simply couldn't. And one of those old regulars, too. A damned shame—I'll say!" He paused for a while, then said: "The others closed up just for an hour, no longer. Then everything was again just as before. A damned shame!"

Then I told him about the visor. He shook his head with a sad smile.

"Well," he said bitterly, "the Major certainly does worry about your welfare—but orders are orders. We'll find some help somehow. Meanwhile look around, maybe you can find something to fix your cap."

Towards evening we passed a wagon train. On the side of a wagon, hung by its chin strap, I saw a heavy shako of a hussar. It was bespattered with mud. I took my knife and cut the visor off and at night I sewed it on my cap as well as I could. It was at least two sizes too large and did not fit at all.

Next morning the Major passed me again. He looked at my visor very sharply, then rode off without a word.

We were to retreat as far as Tarnow. Fresh replacements were waiting there. After a few days' rest, we were to advance again. On the last two days, however, I could not march farther. My wound burned with infection and my foot was swelling rapidly. I was feverish and a surgeon gave me written permit to ride on one of the ammunition wagons. It shook and bumped the breath out of me, but it was better than marching. Now we were with our old regiment again, and it was good to see some of the old comrades.

We camped on the heights above Tarnow. In a few days, the men began to look human again. As soon as they got enough food and sleep, they became carefree and good-humored. Strange creatures, soldiers are!

They scampered down merrily to the brook to wash up and to bathe. And how skinny the poor devils were!

In the evening they would sit around the campfires and sing happy, naughty soldier songs—not caring what tomorrow would bring.

The regimental mess-officer, a captain, walked up whistling to our group, that lay in the shade of some trees.

"Well boys," he said, "good news! I've got a cook now, who used to be four years in the Royal Palace at Buckingham. A regular chef—no dirty army cook. Think of that—what a haul!"

There came a murmur of satisfaction all around.

"We'll start with a nine-course dinner right today," he continued. "Twenty cigars for each of you, cigarettes and cognac—all you can stand. Long live the war!"

So once again we sat at tables, tables covered with regular white tablecloths—it did not seem real! That captain was a sorcerer. Why, of all things, the orderlies who waited on the tables had even coarse white cotton gloves on, just as at home in the garrison! The muddy uniforms were scraped and brushed; everybody was shaved, some even combed. And what food—and how much of it! It was incredible that it should all belong to us.

When the cigars were passed around and black coffee was served, nobody spoke of the war anymore. We had all had it—and we would still have plenty of it. Some of the boys knew such uproariously funny, indecent jokes! Everybody was roaring with laughter. I even forgot that my wound hurt.

1 - Only the cavalry wore soft field caps without visors.

Chapter III

I was in the hospital at Tarnow, in a clean white bed. Previously the nurse had given me a hot bath. I had lain in the tub, thinking of nothing in particular, just enjoying the warm bath—the first in six weeks. I was puzzled, how so much water could turn dark as ink in just a few minutes.

Without any preliminaries the nurse walked in. I felt very uncomfortable in the presence of that pretty young thing—the water was so black. So— I sank still deeper into it.

"Come on," said the nurse, while rolling up her sleeves, "stand up. I'll scrub your back."

"Why, Sister," I started hesitatingly, "I thank you, but I—I can do it myself."

"No, you can't," she came back firmly. By now she was already soaping the big scrubbing brush.

Never before did I feel so uncomfortable. She meant business.

"Really, Sister—I can do it all right—besides I have nothing on—I didn't know you would come in—"

"Well," she said good-naturedly, with a smile, "all right—don't stand up, just kneel up. You're all like big babies. Come on now, be nice!"

When she had scrubbed my shoulders, she stopped.

"Did you get birdshot in your back?" she asked.

"Birdshot? No. It must be those lice."

She was very careful not to hurt as she moved the brush among those burning scars.

Now I was in a rolling train, clattering monotonously over the rails. Tarnow was evacuated in a great hurry and the wounded were transported first. Ordinarily, each man got a slip from the hospital, with orders where to report for further treatment in the hinterland. But there was no time for that now.

So everybody could go where he wished—unless he was taken from the hospital train somewhere.

It occurred to me that I might just as well go home and heal my wound there. And so—home I went. Everybody was so nice—and everybody grew so tiresome after a short while. All wanted to hear about the war and I had to repeat everything a dozen times; it bored me. They were thrilled.

Said a gentleman in a very secure position, with excellent prospects to stick it out there, until the bitter end: "It must be a wonderful sensation to follow the flag, flaming young eyes around, and flashing bayonets—"

He still imagined the war as the war correspondents depicted it. Flaming eyes—yes! Eyes were not flaming after a fortnight of marching without sleep; they burned, sunken deep, and the foreheads did flame. And of course the flag! What did it mean out there where it was raining death? How many saw it, when it was carried unfurled in the very first battles? Half a platoon, maybe—if the interval between the men was not too great. It just drew all the machine-gun fire—and everybody tried to keep as far from it as he could manage. Those flying colors! Flying to the ground as often as the color bearer was shot.

No regiment dared to expose the colors after the first week. They were furled in black oilcloth covers, lying on stacked rifles with the companies alternating to guard them while others could sleep. I never heard so much swearing as when a company was made "color company" for twenty-four hours and had to guard the flag.

Did it mean anything to the men? They were much more interested in a field kitchen, or a dry place to lie down, than in all the flags of the Imperial and Royal Army. And they were better men, too, than all those war correspondents in checkered breeches and immense caps, babbling about flags and the wonderful spirit of troops—and other things they never saw and never knew.

What did those men know about that tragic, vast retreat? Officially it was stated, that "our army was successfully withdrawn after glorious battles, with flying colors"—yes, positively "flying colors"—"unbroken, in excellent spirit—eager for battle."

Just a slight reorganization. Could I tell how it looked in reality? Would they have ever believed?

After six weeks I was with my regiment again. They were much farther back than when I left them. I was promoted to ensign and in another four weeks to second lieutenant. Many of the boys were gone. That good fellow, the captain, had fallen in a night attack upon some village. It was cold now, the middle of November. We were billeted in a small village and the first night we slept fully equipped, awaiting marching orders.

The fact that you know that the order to march may come at any minute does not add to your restlessness; it makes you sleep all the sounder. You get accustomed to the idea that you are here to march. Each minute that you don't have to march is your gain and you use each minute to your advantage. But we did not march that night or the next day. In the morning we took off the equipment and lounged around with nothing to do. We were vaccinated for the eighth time—against, I don't know what!

It went around that we would stay right there for two more days. If the staff assures you that there will be no alarm—then everybody is restless. You get the idea that you are resting now and your rest is totally spoiled by the thought of the possibility of an alarm. When we retired for the night, our new company commander, a first lieutenant, removed his shoes—a very bad omen; it always drew alarm with it. But after a while, we all took off our shoes and blew the candle out.

There goes the bugle!

"Alarm!"

We marched all night, until next day noon; then we were put into the firing line and fought for a week without a let-down.

Now, every man had a spade, and it was no longer considered a shame to dig in. But it was very hard to dig; the earth was frozen so that you could not break it without pickaxes, and there were only four pickaxes to each platoon. We had no trenches here, as we were moving too often to dig trenches.

If a man could lie long enough in one spot, he would throw up a little mound before his head, and gradually, as his mound got higher, his hole got deeper.

Even we officers had our spades now, Russian spades, if possible; they were sharper and better. We didn't have to wear long cumbersome swords anymore, just bayonets; it was so much easier to move unhampered.

On our last march, we picked up a dachshund. To be exact, we did not pick him up; he joined us and, after he had stuck faithfully to our company for a while, he was promoted to "company dog." He was a very friendly little fellow, with a long funnel-like body on very short, crooked and soft little legs. We called him "Russ." At day he bounced merrily among the mounds, behind which the men were shooting, and barked now and then playfully at the Russians. At night he was especially welcome; then he would crawl into our overcoats and out of gratitude keep us warm. He was such a loyal and intelligent little dog. He knew exactly the space covered by our company, and he kept within its boundaries. Never did he go to another company.

On the day he joined us he looked so tired, his short little feet lost in the deep, frozen cart-ruts, that I lifted him into the saddle of our company commander. There he hung for a while, like a long sausage, until he evidently got displeased with the uncomfortable ride and expressed his wish to get back to his feet.

One morning, while trotting peacefully among the mounds, he was shot. It must have been by accident, for he never harmed the Russians or anybody else.

Winter came early that year. The nights were bitterly cold. There was no snow as yet, but everything was frozen stiff and hard. We had good heavy sheepskin vests that kept our bodies warm. We used to wear the sheep-skins right over the body—they were much warmer that way.

But even so, we awoke at night. We could not sleep for our knees were freezing. This was so unbearably painful that one could hardly stand it. Blankets offered little protection against such severe cold. We used to lie around in the morning with our knee-joints so stiff and sore that we could not move.

Freezing, marching, patrolling, skirmishing, battling, advancing, re-treating—forward again.

By now this whole campaign had become a standard routine work—very businesslike. Men went to battle without fear and without enthusiasm, just as they would go at home to their factories or fields. After a while, all were alike. There were no heroes and there were no cowards. The brave men recognized that it was foolish to expose themselves more than was strictly necessary, and the timid ones wouldn't crouch more than the others did.

They were not interested in the possible outcome of the war. Galicia—though belonging to the Monarchy—was a strange country to all of us. What had we in common with those long-coated Jews and filthy Ruthenians?

Each officer had to censor the outgoing mail of his platoon. The men were not allowed to write the place of our location. In most cases they did not know, anyhow, where we stood; and, if they knew, they could not spell it. Furthermore, nobody was supposed to kick or criticize —not even in writing.

They never did. Sometimes they wrote that they did not get enough to eat. As a matter of fact, I never heard a private yet say that he had enough—no matter how much he got. They complained about the cold, and invariably they hoped that soon there would be peace.

Poor fellows—that was in 1914!

One evening I overheard some of my men talking. Corporal Pettenkofer had received the large gold medal for valor that very day, a rare distinction. The corporal had two others besides. The men were lying around and smok-ing. Said a private, a stocky little man, smoking a huge wooden pipe:

"Hey, you Pettenkofer! Suppose the Emperor or some other general came around and asked you what you'd wish? What would you wish then?"

"Yes—the Kaiser coming around here, just to ask Pettenkofer—you saphead!" said a lance-corporal. The others laughed. There was a pause, for it took Pettenkofer always a while before he could think up some good an-swer.

"What I'd wish?" he said. "Well, first I'd wish a good stein o' beer and then I'd want to go home and pitch some manure. Damn it! If they'd only let me, I'd give them all my medals!"

My company was battalion reserve, right behind the front. There was a first aid station in a half-demolished manor house and it was crowded with wounded. It was just a place where bandages were put on hurriedly and then the men would be transported or would walk back to regular dressing stations or field hospitals.

These men who were allowed to lie there were dying; there was no sense in moving them. There was a field curate among them, praying and giving absolutions. Surgeons and sanitary soldiers were working with feverish haste, bandaging our own men and Russians—it did not make any difference.

The priest was bent over a waxen-faced man who was fingering his rosary with grimy weak fingers.

In a corner, propped up against the wall, lay a tall Russian, shot through the lungs. Blood oozed with each breath, but looking at his red cheeks one would not have known how fast he was going. Sometimes he bit his lip and squinted painfully. Then he noticed me.

"Washe Blagorodye,"[1] he said, looking up with a little hope, "please give me a papyrosy," and he held out his hand.

I was stupefied. What—this dying man with his pierced lungs asking for a cigarette?

I went over to the surgeon: "Say, Doctor, may I give a cigarette to that Russian over there? He just asked me for one."

"Let him have it," said the surgeon. "It won't do him more harm—and it will be his last cigarette anyhow."

I lit a cigarette and gave it to the Russian. He inhaled each puff with evident satisfaction and when finally the stub got so short that it was hard to hold, he drew in his lips, so as not to burn them. Then he put out the glimmering stub between his wetted fingers—taking care not to ignite the straw.

Half an hour later I returned. He lay there very limp now, with his head fallen to his chest—and he did not ask for another cigarette.

On a November morning, we were withdrawn from the line, entrained and sent to stem the Russians who were hammering frantically at the Carpathian mountain passes on the Hungarian border. There were some heavy battles and desperate attacks, but we drove them slowly toward the River San.

It began to snow, and an icy wind searched and cut through the mantles. The country was desolate, frozen, dour, raw. The war had such a rude flavor here, among frozen marshes and stubby bogs.

There could be no continuous, closed lines in this terrain. Regiments and battalions fought a guerilla war against similar units, eagerly trying to gain a flank for decisive action.

For weeks we never used a spade—save to dig cooking holes at night. We lived like a horde of tramps; this roving warfare had its own peculiar character.

Our company lay before a thicket in a frozen bog. We pressed our faces into coarse, stubby weeds, for the Russians were spraying us with all the machine-gun fire we could stand. They let us march out into the open first, to have good targets. Opposite was a thickly wooded solitary hillock, from which sputtered the guns.

When it grew dark, the fire ceased and we withdrew to report the affair to the battalion. We also hoped to find the kitchens, but they did not turn up. Once more we supped on potatoes and hardtack and then turned in for a few hours—rather grouchy.

At four in the morning, somebody gently kicked my hobnailed boots. It was the usual way to awaken people. There was no disrespect or rudeness in this habit; it just saved the trouble of stooping down and shaking one with the hands.

"Get up," said the captain, "and wake the men. Assemble the company at four-fifteen, right at that flat rock over there."

It was dark night when we marched off, very sleepy, cold and empty—a little more than sixty men. Half an hour later we still marched in darkness, and the captain swore choice curses at stones and roots that made us stumble.

"Hell of an idea!" he fumed.

"What's wrong, captain?" I ventured. "Where are we walking to this nice morning?"

"Where? You'll be surprised! To that little mountain again. We are to bring in prisoners and possibly those machine-guns that nearly picked off our pants yesterday."

For a while, we stumbled on.

"Tough proposition," I said. "How are we going to do it? We haven't seen any of our artillery for two weeks."

"Well," said the captain, "we'll take it easy—and that's all. I won't have you fellows butchered just to get those cursed guns. Furthermore, my leave is due next week. I'll be going home to get married."

By dawn we reached the thicket and, still recalling the hot reception we got the day before, we proceeded carefully. But that ominous hilltop was quiet. We did not trust it yet, for they might be tricky and let us approach quite near and give it then. But not a shot fell; the hill was deserted; the Russians had left.

"Well," said the captain, with a smile, "we have taken this hill easily enough. This was our objective. Guess we'll rest for a day and make up for the lost sleep. We're all in."

However, to make quite sure, we descended on the opposite slope and then decided to push on four miles farther. We split the company. The captain kept half of the men and went straight ahead, and I swung to the right with the other half, keeping in touch with relays.

It was a regular morning walk, for we did not hurry and were not molested. It was a similar feeling to staying away from school. At ten in the morning I took out my message-pad and sent a runner with a written dispatch to the captain:

"I bought a pig at the farmhouse I have marked red on the map. Thirty kronen—very nice fat. We could rest for the day here. They also have potatoes. Lieutenant H."

Twenty minutes later the captain came with springy steps, followed by his men, with wide grins.

"Where is the pig?"

"Right behind the farmhouse, sir; the men are cleaning it. We had to shoot it first; there was no other way to get the beast; we tried to catch it for ten minutes."

Well, for the rest of the day everybody was happy and greasy as far back as behind the ears, and there was fried pork even in the blouse pockets and in the cartridge belts.

The next morning we strolled back with the notion of reporting to the battalion—provided we found them at the same place, for they might have moved meanwhile.

We rested in a wood and sent out pickets, for surprises are unwholesome. We had been there hardly five minutes when one of the sentries came back panting.

"Sir," he reported to the captain, "there are Russians down in the ravine."

"What the devil! How many?"

The man thought for a while. "About thirty. That's what I saw, sir."

"What were they doing?"

"Nothing. Just lying around."

"Up!" said the captain. The men rose.

Two cadets were to remain with the main force. The captain took six picked men and I did likewise. He was to approach the ravine noiselessly with his men, from the north, while I proceeded at the same height with my men, south of the ravine. As soon as the captain signaled, his party was to start to shoot down into the ravine and we were to join in from the opposite side. However, it was our purpose to frighten and capture them, and we were not to get too rough unless they gave reason.

The wood was clear of underbrush and we marched softly upon a thick carpet of pine needles right up to the border of the ravine where we were able to watch each one of their movements. They were hopelessly trapped in there.

There were the Russians, sitting at a small brook. But not one of them had a rifle. In vain did I look for some rifle stacks—there were none about. I was nonplussed. For a time I waited. Then I saw the captain creep up cautiously on the opposite side and give the signal.

We opened a rapid fire, lying on the edge of the ravine, shooting over the heads of the Russians, down in the hollow.

"Hands up!" yelled the captain as his men started to fire.

There was a wild confusion down there; white handkerchiefs flew out and hands went up.

"Nicht schiessen! Nicht schiessen!" (Don't shoot) came up a trembling voice in German.

They marched out of the ravine, as directed, and then we counted twenty-four of them.

"For two days we have been trying to surrender," said a little German-speaking Jewish soldier of the Tsar.

"Gott sei Dank!"

The battalion was highly pleased with our catch, though they wanted to know what had become of the machine-guns.

I would have given anything to see the fantastic report that the good captain must have conceived.

He just squinted his eye, as he issued his orders to me:

"See that the men keep their mouths shut—or we won't feed them pork the next time."

We reached the river San—and that's where we dug in for the winter. In February our regiment was shifted to build some strong point positions in the Carpathians.

1 - Meaning: Highborn Sir—in the official army term, as Russian soldiers had to address their superiors.

Chapter IV

Our Regiment was entrenched in the Carpathian Mountains. Good entrenchments those were too, for it took months to build them from sturdy turf bricks and heavy timbers. If the Russians wanted to be serious about this thing they would have to move up larger calibers for their destruction. The light field artillery so far had not done much damage.

Three rows of barbed wire were there to make things uncomfortable, with a row of murderous mines sunk invisibly into the ground. Between the parapets and the first stakes of the wire fence, were closely dug, cone-shaped "wolf pits," with sharply pointed stakes extending from their bottoms—a surprise for those who came too near and then wanted to dodge the barking machine-guns.

As a further protection—and very effective too—we had about two thousand yards of distance between the two hostile positions. There was a tendency on the part of the Russians to keep quiet and behave decently, provided we did the same. There was a valley between the two lines, thickly wooded with the most uncomfortable kind of underbrush that grew anywhere, and the going on these steep slopes was anything but a pleasure. Near the top the growth thinned out, leaving the summits bare, with the trenches exposed.

Down in the bottom of the valley, a cold and clear mountain stream kept gurgling its monotonous song, to the ferns and strangely twisted juniper bushes. It ran through the miserable little Ruthenian village of Regetow.

Regetow wasn't much of a village, ever, but now it was no village at all. Its destitute, tumble-down log huts and shacks offered an excellent supply of building material for the trenches and dugouts. There it was—handy—we just had to go down and fetch it, throw ropes around the logs and drag them up to the trenches.

Now, dragging heavy logs through that infernal underbrush, up a steep grade, could not be done effectively without a considerable amount of bad language—and a lot of bad language there was.

It is true, there was a halfway decent road leading down to the village, but this road lay bare all the way and any movement on it should have provoked a furious bombardment. Thus it was reasonable enough to keep off that road—in daylight at least, with such a wonderfully blue sky above us and with excellent visibility.

One day, however, a man of the wrecking party, one of those log drawing champions, getting sick of the pricks and tears of the brush, got a bright idea and struck out for the road. "Damned fool," I thought, "he might be blown to pieces any minute now," but knowing privates as I did, I was not much surprised at the sight of a man risking his hide, if only he could get a wee bit of comfort out of it.

Contrary to expectations, nothing happened; no shrapnel came howling; no shells burst. Very soon the second man was dragging his log on the road and the rest of them followed in no time. On the next day, the house-wrecking party made no bones about it but went down to the village right on the road. To their great surprise, they found another gang working there already. These were Russians, however.

For a moment or two, there was some consternation; no one knew exactly what to do. The Russians kept their rifles on their backs and were in no way hostile. They waved in a friendly way and then got busy with their crowbars on the huts standing on the northern side of the village. The Austrians kept to the southern side and the work went on briskly without any interruption. For a while, both parties kept an eye on each other—still distrustful—but after a few more days, all suspicion vanished.

It was a kind of silent agreement—ours working on the southern end, the Russians on the northern side, nearer to their own lines, with no mean tricks to be played on each other, two hundred yards apart, with a well in the center of the village to be the dead line. Never was this agreement violated—on either side.

Later on, to speed up work, we took down some dynamite sticks and blasted the huts that were to be wrecked. It loosened up the logs, if the dose was not too large; otherwise, we got splinters only.

Very soon the Russians adopted our advanced technique, and now Regetow began to shrink considerably among the merry blasts on both sides. Already we were thinking how to go about the last hut, because it would surely come to that: Who would have it, we or they? We would probably have to match for it.

This was the condition of things toward the middle of April. After all that hell we had been in from the beginning, this seemed a decidedly convenient place to stick it out. The rations were plentiful; we officers had five cigars a day—God knows from what they were made, but we did smoke them occasionally if they were not too green and raw. There was always some strictly prohibited merry card game in one of the dugouts, the only chance to spend our pay, if we did not wish to subscribe to the constantly offered war bonds. And there was plenty of rum and brandy to keep us in good spirits.

There wasn't much firing to speak about—the distance of two thousand yards being a trifle too long for accurate shooting with those worn out rifles—and above all there was a peaceful, if not happy, disposition on both sides, up in this sparkling clean air under that marvelously clear and blue spring sky.

True, we had our sharpshooters at the loopholes to fire a shot now and then conventionally. These were duly answered from far across the Rotunda—as we called the mountain where the Russians were dug in—but these were merely mutual reminders of our presence.

In the morning our batteries fired a round or two—but not unduly early. Then the guns were cleaned, oiled and put away for next day's work. After dinner, the Russians sent over their greetings, and then their gunners called it a day.

The conflagration of the world was reduced to a mere flicker here, to the general satisfaction of all concerned, a real picnic to the front lines— sponsored and paid for by the government—but after a few weeks of this sort of life we began to wonder how long it would go on.

Six hundred yards behind the front line, upon the ridge, were the battalion reserves, one company of each battalion always in readiness. The front could sleep, if they chose, but the reserves had to be constantly on the jump without a moment's let-down. The command certainly had a way to keep these reserves busy.

As a rule they were those who furnished the wrecking gangs, who dug the "wolf-pits," kept the wire entanglements in condition, cut the turf bricks and the timber—kept on coming and going wherever some work was to be done. If there was a night raid or some nasty patrol duty —out marched the reserves. So everybody prayed that he might have the good luck of staying right in the front line and not be called on reserve duty behind the lines.

One morning our batteries failed to discharge their customary rounds, and there was considerable guessing among us why they failed to do so. Soon the telephones in the dugouts were buzzing with orders. Men were greasing their shoes, scraping mud off their puttees, buckling their belts and tidying up the trenches. It looked as if visitors were coming, and some big dogs too.

Towards ten in the morning the Brigadier General, accompanied by a flock of staff officers, the Regimental Commander and the Battalion Commanders, with their adjutants, appeared on the right wing of our regiment, and started the inspection, ducking before each loophole as they passed. There was no special reason for this ducking. We had had—thank God—an exceptionally calm forenoon so far, safe enough for a kindergarten.

Anyhow his Excellency ducked faithfully as often as he saw the butt of a rifle, out of sheer habit maybe, and by the time his party reached the left wing of our regiment, he had ducked about four thousand times—as the regiment happened to have been brought up to the full strength of four thousand men. On the left wing his Excellency was a rather sad looking general and a grumpy one too. Here he held a conference, standing behind a steel-lined loophole, pointing now and then towards the

Russian lines on the Rotunda, making ugly faces at it.

By noon they were gone, through one of the deepest communication trenches. A little later an orderly came and handed me a folded order from the battalion. My company was ordered on battalion reserve—to report at two o'clock. So ended a happy chapter of the war.

That afternoon happened to be a very quiet one for us. There was no timber to be brought in, no turf bricks to be cut—in fact there was not a single thing to be done. And a fine day it was too, the sun shining mildly. On the bottoms of the crevices and deep ravines there was still some hard frozen icy snow, but on the southern slopes the sun shone friendly, radiating a balmy warmth. It was ideal weather for exterminating vermin. Off came the shirts and the hunt was on. It wasn't exactly a hunt—though game was plentiful—it was more a massacre. Then we took a plunge in a little brook that formed a crystal pool in one of those ravines and sat out in the sun to dry. There were still some glittering drops on me when a dispatch carrier asked for me. The battalion commander ordered me to report immediately.

The Major was a rather sociable fellow, but this time he was pretty stiff and formal. It looked like orders. I clicked my heels, saluted and reported as required. A map was spread out on his table and he beckoned me to step nearer. Sure enough there were marked with blue pencil our own lines accurately. Little blue circles with stiff little upright tails marked our outposts in the valley.

A heavy red line marked the Russian trenches on the Rotunda.

"See here, Lieutenant," he said deliberately, "we have information that the Russian regiment opposite our positions was relieved last night, we don't know by which one, though. In order to find out, you are ordered, with half of your company, down to the valley to lay an ambush and bring in information. Bring in at least one of them—dead or alive, I don't care—but bring him in.

Equipment—just light raiding outfit with one hundred rounds of ammunition for each rifle. And don't make much noise with unnecessary shooting; use the bayonet.

Have bayonets fixed before you pass our lines. By the way, have your men do an hour of bayonet drill this afternoon; you have quite a lot of those rookies we got last week." There was a short pause as he searched his mind to see whether he had forgotten anything of importance; then he continued:

"You will leave as soon as it gets dark and return before daybreak. Put down the password; it's 'Lantern.'

The countersign is 'Linz.' Report to me in person immediately after your return. Did you get me right, Lieutenant?" he asked.

"Yes sir, absolutely." I clicked off and made a jerking army bow. He returned the salute and shook hands, dropping his stiffness.

"I hope you'll make a good job of it," he added, more friendly this time. "His Excellency, the Brigadier, is expecting a lot from the Kaiserjaegers, and our regiment is not going to disappoint him."

As I closed the door behind me, I had to stoop down in order not to bump my head against the low door post. A rather miserable hut the Major had picked for his quarters—but then the variety was limited. In the kitchen, the only other room in this wretched hovel, were a few telephonists, some orderlies, a couple of dispatch riders and the Major's adjutant, an ensign, twenty years my senior, a broad-shouldered, gray-bearded gentleman—in civilian life a prominent lawyer in Vienna.

Since I was his superior in rank he clicked his heels and stood at attention.

"Stand at ease, Doctor," I said while we shook hands.

"A hell of a job the Major's given me. Haven't you got better things to think of?"

He tried to console me, saying that the job might prove very simple, as the new Russian regiment also would probably dispatch a patrol. In similar cases they always did, and in that event we might be lucky enough to run into their midst in that pitch dark valley and shoot it out there and then. If so, it might save us all the trouble of looking for them.

A very cheerful prospect, I thought, a dogfight at midnight, taking pot shots at random, not knowing whether you hit friend or foe. A nice little battle that's going to be, with half of my men just arrived, fresh from the drill grounds of the hinterland, inexperienced young rookies, mere boys.

So I left the hut, muttering subdued curses against His Excellency, who had ducked so diligently, the very forenoon of that promising day, wishing he could participate that night as a private soldier in one of my platoons.

First of all, I gathered my platoon commanders and all the noncommissioned officers to give them orders. Then the two platoons I picked out went through an hour of strenuous bayonet work. They were very glad when it was over. And now to the equipment.

This was the ninth month of the war, and leather was already scarce. By some ingenious order, that probably dated back as far as the early part of the

Eighteenth Century, the carrying straps of the ammunition boxes were still made out of excellent leather; but the cartridge belts and the coverings for the field spades were made out of tin. A great idea! Let these unhappy tin soldiers once lie flat on their stomachs, loaded down with all their equipment, weighing around seventy pounds, and these tin cartridge boxes flattened out like so many pancakes.

The hinges broke, and the only way to get the cartridges out of them was to blast them out. If these tin boxes happened to be empty, they were simply flattened into a shapeless mass, fit to be thrown away. And the tin spade casings were just as good.

And how such a tin company would jingle while they were marching! It was superb. Thinking of the proverbial cat, and having no desire to march out to a serious engagement with a bunch of musical clowns, I ordered all the tin-ware to be removed, and started a drive for some leather equipment, which was still to be found here and there in the regiment and which was loaned for this night only, on my solemn pledge that it would be returned the very first thing in the morning.

Before it grew dark, I went up with the Major to the trenches and, looking down into the valley that lay in silence in the depth, he gave me some vague advice as to how to go about this thing.

Just at that moment I did not have the faintest idea what I should do, and, listening to the talk of the Major, I gathered that he knew just as much about this thing as I did.

While my orderly was handing me my equipment, I told him to have some hot tea ready toward two-thirty in the morning.

"I hope, sir," said the faithful soul, "you will return in good health to drink your tea. I will be waiting for you."

Dusk came finally. We had to wait until it got dark enough so that we could pass our lines without being observed by the enemy. Up went the bayonets, snapping to the muzzles. The "Spanish Riders," the moveable parts of the barbed wire fences, were pushed open, and we moved out, down the slope, toward the valley. There was mist below and the Rotunda was in a shroud of haze, dark and misty as a phantom castle. There was a deadly silence, broken only by the shuffle of the feet of a hundred and twenty men. We came to our outposts in a thicket, and were challenged to exchange the password and the countersign; then we proceeded into No Man's Land.

Under the command of my best sergeant, I pushed an advance guard of sixteen men towards the valley. We followed them at an interval of a hundred yards. There was a fairly good highway in the valley, running through Regetow in a northeasterly direction, and my advance guard had orders to push as far as this highway and wait there for me. There I would make final dispositions, setting the trap for the Russians—if they were willing to march in.

God knows, I had been trying hard to think up some kind of a plan all afternoon, how to arrange that ambush, and not a single idea had occurred to me. But now, standing on the spot, with the advance guard waiting as instructed and with the rest of my men standing behind me awaiting orders, I worked quite mechanically.

I ordered my men to take cover in the ditch that ran alongside the highway, took one of my ensigns, the sergeant and a corporal, and struck out for a little scout work. The corporal acted as my special bodyguard. Wild poacher and rascal that he was, he could be trusted in danger. He used to boast that at home, in Tyrol, he picked off chamois from the rock at eight hundred yards, and, knowing his ability with the rifle, I believe he did. Accustomed to hardships, with the eyesight of a lynx, and a deadly aim, he had proved his worth many times, and so far had three medals for valor—Corporal Pilz.

We followed the highway. Three hundred paces ahead we reached a fork. A dilapidated cartway ran to the north, toward the Rotunda. The mountain stream formed a bend here and came to about fifty feet from the highway. That cartway led straight to the creek and went over a wooden bridge. Across the bridge, on the other bank of the stream, half hidden by trees and bushes, stood a shed.

Into this shed I intended to put half a platoon with orders to cut off the retreat of the enemy raiders if they should pass the bridge. A small detachment was to remain in the ditch, alongside the highway, where all my men were standing at present, awaiting further orders.

Then I followed the highway again. Two hundred paces farther on, there was a larger shed, on the southern side of the road. This was to be the key position, the center of the trap, where I wanted to remain personally with the main force, to direct the operations if anything was to happen.

A fourth patrol I pushed out in an easterly direction, just to secure my wing and to cut off the retreat in that direction. Thus we formed a triangle, with my main force placed in the center of the base line.

My plan was very simple; I expected the enemy to approach from the north, from the Rotunda, crossing the bridge, if they wanted to reach the highway. If they did choose this course, my strong northern outpost would be in their back and they were in the center of our trap.

Then, there was a good chance to expect them from the east, coming on the highway, in which case I would permit them to march up to my own main force, to be attacked there under my personal supervision. Thus, they would be surrounded again from all sides—with all the other detachments hurrying to the fight in the center.

In our back, to the south, stood our own lines; it was pretty safe from this side. Westward, there were no roads at all. It was improbable that they would approach from there, but, if they did come, our trap would work that way equally well.

Of course it was against all reason to expect them to use the roads, for it was evident that the roads would be guarded first, but there was also very much in favor of my theory. Knowing soldiers—no matter what kind of uniform they wore—I was pretty sure that they would prefer to take the chance and stick to any kind of road, rather than to grope their way, stumbling in that dark and misty valley, somewhere in the underbrush, with no possibility of keeping their units together.

So I sent my ensign to place the outposts. The movements were executed in utmost silence, practically noiselessly. Strict orders were given not to shoot, unless the Russians started to do so, but to wait for the signal of my whistle and then to attack swiftly with the bayonet.

All outposts were instructed to push towards the center if anything happened there—to close the trap. There was not a whisper to be spoken while lying in wait—absolute silence was of the greatest importance—and they were threatened with court-martial for lighting a match or smoking.

By ten o'clock everybody was in his allotted place, waiting for things to happen.

Everything was quiet. Upon the hillcrest the lines lay in silence, no shot was fired. No light pistols and rockets were shot from our lines, to avoid exposing our movements in the valley. It was significant that that very night the Russians also refrained from any illumination.

This made it probable that they too had to hide something. Very probably their own raiding detachments were on their way toward our lines, feeling their way in the dark. But so far nothing happened. It was dark, but there was now and then a faint moonlight breaking through the clouds. Fog settled in the valley, but a slight breeze kept it shifting all the time, intensifying it sometimes then clearing it away again. At times I heard a faint whistle from the Rotunda—the signals of the Russian outposts, hidden somewhere on the wooded slope—then quietness again with just the faint murmur of the little creek and the light swishing rustle of a dried leaf swept by the breeze over the stones.

Towards midnight, I inspected my three outposts; the boys were silent but rather nervous. Thick clouds drifted across the moon and made it appear always paler—till it was hidden completely. When I returned to my detachment, it was drizzling, one of those fine drizzling rains so common in these high valleys.

The breeze died away and the rain became heavier, beating monotonously on the battered boards of the roof, leaking through the cracks into the shed. The men were sitting with their backs to the wall, waiting patiently for something of more interest, rifles firmly gripped, ready for action. After a while, the rain became lighter, became a drizzle once more and then died altogether.

I was getting stiff from sitting too long in that shack and, together with my sergeant, I went out to look around. There was a reddish glow above the Rotunda which became more intense with time. Probably some miserable village was burning somewhere behind the Russian lines. As the glow grew stronger, the whole valley took on a faint reddish hue.

We were standing in a farmyard, with some coops and sties in the rear, a broken plow nearby and the skeleton of a dilapidated wagon at the far end. Here and there were traces of a low picket fence, running erratically up to the border of a thicket, from which this crude farm was once hewn. The soil was stony, not good for anything except potatoes.

Gradually the glow died away to a very faint pink that settled on the top of the Rotunda, and the valley became gray and dark once more.

At one o'clock I ordered the outposts to relieve their pickets and substitute others for them.

The thing had become tedious by now. I glanced at my wristwatch. The luminous dial showed half past one. I gave myself another half hour. If nothing happened by two o'clock, I would order in my outposts and march home. By the time we got to the wires, it would be three o'clock anyhow— just about the right time to be back.

It was getting very chilly and my men were shivering. They huddled up close to one another in order to keep warm, and most of them were very drowsy. It was a rather trying affair to keep awake after three and a half hours of patient waiting, with no word spoken, sitting motionless in that dark shack.

But those cursed greenish hands on my watch seemed to stand still. One-forty—thank God—twenty minutes to go yet. I was getting very sleepy myself and had to stifle many a yawn. I was shivering with chill and was longing for the tea with an honest dose of rum that I knew was waiting for me. A quarter to two—still fifteen long minutes to wait. Everything was so quiet, just like a vast, silent grave. Suddenly I heard confused yells, then the loud bark of a rifle, and in rapid succession two more.

I whisked out my automatic and dashed out to the road. My men jumped to their feet in great excitement.

As fast as my legs could carry me, I ran toward the bridge, to my northern outpost, where the trouble had started. There was a furious fusillade now; bullets whizzed by from every direction. Those idiotic outposts of mine, disregarding all orders, were firing furiously in our direction. I was standing in a crossfire from three different sides, with the Russians shooting frantically out of the darkness. Hissing bullets spattered on the road and ricocheted on the stones, howling hideously.

Both lines, high upon the crests, aroused by this lively shooting, started a nervous fire, accompanied by dozens of machine-guns, and very soon the guns were booming too. Tiny red flashes of thousands of rifles appeared on the dark horizon, far above our heads, and gave the appearance of a huge fiery serpent writhing in the night.

Light rockets shot upon both sides in blazing parabolical curves, and the dance was on.

Right at the fork, in the middle of the highway, completely ignoring the buzzing slugs, stood Corporal Pilz, facing eastward, ready to shoot.

"What the hell is it, Pilz?" I asked.

He let go the trigger and pointed to the sharp curve of the highway, where stood a mud hut with whitewashed walls. "I got one of them, sir," he said very calmly. Sure enough, right below the white wall, sunk into a shapeless heap, there lay something.

I tried to piece together what had happened. Well, the Russians did come; not on the cartway, nor on the high-way, and not through the underbrush, but—confound them—in the bed of the creek. This possibility I had overlooked entirely.

The creek was low and could be forded easily; in many places the water did not reach above the knees. The last time I had seen that creek it was a rough torrent, swelled by melting snow. Now, they simply walked upstream in the shallow water—completely covered by the overhanging thick brush and trees.

As fate would have it, their most advanced picket left the river bed just before he came under the bridge, exactly where my northern outpost was stationed for such emergency. He probably was one of those dumb and inexperienced rookies—exactly like one of my own men that stood for a picket on the northern post. Thus, as he sneaked carefully upon the soft banks, he bumped squarely into my picket hidden in the brush, probably dozing. Both of them, scared out of their wits, let out a howl and jumped back, the Russian firing once in the air and my picket twice.

In an instant the creek was alive with Russians, scampering to the banks, running in all directions, shooting wildly. By this time my other outposts were doing their best to make the confusion complete. Some of the fleeing raiders reached the highway—about a dozen of them—and ran in wild confusion toward the eastern curve. But Corporal Pilz was already on the highway waiting to do his stuff. As soon as the first running figure came to that white wall, offering a fairly good target in that misty darkness, he put two bullets into him with deadly accuracy.

There was nothing to fire at now, but it took some time before I could stop all that foolish shooting. Gradually the violent firing of the lines above also slowed down into spasmodic bursts with an occasional Russian salvo rolling over. Then, together with the dying light rockets, the fire ceased altogether. I ordered my outposts back to their locations and sent Pilz with five men to bring in that vague figure that was lying at the bottom of the whitewashed hut.

They brought him in on their rifles and placed him in the center of that gloomy shed, on a thin layer of damp straw. He was still alive but seemed to be unconscious. I switched my flashlight on and, together with the ensign and the sergeant, made a hurried examination of him, hoping that we still might save him.

There he lay on the straw, pale and bloody, amidst my wide-eyed, horror-stricken rookies, with his life rapidly ebbing away. He came to after a while and opened his eyes. We gave him some rum which he drank slowly. He was obviously in great pain, for his contorted expression told of his suffering. His right hand groped vaguely in the damp straw and he made some feeble efforts to lift his hand. The left arm lay limp at his side, shattered completely by a bullet. But this shot could not possibly have caused all the suffering of this blond giant—there must have been something much more serious to bring him down. We unbuckled his cartridge belt and unhooked his long coarse mantle. There were large bloodstains on his green tunic and his shirt was drenched with blood. There I found a second shot through his groin. There was no help for this—most deadly of all wounds. There was just one thing to do—to hook his mantle again and wait for the end.

I rose utterly sick from the thought of the impossibility of any help. I have seen men die—dozens of them, I have seen men suffer—hundreds of them, but never did one impress me so much as this poor dying soldier here, amongst his enemies, in that miserable gloomy shack in the midst of the night.

It was quite impossible to move him up to our positions in such a hopeless condition when I knew that the slightest movement caused him unbearable suffering. I was pretty sure he would not be alive by the time we got him to the trenches. But I simply could not leave him here to die alone beside the road like some filthy animal.

We would stand by his side—helpless, though—till he breathed his last. It was well after two now. At four o'clock it would be bright day, and I was supposed to return with my detachment before daybreak. Orders or no orders, I decided not to leave this man as long as there was any trace of life in him. Above the Rotunda, there was again that reddish gleam, even stronger than before. Another conflagration, some other wretched huts crumbling in the flames. Outside in that little potato field, right behind the shack—scarcely twenty paces from the spot where the man lay in his last agonies—worked four of my soldiers with hand spades, digging a grave.

"Juro," I told my ensign, "listen to what he is saying. You know a little Russian."

Juro went down on his knees and bent over the man to catch his whispers. Right then he wasn't whispering at all. His eyes were closed and his blond bushy beard was soaked with bloody froth. Now and then a slight spasm shook his once powerful frame. His features were calm now, such a kindly face he had.

Juro listened. His lips were silent, his breath came irregularly. It was so quiet; from the potato field one could hear the soft dull thuds of the earth thrown up from the grave; now and then the steel spades ground against stones. We lit a candle; the battery of my flashlight was giving out. Juro was down on his knees.

"Gospodi," muttered the dying man, "Gospodi pomilooy." (God, oh God have Mercy.)

The end came. His chest moved, barely rising.

"Masha," he whispered, *"moya Mashenjka."* (Masha, my little Mashenjka). Then he whispered no more and he breathed no more.

Juro got up slowly.

"Sir," he said in a husky voice, with a lump in his throat, "he is dead."

Into the flame of the candle, held by one of my men, dropped an uncontrolled tear, causing the wick to sizzle. There we buried him in that grave, four feet deep. What he had in his pockets we emptied into his cap. His identification tag was cut from a cord around his neck, his equipment gathered, the epaulets cut from his overcoat and from his tunic.

While a dozen of my men were filling up the grave and forming a mound, somebody made a crude cross out of that picket fence nearby and stuck it down where his head was. I removed my cap; so did my men.

"Now, boys," I said quietly, "say a prayer for this poor fellow."

Far behind the Rotunda, that burning village cast its reddish gleam faintly upon the bowed, unkempt heads of my rookies, crossing their clumsy fingers over the muzzles of their rifles, murmuring the Lord's Prayer.

It was just beginning to dawn as we crossed our trenches, and I sent my men to sleep. I went straight to the dark hut of the Major. I rapped on the window and his adjutant opened.

"Wake the Major," I ordered, "I have to report."

The Major was sitting on his cot in his breeches, his grayish hair tousled on his forehead, blinking sleepily. I saluted. "Sir, the hundred and thirty-fourth Siberian Rifle Regiment is holding the Rotunda. We shot a raider; we had no loss of life; two of my men are slightly wounded."

"Very well, Lieutenant," he said, putting his feet again under the coarse blanket. "Report in detail in the morning. Good night."

"Come on, Juro," I said to my ensign, waiting outside, "have tea with me. It will do us lots of good. We'll put plenty of rum into it."

My cadets were already waiting for our return; my faithful orderly stood smiling, much relieved, at the door of our hut. After several big mugs of tea, we lit our pipes and then went over the contents of the dead soldier's cap. There was a clumsy, cheap watch with broken hands, a little triangular brass icon of St. Nicholas, the Patron Saint of the Russians, a wooden spoon, a shabby black leather purse with some money in it, and a very worn pocket-book with curled leaves.

There Private Wassilij Alexandrowitch Haritonoff wrote down in his own simple words, printed in a clumsy awkward type, such things as he wanted to remember.

And other things too—things he hoped for dearly. Private Wassilij— lying with a hole through his belly in that little potato field, muttering the name of Masha with his faithful last mutter...

Who was Masha, or Mashenjka, as he said, endearingly? God knows. His wife? His little daughter? Maybe his sweetheart. Masha will anxiously await his return, and will never know that Wassilij is covered with four feet of cold earth for the greater glory of the Little Father and the inquisitiveness of His Excellency, the Austrian Brigadier General—and, of course, mainly because Corporal Pilz, with that devilish black beard, was such a crack shot.

Some seer, that simple Siberian farmer Wassilij was!

Among other notes he put down in that battered little notebook, there was one that said: "Woina konchitsya—The War ends on the 21st of April in the year of our Lord 1915."

And truly, the war ended—for Wassilij at least—on the twenty-first of April, just as he secretly hoped—at three o'clock in the morning, to be exact.

Chapter V

Three days after we shot Wassilij, we rolled our coats over our knapsacks, buckled the straps and marched off into the night. This was a quiet sector, here, that could be held safely by old landsturm men. Our presence was needed on a spot where there was to be plenty of action.

For seven nights we marched. It was to be a great surprise for the Russians. By day, we rested in billets and were not allowed to be seen outside. Then we stopped southwest from Tarnow, and had two days' rest. On the second day, there was a field-mass and general absolution. There were many to die; it had to be done wholesale. We did not like field-masses. It was not the field-masses themselves that we did not like; those were inspiring and beautiful affairs, and even soldiers are willing to bow their heads to God, but masses always meant something—and never anything good.

When it grew dark, we drew double rations, and double rations always made you think of the Last Meal. After that, every man got as much ammunition as he was able to carry. Mounds of ammunition were there. We got bags, also, for hand grenades, and enough grenades to fill each bag to its brim. Each officer received six signal-rockets, with which we were to signal our artillery to lift the barrage. Furthermore, everybody got white head flaps, which were tied over the backs of our caps, like little aprons. They hung down the neck, like those sun-guards worn by colonial troops. However, they were not to protect us from the sun; they were to help the artillery observers to denote the exact location of our lines—once everything got mixed up during the fight.

Then we relieved a regiment in the first line and cut our own wires in many places. In the night we sent our sappers to blast the Russian wire entanglements—there were forests of them. The sappers crept out behind steel shields, which they rolled before them. The dynamite was attached to long poles, which were to be pushed among the supporting stakes of the wire fence. It was a one way trip for many of those poor devils, for few came back. But some blasts went off beautifully. This was the first of May—usually the day for May-poles and May games, back in the good old days. It was to be a memorable day out here.

At two in the morning, sharp, seven hundred guns turned the front, on a section of forty miles, into a veritable hell. There was no caliber, from the lean muzzled 75's to the 32.5 siege guns that did not spit fire and steel for four solid hours. The air vibrated and the earth shook. We were completely deafened.

Behind this black and red curtain of death, we worked up to storming distance. At six sharp, the artillery ceased fire and we stormed.

There was not much to be taken, and whatever remained was pounded to a pulp. Shell holes and craters, deep enough for cottages, yawned where the 32.5's established contact with the ground. Everything was churned into a powdery, splintered, bloody mass.

In some deep craters we found a few crazed moujiks, kneeling and praying—trying to kiss our hands; but otherwise, nothing was left of that formidable first line, with its barbed wire glacis eighty yards deep, just here and there a fragment of wire sticking out of the soft muck—a boot with a stump in it, heads, caps, rifles, hands and forms that may have been human beings once. Then we went to work on the second line. This fought back like the very devil himself, but in the afternoon we had it, also several machine-guns, which we turned promptly. While we rested a bit, we gave the third line a taste from their own machine-guns. Reinforcements came up, for we had lost half of our men already.

Then we bit into the third line, and we nearly broke all our remaining teeth. We attacked and counterattacked, and there was a vicious murder with detached bayonets. We were in and then thrown out again. Then we were in once more, to be thrown out. There were no units now and no command any longer; there were no lines of ours or theirs. Each man was shooting at the next best target—a very personal and individual battle. There was no time to dig rifle pits. If one was needed—and it certainly was needed—the useless dead was dragged out of it and his place taken. His blood did not matter on the uniforms; they were hopelessly dirty anyhow.

You could shoot Russians from the flank, right into the ear from forty yards, and they could fire right into our armpits from the same distance. We started out with plenty of hand grenades and still there were not enough.

When night fell, the Russians drew back a little to form a semblance of a line and we did likewise. We dug in hastily. It was hard to dig, for here we had clay, instead of soft muck. When we were deep enough, we ate some hardtack and bread, as we did not expect that any food would be sent to this place. There is no army cook who will expose perfectly good kettles to such murderous fire. Our hands were very dirty; we cleaned them before eating with a little spittle. Only the palms, of course.

Drinking water from the canteens is much too precious for washing purposes if you do not expect to get water for two or three days. Furthermore, my canteen was empty; there were two holes in it.

In the night it rained. To be exact, it poured; and our pits filled with water. That clay held the water, as any good pitcher would. It was a high grade clay, to our utter dismay, for not a drop leaked out. There we sat in the water holes like frogs, only very silent. The shooting stopped. Frogs don't shoot—that's clear. Those Russians were just as badly soaked as we. Later, when the rain stopped, we ladled out the water with caps and mess kits—whatever was handy.

Dawn broke slowly, steaming and gray. Over there, the Russian rifle pits were empty; so was the line behind. Dead lay all around.

We did not follow, for a few hours. The sun broke through the clouds and the drenched, heavy uniforms began to steam. We got coffee and yesterday's rations. There was plenty to eat, we got all the dead men's rations and then we marched off east, for fresh battles. And we drove them hereafter in daily battles, for two months to follow, through Galicia, towards Lublin.

For two weeks we were stopped in the vast pine forests on the river San, where we promptly dug in to beat off several desperate counterattacks of the Russian rear-guards. They tried everything to check our advance. They even set the forest afire, and Hell cannot be much worse than that burning forest was for two weeks. When we dug in here, we hoped to get a little rest for a while, for we had never been relieved for a single hour since we smashed their front. For two weeks it was a dead-lock, with furious trench raids on both sides. Things were made pleasant with *minenwerfers* and even liquid flame sprayers.

While our battered and thinned out ranks were filled up with replacements, the Russians hurled each day increasing masses to renewed attacks. They never got farther than our wire and those who reached it hung there, black and limp. Dead lay scattered everywhere, pea-green dots mottled the ground, which became more black and gray each day, coated with soot and dust.

On one early morning, there were no Russians in the trenches. Again they had cleared them in the night. The advance of our southern wing in eastern Galicia made their positions on the San untenable.

Once more the daily routine of the pursuit started. We marched for several hours until we were fired on. Then we spread out and sent the message back, stating where the enemy lay. By the time our main force developed into fighting formation, and the battle of the day started in earnest, it was generally broad daylight. There wasn't much action of the artillery on either side; ammunition was scarce and saved for positions at which it was worthwhile to shoot. The Russians started to fire at anywhere from twenty-six to twenty-four hundred yards. We advanced, disregarding their fire, up to fourteen hundred yards. Only then did we open fire and start to move forward in short jumps. Machine-guns were set up and under their protecting fire we kept pressing on. By mid-afternoon, as a rule we were not farther than three or four hundred yards. Then, in the baking July sun, we would wiggle up, one by one, still closer.

Men fell and died, weighed down by heavy knapsacks, their faces gray with dust and grime, clawing the dust with stiffening fingers. On average, I lost from ten to fourteen men a day from my company—if the resistance was not too stubborn and we were not facing machine-guns frontally.

By sunset, we came near enough to settle the issue for the day. If they still showed some fight, we charged, with the bayonet, those who still survived. But in most instances it did not come to this. Whenever we managed to approach the proper distance, for the final charge, they were generally sufficiently demoralized to throw their rifles down and put their hands up.

Poor wretched devils those were, tired with the stiffness of crouching for ten or twelve hours in some hole, far too small for them, with aching shoulders, hammered blue by the butt of the rifle, their brains sunbaked into dizziness, seeing with sinking hearts the ever oncoming, on-creeping foe, thirsty and hungry, vermin tortured, with bullets spattering around them, day in day out—for weeks and months—with the same prospect for the next day and the day after—to be done all over again in some other miserable hole.

If their fire was too ravaging, we dug in for the night and waited for them to clear their positions while it was dark. In the darkness of the night, our field-kitchens drove up near enough so that the men could be fed. Crumbling, evil tasting, greenish-brown bread rations consisting in large part of maize, were distributed. Tobacco was drawn—always less than due—and if the mail could catch up with our advance, it was delivered. Canteens were filled with greasy water from the soup kettles, and ammunition was replenished.

After the pickets were posted for the night watch, we would fall into a deathlike sleep for three or four hours amidst the straggling straps of the packs, just the blouse collars unhooked. If there was no night alarm, we would proceed in the dawn to repeat the day's work against some other hastily erected rear-guard position—ten or twelve miles farther.

Our reserves were used up in this gigantic drive; there were no rested troops to relieve us. We did not have a chance to wash for weeks, not even our hands. Our eyes were bleary with dust, our ears scratchy; sand and dust clogged our hair into thick mats and made us look gray; our pores were plastered with dust, and salty tasting sand ground under our teeth.

But on the next day we straggled on; with sore feet, wrapped in dirty rags, worn to frazzles; with stooped shoulders, smarting under the cruel straps of the knapsack; deadly tired, with glassy eyes, swallowing more dust and stench—clattering, slouching, marching to some other fray.

In the Official Communique we read: "Our heroic troops continue to pursue the beaten foe in excellent spirits, with flying banners."

After ten more days, all in "excellent spirits, with flying banners" to be sure, but with hanging tongues, emaciated bodies and parched brains, we suddenly stopped. Warsaw was menaced and the Russians brought up tremendous reinforcements that nearly stifled us. The banners were furled and we dug in once more. A new battalion arrived for our regiment to fill up the gaps again. Thus my company, numbering two hundred and forty men at the beginning of the drive, eight weeks ago, was brought back again to one hundred rifles. We had crossed the river Vistula and stood in a south-easterly direction from Warsaw, pressing toward the southern end of the semicircular salient protecting the city. The Russians were determined to defend this sore point to the bitter end, and they suddenly went into furious counterattacks. Heavy artillery was brought upon both sides and for a few days the battle raged undecided. We managed to repulse all counterattacks, and there was a deadlock again. We were fighting in a rather open country now. The wooded hills were left behind us, but we stood among low hillocks, covered at this time of the year with high ripe wheat, wherever we looked.

Both fighting lines were upon the crest, not more than a few hundred yards apart, and so long as we could shoot directly at the positions, which stood clear and sharp on the horizon, we saw what we were shooting at; but as soon as they went over the top, toward the shallow valley that separated the two positions, they were completely covered by the crops. All we could do was to spray the crops at random with our fire. On the slope, ascending our positions, they were lost entirely to our sight. At night we tried to set fire to the crops, but the vegetation wasn't dry enough to burst into flame. Then we tried to trample down as much as we could, to lose some of the fatal dead space. In the night I received written orders to spread out on both of my wings. I held about three hundred yards; it would be six hundred now, but we extended, making a weak position still weaker.

On my left, were the ruins of a village, on my right, between my right wing and the neighbor company, was an unoccupied gap of two hundred yards. One rifle, approximately, for six yards.

We got some ammunition and also a promise that sappers would come in the night, to help us with digging, and to put up hastily some barbed wire. The captain commanding the battalion said that our fliers reported great masses of infantry and that we might expect an attack in the morning.

With full equipment we started to dig in on the extended flanks. I gave orders to each man to dig a three-foot hole and, when this was done, to start digging toward each other, linking the holes to form a trench. Toward dawn the work was finished and we started to dig deeper. The soil was very soft, and digging would not have caused any trouble, but my men were completely exhausted and ready to drop. The sappers who had been promised did not turn up.

At three in the morning we got coffee. At least, officially it was rated as coffee, but I do not know from what it was concocted. Bitter, very thin, and greasy from the soup-kettle, but at least warm. We were freezing at night, to be boiled by day by a sun that made us half crazy.

The sun rose right behind the Russian positions, flashing through their loopholes in a scarlet blaze. Even the sun was against us with its blinding rays. By nine o'clock it was hot, and there wasn't a drop of coffee left in our canteens. I ordered six men to gather all the canteens from the company and fetch water for the day. But it was already impossible to leave the trenches. There was a furious fire as soon as a head popped up behind our parapet. Russian machine-gunners sprayed our line with an uncanny accuracy; bullets ripped and gnawed the earthen rim, whistling menacingly, spattering dust and swishing among the stalks. There was no way to get water before darkness fell again. Suddenly the pent-up fury of the Russian artillery broke loose. On my adjoining left wing, our sister regiment, the Brixen Kaiserjaegers, were attacked on their entire front. Heavy shells burst in the flimsy trenches, obliterating them completely. After ten minutes, the bombardment became a regular drum fire. The Brixen regiment suffered heavy losses and started to drift back from their completely demolished positions toward a thicket.

From my trenches, which overlooked theirs, I had an excellent view and could observe how the whole attack unfurled. While the artillery fire was at its height, the first wave of the Russians went over the top. Their gunfire ceased and now our artillery started to shower shrapnel on them. The Brixeners broke anew from the thicket, advancing with reinforcements towards their deserted positions, mowing the attackers with machine-gun fire.

The few who survived fled in wild disorder, and the attack broke, but the fate of the Brixen regiment was sealed. As soon as they got back to their former positions, another drum fire broke loose over their heads, worse than the previous one. A second wave of Russian infantry advanced, followed at intervals by third, fourth and fifth lines. Among dense clouds of dust, whirled up by bursting shells, I saw our lines crumble, to be definitely repulsed into the thicket. For a while sounds of fierce fighting came from there. All morning we had rifle fire, which grew stronger all the while. As soon as the Brixen regiment's fate had been sealed, the Russians turned their attention to our sector. Heavy shells started to spot our trenches, which began to crumble under the strong fire. Wherever a shell buried itself, the ground buckled, and a thick column of black earth spouted towards the sky. Black mist drizzled down, like a fine rain, blinding us. Sand drifted from the parapets in a steady stream. It was noon. Dimmed by clouds of dust, which veiled us in a misty haze, the sun blazed in the zenith, burning like the fire of Hell. Already at several places my trench was torn by huge gaps; dead soldiers lay half obliterated in the filling craters. The heat became a torture. My men knelt panting, behind the crumbling, ragged parapet, with the sweat running in dirty streams down their grimy faces, shooting with overheated rifles. Our throats were dry, our lips parched. Then the telephone buzzed and the captain gave orders.

"Lieutenant," he said, very excitedly, "the Russians broke through on our left and our regiment is ordered back. You with your company are to cover our retreat and hold on to the last man."

I could hardly hear his voice in that infernal din.

"Sir," I shouted into the speaker, "send me reinforcements. I have lost thirty men already; our ammunition is running low; we also need water for the machine-gun; it's overheated and jamming—"

"I have no reserves left," snapped the captain. "I can't spare a man. Get ammunition from the—" The telephone was silent, he did not finish the sentence. I frantically pressed the switch on the handle. No use. It was dead. The line had been shot.

"Repair the wire!" I called to the telephonist. He crept out of the shallow trench, crawling on his stomach, feeling with one hand the wire leading to the battalion. He was scarcely twenty feet away when he was shot through the head. Now we were cut off entirely, left in this hell-hole to our fate.

"Fix bayonets!" I ordered.

Our ammunition was diminishing rapidly. The dead were stripped of their supplies. The rifles were burning hot; some of the bolts were clogged by the whirling dust and did not work. The machine-gun was steaming and sizzling with heat. It jammed and worked irregularly. A corporal came from my left wing, crawling through the trench to my position in the center. He was exhausted, on the verge of collapse. I hardly recognized his face, gray with dust and muddy perspiration. "Sir!" he panted, while he tried to lift his body with his hands, "the ensign begs to report that our ammunition is nearly gone. The Russians are shooting from the houses in the village in our backs. Cadet Segalla, from the second platoon is dead."

"Tell the ensign I will send for ammunition immediately. Meanwhile gather the ammunition from the dead and wounded and give it to the best shots only.

Tell Sergeant Hilt to take over the command of the second platoon and let him report to me. Now get back to your place."

It was plain murder to dispatch somebody to get the ammunition, but I had no choice. The worst part of it was that the ammunition cases were much too heavy for one man, and there were always two men needed to carry a case. I turned to the men, nearest to me:

"Who of you volunteers to get ammunition from the battalion? I will recommend him for the Silver Medal."

After some deliberation, two boys, inseparable friends, reported that they were ready to go. Neither of them was over eighteen, sturdy Tyrolean mountaineers. How proud they would be to show the Medals for Valor to their sweethearts when they went back for a furlough! Be sides it meant a yearly bonus of seven and a half kronen (about a dollar and a half) with which they could buy enough tobacco to keep their large porcelain pipes burning for quite a while. I ordered them to unbuckle their knapsacks and take just the cartridge belts and rifles along. While my machine-gun started to spray the enemy's parapet, in order to keep them down for a while, these boys crept carefully out of the trench and started to crawl rapidly backward. The wheat was trodden down there; they were exposed for fully thirty yards before they would reach the upstanding stalks—and then be lost to the sight of the enemy. They were halfway by now. My heart stood still, watching those two boys. Then suddenly the Russian machine-gun popped up and opened fire. The first burst was too short.

"Get that cursed gun!" I yelled to my gunner. He trained his gun on the Russian machine. His bullets spattered on the heavy steel shield of the hostile gun, but could not do any serious damage to it.

It kept on shooting, vibrating and shaking as with some hideous laughter, and stretched my two boys to the ground, just as they were about to creep among the stalks.

There lay those two brave kids, motionless. Our situation was getting more desperate with each minute and I simply could not give the order for two other men to try again.

But we had to get ammunition somehow. We were sacrificed and lost anyway—this stood clear before me—but we were supposed to sell our lives dearly, that the regiment might retreat safely. It would not do the regiment much good if we stuck to the very end with empty rifles.

I turned to my orderly: "Go up to the right wing and tell Cadet Schroeder to send two men for ammunition immediately. Report back at once!"

This was my last hope. If this failed, there was nothing else to be done. Upon my right wing the terrain was slightly more in our favor. As I looked in that direction, I could see our lines go back. Not much could be seen of the men, on account of the high crops, which covered them nearly to the shoulders. Now and then they stopped and turned to shoot at the Russians, who were after them. Thus, my right wing hung in the air too. The man I dispatched returned and reported that the cadet lay severely wounded, unconscious. The orderly had had enough brains though to give the order to the cadet's proxy—a corporal.

By some miracle, the two men sent for ammunition got back. When they were returning, carrying the case, one was wounded. The other man could not carry the case alone, so he pried open the lid, filled his pouch, his pockets, his blouse and his cap with as much ammunition as they would hold, and then dragged in the half empty case somehow.

Out of this supply, I ordered the empty machine-gun belts filled, so that at least the machine-gun would be fit for action in the decisive moment that seemed to be near.

Our artillery was silent; through my field glasses I could see them limber up and then gallop away at break-neck speed.

Wherever I looked, I saw the advancing Russian infantry. Down to my left, the village was swarming with them; up toward my right wing, patrols were already sneaking in the wheat fields to get us from the back. I dispatched orderlies to my outlaying platoons and ordered the wings to contract toward the center, thus shortening my front to half of its former extension. There were only sixty men left now, out of the hundred.

Then our opponents went over the top and charged. They seemed to grow out of the earth, in such overwhelming masses did they come. I jumped over to the machine-gun. It danced and trembled like a venomous demon, spitting fire and destruction. A dozen of the charging men fell and sank on the parapet, but the others came rolling on with long drawn yells, in batches and droves, leaping and driving on the declining slope—seeming to swim in the rippling wheat. More of them fell, sinking into that yellow sea of ripe wheat, and still more. His Majesty, Death, was harvesting with modern efficiency! Ra-tat-tatt-ta—and the ripe human crop fell, mowed down as by some invisible scythe. Tiny leaden wasps in shiny steel jackets pricked small holes into madly throbbing hearts, cutting small exits for the soul to escape from this human made hell. My men jumped up and were standing in the half obliterated, low trench, firing the very last cartridges.

By this time the Russians had reached the bottom of the shallow hollow that separated the two positions and were safe from our bullets in that dead space. In our rear, already a closed Russian line was advancing—we were cut off completely. To make things worse patrols were shooting from the rear. Then came the end. That mass, outnumbering us several times, started its final assault up the grade. My machine-gunner put the last belt into his gun, waiting for new targets, that would emerge from the dead space.

Left behind on the parapet, the Russian machine-gun started to shoot in support of the ascending, storming troops—right over their heads. It caught the remnants of my right wing and annihilated it completely. Suddenly, it stopped its fire; the assailants had reached a height on the ascending grade where they would have been endangered by their own gun.

Then, for the last time, my gunner pressed the button, firing into the dense crowd, not more than fifty yards away. The belt withered like a serpent into the feed, vomiting steel and fire; empty yellow brass cartridges flew clicking from the gun.

Bullets are made to pass through four men, and these last bullets were not wasted to snuff out single lives. In that terrible carnage among those wild-eyed, half-crazed, panting creatures—the attack crumbled. Men fell, groaning and screaming, the slope was thickly dotted with fallen men.

But our fate was sealed. Already my wings were taken, and new masses emerged from the wheat to crush the life out of us. My gun was silent—the last cartridge had been shot, the gunner lay dead, limply hugging his gun, shot from the rear.

I shoved him aside with feverish haste, tore open the feed, jerked out the feeding joint and flung it far away, to make the gun useless.

By this time they were upon us from all sides. There were curses, shrieks and groans, the clatter of steel. Heavy steel lined rifle butts came down crashing. A huge fellow aimed at me from a distance of a few yards. I ducked. His bullet grazed my cap and tore through the rolled blanket behind my neck. In answer, I shot at him twice with my automatic—missing him both times. Then one of those wildly swinging butts came down, sinking him with a crushing blow, cracking his skull.

After this, I have only a hazy recollection of what happened. I know my empty gun was torn from my neck by a white-faced, excited Russian officer, with chattering teeth, and those of my men who were still alive stood on the trampled parapet, utterly dejected, trying to hold up their dirty, trembling hands. Rifles, with their butts up, were stuck in the ground—meaning capitulation. Masses rushed by, continuing their pursuit. My orderly was standing beside me, sobbing, gasping for breath.

"Sir," he said with an effort to smile, "we are saved."

And then he crossed himself.

Chapter VI

Six men were left behind to guard us. We were to throw off our equipment and then march immediately. We were allowed to take our overcoats, blankets, mess kits and canteens; everything else was to remain there. As we marched back—forty-two of us, not counting the Russian guards—I saw what tremendous losses we had inflicted in our last stand. The slopes and the valley were strewn with wounded and dead, and they had plenty of dead in their trenches on the summit and still more behind.

Cossacks rode through the village in long columns, at a fast trot, savage-looking warriors, who shook their lances at us. After marching half an hour, we came to a clear creek and we made signs to our guards that we wanted to drink. We stopped and all of us—prisoners and guards—went down flat to drink. After that sweltering day in the blistering sun, our throats were utterly dry. We bathed our faces and washed our hands, even dipped our heads under the water. It refreshed us a little. Then we continued our march.

After three more hours we were commanded to halt on the marketplace of a little village. There were more prisoners here. The men got some soup and bread and could rest for a while. Together with my ensign, I was taken to the divisional command to be questioned.

The command was in a very comfortable manor house, shaded by large trees. The shades were drawn; it was nice and cool behind the thick walls. There were several Russian officers in the room. I saluted and they bowed courteously. Our regimental number was taken, then our ranks, names and age.

The officer who questioned us spoke fluent German, others seemed to understand too. When he had all the data concerning us, he tried to get some information regarding the strength of our regiment, whether we belonged to the so-called "Flying Brigade," where we were before, and other questions that seemed to be important to them. Other Russian officers were standing around us.

"Gentlemen," I said with a short bow, "I wish to thank you for the courteous treatment you have so kindly shown me, but I am not allowed to give you information about our army."

"Perfectly all right, Lieutenant," said the questioning captain. "It is my duty to ask you, but we recognize your privilege to refuse answer." Then he introduced himself and added: "You are invited to have tea with us, gentlemen—out on the porch—if you please," I accepted with thanks. Some other young officers introduced themselves. Counts and barons, in well-polished high boots, well groomed, looking very spic and span. There were cordial handshakes and absolutely no hostile feelings. Heels clicked and spurs jingled.

Tea was served on the porch—in a large samovar—with some cake and jam. They offered us cigarettes. I could never have got a better reception at our own mess.

A half hour later we were marched off. Toward evening we came to a large village, where more prisoners were waiting. The infantrymen who had brought us thus far were relieved by Cossacks, who were much more disagreeable. All night we marched, without rest.

Toward daybreak, we stopped on a large meadow, on top of a gently declining hill. Far down, in the valley, we saw the lights of a large city and some smokestacks. It was Lublin. We slept for three hours, then we marched into one of the large barracks in Lublin.

Our fliers were dropping bombs; there was great excitement everywhere. Troops were marching, artillery and wagon train. Lublin was evacuated. We were to be transported into the interior somewhere that same afternoon.

The barracks were filled with our officers, and there were thousands of privates in the yards. When night came, we were marched off to the railroad station and ordered into boxcars—forty men into each. We crowded and sweltered in the heat. Two armed guards sat at the doors, which were not allowed to be opened. At the stations we were kept in the cars and fed once a day, like animals, all eating from the same pot.

For each day on the journey, when we were not fed, each officer was to receive a rouble and a half; but there were days when we did not get so much as a crumb, and not so much as a red kopeck.

Withholding these payments, the transport commander could make as much as 450 roubles a day, for there were three hundred officers transported on this train alone. At one of the stations, where we stood for several hours, we got permission to leave the boxcars and, accompanied by the guards, we went to the buffet to get a drink. Several Russian officers of high rank, who sat at the tables, ordered us out rudely, shaking their riding crops at us. There was great indignation, but we were powerless.

The farther we got back into the interior of Russia, the worse it became. It was the same here as everywhere else; intendants, military officials and officers, sitting pretty, at a safe distance, were much more bloodthirsty than the best shock troops in the field. Insignificant little army clerks, meek little bookkeepers got drunk with power and ordered us about, yelling at the top of their voices.

In six days we reached Moscow; in three more days, Kazan, the Tartar capital on the Volga. From here we were to be distributed to the large prison camps along the Volga and the Ural mountains.

We had traveled twelve hundred miles in boxcars and, by now, one could feel each bone in the body hurt separately.

For two days we were in Kazan, kept in a closed down brewery. There was prohibition since the outbreak of the war, and breweries were no longer needed.

First of all, we were ordered to remove all our rank marks—stars and stripes and gold buttons—everything that marked us as officers. After a good wash-up in the wide yard, we went to inspect the barracks. We got a hearty reception from a large group of officers, who had reached here before us, and questions were raining upon our heads.

The barrack buildings themselves were deserted; they did not seem to be inhabited by those whom we found at our arrival. No things lay scattered around; there were no ashes or cigarette butts anywhere. One could see that those outside never went near this place.

I asked a lieutenant for the reason. He laughed and told me to follow. Inside, he lifted a slanting board that served as a headrest on a long row of bunks. Thousands of bugs scrambled in wild confusion.

"That'll give you an idea what's beneath the other boards," he said. "We all sleep outside in the yard, in empty kegs. You can rent a keg for ten kopecks from the caretaker, but better hurry before they're all gone."

For two nights we slept in kegs. They reeked with the smell of stale beer, but we slept very well.

On the third day the brewery was cleared of all officers. Together with two hundred others I was marched to a landing stage, put on a riverboat and sent to a small county seat on a tributary of the Volga. Here we were checked up and then searched once more, for the tenth, but not the last, time. However, nothing was found; everything worthwhile had been taken on previous searches; and these fellows were out of luck. Several whistles they got. All they could do was to rip open some rubber cushions, but after these showed negative results, they were returned.

At the barracks, we were ushered into the presence of the commander, a Russian colonel, who looked for all the world like one of those characters that since have become standardized in Hollywood productions. He had gray whiskers, parted in the middle of the chin, and trained to flow parallel with the epaulets. His tremendously baggy pants were tucked into elephantine boots, and across his considerable girth dangled a long scimitar pointing forward.

He asked if anybody among us knew Russian. There was a cadet who spoke pretty well, and he was appointed interpreter for the Colonel.

We were told to keep discipline among us and to behave decently. There was no place in his barracks for us. He was at a loss to understand why, in the name of the devil, the Kazan Corps Command sent him our transport, when he was overcrowded without us. Empty buildings would be requisitioned in the city, where we would be billeted if we paid the monthly rent, and paid it on time.

Groups of twenty or thirty officers were to be formed for each billet, according to its capacity, and each group was to have its special Russian guard—one private for six officers, the eldest, the "Starshy" to be the guard-commander, from whom we were to take orders.

We would have to pay for our food, also for firewood and kerosene—and four officers were allowed to have an orderly, who could be picked from our captive privates. Each subaltern officer was to receive fifty roubles (about twenty-five dollars) a month. There were no newspapers whatever to be read and no books to be bought, with the exception of dictionaries, grammars and the Russian Bible. We were to rise at seven in the morning, and lights had to be put out at ten at night sharp.

Then again, we must not dare to talk to any civilians, males or fe-males—females especially—for they would be fined three thousand roubles or given three months in jail, and we would go to prison for the rest of the war. Further orders would come from time to time to the billets. The cadet reported that he had told all, and after that, the Colonel withdrew promptly. Groups were formed and after several hours of search we were billeted and left with our guards.

So once again we had a roof over our heads and we could call it our home if we wanted to.

A feeling of quietness and security cast its spell over our small group of twenty, whirled from those trying events, after months of hardship and danger. For the time we did not feel unhappy at all. The consciousness of our captivity was suppressed by the thought that we were going to run our own household, now. True, we did not have the slightest idea how to tackle such a thing, but, of all things, we would have plenty of time to think that out.

We were all young, bubbling with life, hardened by service, and we were to get fifty roubles a month! It looked like a welcome rest—a sort of a long vacation, paid by the Russian treasury. Why worry? We had three small rooms and a kitchen. There was no furniture whatever—just the bare walls. For a week we slept on the naked floor and after that we found it very uncomfortable. We expected to get money from the command, but it was postponed from one day to the other.

Everybody had still some money—we could not spend our pay during those active weeks at the front—and so we decided that it was about time to think of furnishing our home and starting housekeeping. Giving a thought to our aching bones, we decided to order mattresses. Mattresses in Russia—at least those for which we could afford to pay—are by no means such elaborate, springy, fluffy delights as are endorsed here by reputable society matrons.

They are made out of bast—a crude plant, cut into thick strips, with very unelastic fibers—three fingers thick when brand new and only one finger thick after one has slept on them for a week. They were promised to be delivered within a week. The upholsterer swore by God—and after two weeks he really delivered half of them. For these we raffled. The losers slept two more weeks on the floor and used a lot of bad language.

Then we bought a saw, some boards and nails, and made tables and benches. Nobody was to sit on the table itself, and no horseplay was to be practiced on the benches—for they were shaky and, being made out of unplaned boards, rather prickly too. This, however, we felt sure would wear off after a while. Then we had to have shelves if we didn't want to stumble any longer among the shoes, caps, pipes, tin kettles and other things scattered on the floor.

We did not buy a wash basin, because, as long as the weather was warm, we could wash at the pump in the yard; but we did buy pots and pans, and took up the problem of housekeeping in all seriousness.

Fortunately, there was a married man among us, and it was evident that he was to become the mess-officer.

First, he did not want to accept such responsibilities—saying that he did not know a thing about it—that his wife ran his household at home. But he was unanimously elected by nineteen others and had to capitulate. The next thing was to get a cook. So the mess-lieutenant went to the barracks and announced to the captive privates that he wanted a cook—and a good one, too.

There followed a wild stampede and, out of the thirty men milling around him, he picked out the one that looked most promising. Three days after, we fired him back to the barracks. Before he went, he admitted that he had been a traveling dry goods salesman.

When he was gone, we held a conference. It occurred to us that the trouble might not have been caused solely by the one-sided talent of the salesman, but by the huge baking oven he had to use for a hearth and which none of us could handle.

It was clear that we had to have a regular hearth—of the kind we were accustomed to—and so we decided to build one. We had an architect; he said he could do it. We got bricks, lime and mortar, everything he said would be necessary, and the architect started to build; all others helped. In half a day the hearth was finished—even whitewashed. Mortar was in our ears and in our hair.

There was a second stampede up at the barracks, much worse than the first time, and the lieutenant returned with another aspirant, but after a week we wished we had not been so abrupt with the salesman.

This one was a bricklayer. Before he went he said that the hearth was a bum piece of work, no matter who had made it; and we thought it wiser not to tell him. We could not well argue, for he was an expert bricklayer.

The architect was very quiet.

Our next cook was a longshoreman, but he said so immediately. Furthermore, he asserted that he had learned to cook on tramp steamers. He had muscles like an ox, and for that reason we took him. His dumplings were very solid, extremely solid, like cannonballs.

However, the Russian guards respected his bulging arms—and so he stuck for a while.

For a few weeks we just slept and kept sitting around without doing a thing, but when we were fully rested and restored, it began to be tedious. We had already heard, a dozen times, the most minute details of how each one of our group was captured—stories and events from the front—till we all grew tired of listening.

Each morning we were led for an hour's walk somewhere outside the city. A guard with fixed bayonet on his long rifle trotted after us and kept us from using the sidewalk, where we were not allowed to go.

In the morning, accompanied by a guard, the mess-officer went to the market and bought the supplies for the day. The guards were always willing to go, for it meant money for them. They got ten kopecks from the mess-officer, and they got a small tip also from the merchant where he gave his permission to buy.

Altogether it was not such a bad business for them to guard captive officers. The guards were older men from the landsturm, unfit for front service, peaceable, ignorant moujiks, with whom it was not difficult to get along.

They preferred this service—where they could drink their tea in peace and sleep comfortably on top of the baking oven—to digging trenches behind the front or to unloading supplies.

True enough, the Little Father did not pay them more than fifty-two kopecks a month for their services, which did not amount to quite a cent a day, but they never grumbled at being underpaid.

They made a little on the side by running errands for us and not seeing things they should have seen. Furthermore, as long as they behaved decently and did not give trouble, they were to receive regular pay from us, which amounted to considerably more than they got from the Tsar. So, for a while, the entire guard got five roubles a month, from which one third was to go to the commander and two thirds to the men.

However, things were not always smooth, for the guards were often relieved so that they would not become too friendly with the prisoners. Besides, we were frequently examined by the Colonel's staff, who never failed to raise the lid and make the guards grouchy.

Sometimes it happened that not one of the guards could read or write, and then they would stand in the kitchen, thickly plastered with daily incoming written orders from the command, and ask us what was written there.

In the morning and at night we were counted, and the "Starshy" had to report twice a day at the barracks that nobody had escaped and everything was in good order.

On such occasions they were instructed as to what stood in the written orders, which they could not read themselves, but while they were returning they promptly forgot what was said at the barracks. If they did not forget completely, they mixed it up in a hopeless way.

There was great trouble with the morning shave. In fact, the morning shaves had to be changed to half-weekly shaves. True enough, everybody had safety razors, but nobody had blades—and no such things as safety blades could be bought in the forelands of the Ural mountains. The true Russians wore whiskers, and so did the Tartars. We got a straight blade and started to shave each other with the most disastrous results.

In order not to cause more bloodshed and hard feelings, we again went up to the barracks and searched our men for a barber. But there was none.

Good barbers and cooks were precious assets to the army, and were not exposed to the dangers of the firing line, but were kept at a safe distance at brigades and divisions. That explains the fact that, unless there was a fateful breach somewhere, deep enough to shake the front, there were no worthwhile cooks and barbers captured.

After a long search we found a man who said he could wield a razor—so, together with a guard, he was brought along to make good his boast.

With devilish ingenuity he somehow managed to cut away the flesh from between the stubbles and leave the stubbles on the bone. However, he learned fast, and after a few weeks he did not draw blood worth speaking of.

The house where we lived belonged to a woman by the name of Alexandra Yefimowna. It was a small two-story building, made of logs, and we occupied the upper floor. It had a long, narrow yard, completely surrounded by a high fence, sheds and barns. Alexandra herself lived in a small cottage opposite the main building, and was a kind-hearted soul. The logs of her hut had become loose with time, and the heavy roof had pulled the whole cabin out of shape. There it stood slouching and tilting as if ready to topple over every minute.

All the time we were on excellent terms with her. We would buy her some pastry or macaroons and then, when the guard was not looking, she would produce a newspaper from under her apron, from the day before or the week before, and give it to us to read.

She darned our socks, which looked to us beyond repair, and mended our shirts. She was like a kind old mother, who loaned her samovar to the guards, and who took care of us as if we were her sons.

We were allowed to write four postal cards each month, and also two letters. As often as she knew that we were writing home, she would come and ask each one of us to send her kisses to her son, who was a prisoner of war in Austria. She did not know exactly where, but she charged us to ask the commander there to take good care of her Grishka.

Months passed. The gayety and ease of the first weeks gave way to a gloomy and disheartening feeling. It was September now and the war had been raging fourteen months—would it never end? The news that came from the Russian front was favorable to our cause; one fortress after the other fell, but still there was no talk of peace.

True enough, we prisoners had little cause to rejoice over the victories at the front. As often as something happened there that was disagreeable to the Russians, the thumbscrews were put on the prisoners of war. New restrictions came each day; we were not to do this and not to do that. We were not to go to the windows, and must keep as much out of sight as possible. Our payments were delayed so often that we finally ran out of our very last kopecks, and we revolted in such a way that the Colonel was forced to wire to Kazan for money. Finally we got partial payments on our overdue salaries, so small that they could hardly keep us alive.

We expected the arrival of a German-Danish Red Cross delegation, and we threatened to report, so that suitable reprisals could be taken against Russian prisoners at home. That brought them to their senses, and once again we got our dues.

Parcels that were sent through charitable organizations were plundered at the command, and more often we did not receive them at all. It was a thing that could not be proved, and they knew it perfectly.

Our uniforms, already very threadbare at our capture, started to peel off in rags, the pants especially. There were boys in seatless pants, who could not go out unless they wore coats.

Meanwhile, a new industry sprang up among our captive privates in the barracks; the guild of the cleaners and tailors was formed. Our soldiers were dying by the dozens of typhoid fever and scurvy. Before they were sprinkled with lime and buried, the members of the guild divested them of their uniforms and mantles. It was something like robbing the dead, but it was done everywhere.

Those uniforms, peeled off the dead, were boiled, scrubbed and cleaned, and then offered us for sale. First we hesitated. Then, as we learned that the Russian moujiks were only too eager to buy them, we had to change our minds, so much the more, that there was no other cloth to be bought there. Overcoats, especially, fetched good prices. Out of these blouses could be made, and good sturdy breeches.

The same as with any other merchandise, the prices were governed by the supply and demand. If there were many dead, the price dropped; if there were few, it rose immediately.

Many of our privates worked on farms. These were, comparatively, much better off than those at the barracks. At least they were fed decently, lived with the peasant's family on the farm, and even dressed like moujiks themselves.

But the rest, confined to the barracks, were in a pitiable state. They were underfed, and most of them were sick. Epidemics were ravaging and, except for the few who were able to make some money as craftsmen, they were a hungry and miserable lot, clad in rags—a veritable army of beggars. We tried to help, wherever we could; but there were too many needy, and the little help we could give now and then was scarcely felt. There were not more than two hundred officers and at least ten times as many privates.

We spent the days trying to invent things with which to kill time. We carved crude chessmen and spent long hours over the chessboard; we drew and painted playing cards and played card games until we didn't want to see any more cards. Besides, at that time it did not seem fair to us to play for money. Not because it was strictly forbidden; we wouldn't have cared much about that. But we were in the most extraordinary circumstances, never knowing what the future might bring, and we were fully aware of the fact that gambling would sooner or later disrupt good comradeship, which we were only too anxious to keep up. We invented new games of all kinds. Many of us started to take up Russian in a serious way, and we studied diligently.

But no matter how hard we tried to keep ourselves busy, the days seemed tremendously long. The ban on newspapers and especially on books seemed to us the most cruel measure that could have been adopted to crush our spirits. We started to feel empty and we felt a change in our manners that was not to our advantage. It was the inevitable result of the war and, still much more, of the captivity. This forced association of young boys was quite entertaining for a while—but now we started to get tired of one another's company. Deep in our hearts we craved for love. After all those rough adventures we longed for some delicate romance—if not more—some platonic love at least. We would have bartered our souls to speak a word to some girl, just to touch a soft warm hand again.

There was a high school for girls in the town. We passed the large building whenever we went on our daily walk. We used to crane our necks, just to catch a glimpse of those pretty little things, who crowded to the windows to watch us pass by. Sometimes we were lucky enough to time our appearance with the short recess they had between hours, for then they certainly would be at the windows awaiting us—and then we were happy. For a while this was all, and we never hoped to achieve more.

Then suddenly unexpected things happened. Families, living on their farms in the neighborhood, sent in their daughters to board near their schools during the terms. Alexandra Yefimowna used to accommodate boarders every year, and got her share this time again. In fact, she got three girls, whom she had boarded before.

At the far end of our yard stood a dilapidated small cabin, inhabited by a toothless hag who swept the yard and took care of Alexandra's pigs. She used to cast murderous glances at us, for no special reason at all, and we always stepped aside, fearing the broom, which looked very formidable in her hands. This was Babushka. Right in front of her cabin, forming a small creek, stood a muddy mixture of the wastewater of the pump and the drainage of the pigsty. Across this moat lay a plank, which served as a bridge to the cabin. To us it looked like a fairy castle, with a regular moat around it and a veritable dragon guarding the three Princesses.

They arrived one morning on a rack-wagon, driven by a bewhiskered moujik, and moved in across the moat.

We were in great turmoil. For hours we sat on the steep wooden stairs leading to our rooms, just to catch a glimpse of them, but during the day they did not show up. Every morning they glided out with downcast eyes, and returned in the same manner when it grew dark.

After their arrival our guards were very alert and their guardian, armed with her broom, looked too dangerous to take chances with. This silent watch lasted for two weeks. The barber had to come down each day now, and we took up the study of Russian with redoubled vigor.

Then we held a war council, for something had to be done. Sitting on the steps was good enough for a while, but got us nowhere. They never looked and never stopped; we had to find a way to hold their attention.

Then somebody hit on a very bright idea.

"Let's make an orchestra," he suggested.

"Great!" said all.

"Orpheus tamed wild beasts with a measly harp," said an ensign. "We ought to get some results with an orchestra."

So we immediately checked upon our prospective musicians. There were three guitar players and two fiddlers.

The mess-lieutenant was an excellent musician, and he volunteered to take charge of the rehearsals and lead the orchestra.

"Very well," we said, "we'll appoint you leader, but you must promise to keep away from the girls—you're a married man."

We dug into our pockets and somehow raised twelve roubles. Out of this we bought two second-hand guitars, two violins and a mandolin with a broken neck. Within two days we fixed the broken neck and also repaired the battered guitars, so that they could proceed with the rehearsals. After three days of hard labor, the guitar players had no fingernails, but the orchestra pronounced itself ready to perform.

Alexandra Yefimowna got an extra-large supply of pastry and was told to give word to the girls to come earlier that evening; there would be a surprise for them. When dusk came, we brought the benches to the yard and the orchestra struck up. Alexandra had sent Babushka on an errand, and the girls sat behind the half-opened door and listened. When the orchestra stopped playing they applauded and asked for an encore. The orchestra had served its purpose and it was to remain a permanent institution.

A few days later the girls sent word through Alexandra that they would have a surprise for us, in the evening. So we gathered in the yard. Again they sat in their dark cabin, behind the half-closed door. Then they sang, to the accompaniment of their balalaikas.

Choral singing seems to be an inborn gift to all Russians. They sang softly, with clear girlish voices, those beautifully melodious folk songs of which we did not understand a word—of which one need not understand a word. A wonderfully large moon hung in the Heaven and the stars sparkled like gems in the chilly September night. Around us loomed, silvery black, the curiously slanting gabled roofs with slender chimneys, looking so unreal in the moonshine. We could follow those soft melodies to the dark waters of the Volga, to the windy steppes and to the sunlit fields on the river Don. We crossed our fingers below our knees and gazed up at the stars—those very stars we had used as directions on dark nights in the field.

Then we looked to them to show us the way, not to get lost—now we gazed up to them to get lost—lost for a while at least. For they could make one forget the present.

So, now that the contact was established, we kept the half-weekly concerts up. Other girls moved into the neighboring house, beside Alexandra's, and, as there was a high fence between our yard and their garden, they put up stepladders and climbed to the top while the music played.

Sometimes the guard used to protest against their presence, but for such emergencies we always had a few kopecks at hand. In this way, we already knew many girls by sight, but it was still impossible to exchange a word with the Princesses across the moat. True enough they did not cast their eyes down so conscientiously as before, but they never dared to stop.

Sometimes we would ask in a whisper if they liked the concert, and then they nodded, smiling. So—here were the girls now, and it was worse than before! How could we talk to them, just once? We made a hundred plans, but none was practical; they were dropped without a trial.

Then suddenly I got an idea. I had a lady's ring, made in the field, out of the aluminum nose cap of a Russian shrapnel. We picked up dozens of those nose caps and those which were not too much deformed by explosion we filed into rings. With infinite patience we even applied copper ornaments made of copper from the shells.

So I retired to a silent corner of the yard and, with the help of the dictionary, I composed a letter to Olga, the prettiest of the three Princesses, offering her my "shrapnel ring" with my most devout compliments. It was no easy matter to write a letter in Russian—it took a forenoon. I had to print each type, for I had not yet mastered those complicated italics. Then I enclosed the ring and, under a pretty seal, gave it to Alexandra to slip to Olga.

Alexandra was scared; the thought of the consequences, of three thousand roubles or three months in jail, made her shudder. And she certainly had no three thousand roubles. It took some time to brace her up, but finally she consented to take the letter.

Next day I got the answer in the same way. It took me another half day to look up all those unknown words in the dictionary. Then I wrote her again and she answered promptly. After a few days, when the correspondence with Olga was an established matter, I enclosed a letter from another lieutenant, to be given to her friend Tania. Sure enough, Tama lost no time in sending her answer. Very soon Olga was asked again to slip a letter to Masha, from an ensign.

Alexandra grew stout on our pastry, but she delivered our mail and brought the answers with a laudable regularity. Gradually the writings became cordial, then sentimental and finally, of course, regular love letters. And now it was time to ask for a rendezvous.

It took three letters to break down their resistance, and the dictionaries began more to look like artichokes than books. The rendezvous was fixed for eleven o'clock that night, at the far end of the yard, where the low steam-bath hut stood, half sunk in the ground. The high fence lowered here to a height of about eight feet, and there was also a very narrow space between the fence and the wall of the bath hut. We could squeeze in here and wait for them; nobody would see us.

They told Babushka they were going to a dance and would not return before midnight. So they had a chance to evade her, walk through the yard to the street and from there enter the neighboring house, where they could wait with their friends until the hour had come. Then they would sneak along on the other side of the fence in the garden until they reached the spot where we were squeezed in—and there we could whisper for a while.

At nine o'clock the "Starshy" counted us and at ten blew out the lamp. He posted the night guard on the small bench outside the entrance to the yard and then retired on top of the oven.

We lay low until a few minutes before eleven, and then all three of us sneaked out carefully. Our blankets were carefully stuffed with shoes and clothes to resemble human figures, so that, if a night control came from the barracks, everything would be found as it should be.

There are no door locks or keys in Russia. Doors are padded on the inside with a heavy felt, which is turned around the edges to keep the cold out. This keeps the doors tightly closed, without locks, and makes them noiseless, too. To make sure, we greased the hinges thoroughly.

As the wooden stairs creaked under each step, we had to avoid them, and so slid down the railing.

The yard was empty. Pressing close to the fence we reached the bath hut and squeezed in. The great clock on the marketplace struck eleven. Half an hour later we heard fleeting steps and, through the splits in the fence, we saw three shadows approaching. We rapped gently.

They stopped and came to the fence.

For ten minutes we squeezed our fingers through the fissures to touch their hands and they poked their fingers through, so that their tips could be kissed. There were delighted low giggles, and everybody had a good time. We burst forth with our accumulated Russian knowledge, and they seemed to get immense fun out of the maze of mispronounced and unintelligible words with which we were eager to express our love. After ten minutes they went and promised to meet us there again. We were numb with cold, but too happy to notice it.

We met another time at the fence, but it was evident that it was much too cold outside.

At the end of their garden, among the bare fruit trees, stood a low hut, where they stored the fruit; and, embedded in a fireplace, stood a large cauldron. Here, if they arranged for a rendezvous for the evening, they would make a fire in the afternoon and the brick hearth would keep the hut warm enough throughout the night. There we sat for hours, just holding hands, whispering and snuggling up close to each other. Through the slits of the grating flickered a mellow reddish gleam, coloring their raptured faces, vibrating on their golden hair. Now and then the embers rustled with a faint swishing breath, as they crumbled.

By this time the whole high school was in a turmoil.

Correspondence had spread rapidly, and there was no pretty girl in the upper grades who did not have a secret beau among the captive officers.

The game was dangerous but thrilling. The directress of the high school could not help noticing that her pupils had changed. They grew inattentive and got bad marks.

Her best pupils were lovesick, and some drastic remedy had to be found to cure them.

Of course no public scandal could be made, for there were too many girls involved, daughters of highly respectable families—among others, the daughter of the chief-of-police. They could not well lock up this little lady for three months.

The boy students, who had taken the only places in their hearts before our arrival, were our most deadly enemies, and gave us dirty looks whenever they had a chance to do so.

The Colonel got anonymous letters denouncing us, and finally the directress went up to the barracks and demanded that immediate action be taken.

One morning all the officer-groups were ordered to the barracks. For an hour we stood waiting for the Colonel, in a biting wind that went through everything. When he finally appeared, he was in a murderous mood. He did not say much, but what he said was very unpleasant.

There were certain complaints against us; what they were he thought it wise not to specify. Therefore, our billets would be abolished, and we were ordered to move into one of the wooden buildings that formed a part of the barracks.

Our major and several of the captains were ordered to inspect the allotted barrack and divide the space among us as they saw fit. There was great consternation, and while the Major's group went to inspect the barrack, we stood there perplexed.

They returned after a short while, and the Major asked us to form a circle around him. He said that the barrack would not hold more than eighty men at most; it would be impossible to put two hundred officers there. Furthermore, it was filthy beyond description, teeming with vermin, and in the basement there was a bakery working day and night, which made a regular Turkish bath out of the barrack. It was no place to house human beings, and certainly no place for officers.

So the Major told the Colonel that all of us had resolved to protest against it, and we would refuse to move in, unless we were moved by force. Whereupon the Colonel gave us ten minutes to think it over; after that he would call out the guards and we would take the consequences. We held a hurried conference and, before the time was up, the Major asked for permission to see the Colonel in his office. He returned after a short while.

"Gentlemen!" said he, "I have settled the matter this time, and we may return to our billets. But I want to warn everybody—and that goes especially for the younger set—that if I catch anybody hereafter fooling around with girls I'll have him court-martialed as soon as we return to our country. You are not to forget that you are Austro-Hungarian officers, and I expect that each one of you will know how to keep up the prestige of our army and not degrade himself by associating with Russian women. The commanders of each group will now collect one rouble from each of you and then hand it to me. I thank you."

The roubles were collected—two hundred altogether—and the Major handed them over to the Colonel. Together with the money went a petition appealing to the chivalrous spirit of the Russians, asking them to reconsider their plan to put us into unsanitary barracks. In recognition of our heroic adversaries, we would ask to be permitted to contribute two hundred roubles to the Russian Red Cross.

The Colonel took the money from our major, counted it and, with a forgiving smile, slipped it into his pocket.

He thanked us in the name of the Red Cross and said that the Major would receive the receipt within a week. Then we were dismissed, and each group went back to its billets.

For some days we lay low, trying very hard to keep up the prestige of our army by not seeing our loves. We tried and failed miserably. A veritable flood of letters came, asking what the trouble was, letters written by those "degrading" Russian girls, with rosy cheeks, soft lips and fragrant blond hair. It was hard to tell them that the wiry little major with the limping walk thought that they were degrading—it was so hard that we could not manage to do it. It was true that we were gambling with the prestige of our army, but it was equally true that they were gambling with three thousand roubles or three months in jail. And so, for a further six weeks, the secret correspondence and the clandestine meetings continued.

Then an order came from the corps-command in Kazan, that all the captive officers were to be transported immediately to the great concentration camp at Syzran, to be pushed off from there to Siberia. And the receipt of the Red Cross never came.

We were loaded on peasant carts and transported in this way for days,untilwe reached the Volga, where the carts were left behind and we were ferried across the river in small rowboats. Huge ice floes drifted, grinding and crushing, and ferrymen stood on the bow of each boat, with long boat-hooks, shoving the most menacing floes away and pulling the boat swiftly into open channels between the floes, which kept on opening and closing all the time. Sometimes the frail little craft got caught between the icy sides of two milling floes and then it creaked so menacingly that we grabbed the gunwales, gasping. I never thought it could be done, and we got out with a sigh of relief on the other bank, to await the arrival of the steamer which was to take us to Syzran.

There were about twelve hundred officers at the large barracks when we arrived at Syzran, and the Russian commander was more than displeased with our arrival.

He assigned a barrack, a huge log building, with two rows of shelves, placed on top of each other, on which to sleep. We asked for some straw, which he declined, with the remark that his barracks were no stables. Furthermore he said that the bunks were not made out of hardwood, but out of ordinary whitewood and we might rest on them easily if we avoided the knots.

Anyhow, we were to remain here for a few days only. After a week, we wished we were horses and had some good straw to sleep on. Whitewood might be very practical for lots of things, but certainly not for mattresses.

This was a regular prison camp with hard bunks, bad food and no moonshine and girls. Those officer-groups that were here permanently lay on iron cots and were furnished as well as they could with homemade furniture.

There was a large group of German officers in a barrack all to themselves, which they kept immaculately clean and orderly. They were under command of one of their majors who kept a rigid discipline, and they were regarded as a model group by the Russians.

Separated, in another building, were the Slavish officers of our army, among whom the Russians were recruiting fervently and with good results.

They were regarded as allies already. The nucleus of the Czech Legions was formed here—those legions that afterward fought so bitterly against us.

At that time we regarded them as traitors, whom we usually simply ignored, but sometimes it came to violent scenes and riotous fights, which were then quickly quelled by the Russians, and the non-Slavs went to jail. Our relations with the Germans were not exactly cordial, but good enough. They thought themselves superior to us, just as to any other nation of the world. They tried not to show it too much, but were not very good at concealing their feelings. However, they invited us sometimes to their barrack to evening concerts and entertainments and were in turn invited to our barrack to play roulette.

Things were done on a large scale in this camp. Backed by some unknown capitalists, who furnished the accessories, a roulette bank was set up each night in our barrack by an ensign, who also acted as chief croupier.

Of course, gambling was strictly forbidden by the Russians, so the roulette bank had its own guard, in the very person of the guard commander, who received five roubles for each evening that there was no interruption in the game. This was a trivial outlay for the bank, which made hundreds of roubles each night.

The ensign himself did not live in the barracks, but had a luxurious apartment somewhere in the city, and the most beautiful mistress in the town. His henchmen set up the table in the aisle between the bunks, covered it with the linoleum roulette board, placed the roulette wheel in the center, posted the guards and then waited for his appearance.

When everything was set, he appeared, immaculately dressed, in high patent leather boots. He gave out the chips, twirled the wheel and threw in the ball. As there were no lights in the barrack, we had to supply our own illumination; and there were dozens of candles of various lengths stuck on the table, flickering and smoking, spreading large pools of molten stearine on the board.

There were hundreds milling around the table, those too poor to play just standing there to watch the others lose their money.

Dense crowds sat on the cross beams of the roof support and also on the upper row of bunks, craning their necks; and serious-faced German professors sat with legs folded under, making careful notes of the winning numbers, trying to figure out schemes which could be used with advantage.

The air was thick with tobacco smoke and the smoke of candles. There was a tropical heat from overcrowding and the excited faces were glistening with perspiration.

Often the game would go on for five or six hours. Candles burned down and were replaced by others. Sometimes pools were formed to break up the bank, and when they succeeded a triumphant howl went up. However, it was always the bank that won in the long run. After a winning pool had split up its winnings, it soon trickled back again.

Otherwise life was pretty drab in this camp. We were allowed to walk in the wide yard as long as it was light, but there was little pleasure in this. It was too cold to spend much time outside, and what we saw was an overcast, leaden sky above our heads, and a tall wire fence all around us. For hours and hours we lay on our bunks in the dark barrack, gazing at the slanting beams which supported the roof, and at the heavy rafters, from which the air current whiffed up small puffs of dust. It was dark after four o'clock, and candles cost money.

Now and then, those who were lying on the lower bunks would protest that those above were spilling dust into their eyes, through the fissures among the boards.

Some kept up a steady whistling from early in the morning until late at night, quite automatically, always the same tunes. Others sat with crossed legs, holding their knees and rocking their bodies absentmindedly, with a vacant look in their eyes.

Each day we waited for the order to be transported to Siberia. As often as we asked the guards when we would be taken away from here, they gave the stereotyped answer: Tomorrow!

We would have preferred any place to this. The information we had about the large Siberian prison camps was not unfavorable. There each prisoner had plenty of space, a reasonable amount of liberty, and was unmolested. The dreaded cold of Siberia was not worse than in the other northern parts of Russia.

One day after another passed, and nothing happened. Then, at the end of the third week, the long-awaited order came. But we were not sent to Siberia—there was no place there for us. Each group was sent back to the camp from which it had originally been sent to Syzran, three weeks ago.

Once more we were hauled on peasant carts back to the Colonel who had failed to produce the Red Cross receipt. He was rather annoyed to see us come back. His pet barrack, with the bakery in the basement, which he had held in readiness for our arrival, was not there. It had burned one night—all that remained was a heap of ashes and some charred beams leaning against the chimney.

Very much against his wish he had to put us back into our old billets. However, he asserted that if there was just one complaint forthcoming against us in the future, we would not go to the barracks—but straight to the jail. Things were not now as they had been before. While we had been away, the girls had moved from the log cabin to some other quarters, and letters came irregularly. It became more difficult with each day and finally we were not allowed to speak even to Alexandra.

Meeting the girls was out of the question. There was a checkup every few hours, and we were counted by the heads now, and not any longer by the bulging blankets, which in the past we could stuff with anything. It was worse than ever. A feeling of impotence crept over our minds and made us feel like caged wild animals.

Christmas came and we were not allowed to have even a small Christmas tree. It made us rebellious, but that did not help. Then three months after our return, we were packed on sleighs and ordered to a camp, in another state, bordering the Government of Kazan. We were rather satisfied with this decision. The journey was to last for ten or twelve days at least, and the prospect of traveling so long in this primitive way came as a welcome change to our dreary existence of the past months.

It was mid-winter, being the month of February, and it was extremely cold, sometimes as much as 40° F. below zero, and deep snow lay everywhere.

Peasant sleighs were ordered to the barracks, and the moujiks swore all they could. Each driver was paid three kopecks for each werst with a loaded sleigh, and that meant that he did not receive a red farthing for all the way back. In other words, he had to furnish a sleigh, a horse and himself, to drive for a full day for the staggering amount of forty or fifty kopecks, and then turn around and drive all the way home for nothing.

Two prisoners were seated in each sleigh. In addition to all their guards and orderlies, everything they possessed had to be placed there. The driver perched on the high bow in front. We sat on our bundles and buried our feet in the hay to keep them from freezing. It was rather crowded with all those guards, orderlies and sacks. We drove all day, and when it grew dark we stopped in the marketplace of a village. It was a fairly large village, where we were to spend the night.

No guards molested us here, though in this instance their presence would have been welcome. The drivers unloaded our packs, and we were left there to find such quarters as we could. We formed small groups of four and five and asked in several houses to be sheltered for the night, saying that we would pay for it.

We were not admitted to the first house, but the second moujik took us in. He brought us a samovar, some milk and fresh eggs, spread some straw on the floor and behaved as a good host. In the morning our group paid him two roubles for all he had given us, and he was well pleased. As soon as our transport commander produced enough new sleighs for the next lap, we started the day's journey.

There was no trace of a road anywhere. Everything lay under a thick blanket of snow and in many places the wind had piled up snowdrifts nearly touching the telegraph wires. The snow had set and had become as hard as ice. In most places the stubby little ponies did not have any difficulty moving the heavily loaded sleighs. On open stretches, the wind-blown, sharp, white snow crests looked like a frozen ocean. Here and there—especially among forests, where there was no wind—the sleighs cut deep tracks in the snow, and for long stretches we drove amidst snow walls that rose on both sides of us and hid the sleighs completely.

In the evenings it was always much the same. As a rule, we stopped at large villages, where it would be possible to get enough sleighs for the next day. We got our samovar and straw, sat around the huge baking ovens they had in each hut, and enjoyed the warmth after freezing all day long. The moujik host would sit with us, smoke and drink innumerable glasses of weak tea and ask a thousand questions about how things were in our own far away country.

And never did they fail to ask when the war would end. They were a kindly lot, these bearish looking, sluggish moujiks, peaceable as lambs. Sometimes they asked us to write a card to their captured sons in our prison camps, saying that they hoped they were in good health and would return soon. There were cottages where they even gave us heavy, coarse woolen socks, that we might not freeze. In the morning we always left with the hearty handshakes of the whole family, wishing us God's blessing for the day's journey.

On the fourth day we crossed the Volga. If the driver had not said so, we never would have known. There was no difference whatever between the fields and the frozen river. The snow completely hid the ice floes and made a smooth surface, which inclined gently on the banks. The driving became a greater strain every day, and we came into open country where there were no obstacles to the wind. True enough, it had been cold all the way, so far, and we had climbed very stiff every evening from the sleighs, but as long as we were not fully exposed to the icy fury of the winter storms, the cold could be endured.

Now the wind came howling, driving great clouds of snow, and we could not stand more than a few hours each day of this ordeal. The wind brought tears to our eyes. These froze there promptly and glued the eyelashes together. Piercing tiny ice crystals stung the eyelids and the hot breath froze to our cheeks. Our mufflers were stiff with frozen breath and, with our heavy mittens, we had to rub our faces and noses constantly to keep up the circulation.

We had none of those greasy but warm sheepskin coats of which each driver wore two, one on top of the other, with a tremendously heavy felt windbreaker above both. They wore finger-thick heavy felt boots, reaching up to their thighs and, thus dressed, they did not seem to mind those arctic blasts.

The shaggy little horses, furry like brown bears, were covered by a hoary coat of white frost. They kept on plugging bravely against the furious wind, releasing large puffs of steam from their nostrils. They seemed diabolic, these sturdy little beasts, with broad chests working like bellows, with their thick short feet stamping the snow in an untiring fashion.

They were never kept in closed stables, no matter how cold it was. They remained outside, under some flimsy open shed, with some kind of a roof above them, and fed with all the oats they wanted to have. No other kind of horse could endure this strain.

There were some extremely bad days, when our caravan did not make more than ten or twelve wersts. We would arrive at a village, more dead than alive, our fingers frozen stiff, our legs lifeless, and then some kind moujik would help us to unbutton our coats and give us a drink of hot tea.

Everything changed, however, when on the last lap of our journey we came to Tartar villages. These were hostile to our Russian guards, and despised us still more. In many places they blocked the doors, and said that they would not permit infidel "Giaours" to enter their house. When the guards finally talked with their rifle butts, they became more reasonable. However, we were told to take off our boots and walk in our stockings.

After paying, in advance, three times as much as in the Russian villages, they were willing to give us some tea and an evil-smelling soup made out of tallowy mutton. For straw they charged us extra, and we were always glad to relieve them of our presence in the morning. On the eleventh day of our journey we arrived at our place of destination, a small district town of about six thousand souls, half of them Tartars.

We were delivered to the command, searched again and then billeted in the customary fashion.

Chapter VII

There were other groups of officers here already and we were divided among them. They were not charmed by our appearance; it meant more crowding for them; nor were we too happy to be required to live together with strange groups, where evidently we were not welcome.

Five billets were in this miserable little place. A large part of our transport had branched off on the last day and had been taken to another camp. The billets were very poor, much worse than those we had had before. There were about thirty officers where I was to live, mostly very young boys, scarcely past the school age, and there was a nerve-wracking racket all day long. The building was a low ground floor affair, built of logs; it had a small room and a larger room and a kitchen. Two rows of double bunks stood along the walls.

Bunks, tables and benches were of the homemade kind, all very crude, slipshod and shaky. There were some heavy logs, sawed to the height of chairs, for which purpose they served.

The fissures between the logs were stuffed with hemp and moss, and once, very long ago, the walls had been papered. Now the paper hung in dirty strips and, where it still clung to the logs, it formed huge blisters. Logs, blisters and the hanging strips were whitewashed with a thick, pasty lime that was gray with smoke and dirt. Every window was cracked and the cracks pasted with strips of paste.

Here we were guarded very strictly. Day and night an armed guard sat in the large room, near the entrance, never leaving the room. At night a small oil lantern flickered at his feet, with which the inspecting night watch from the command could count us.

Once a week, all the bunks were taken to the yard. Kerosene was poured into the cracks and joints and, while we stood by with buckets, they were set afire. Thus we tried to exterminate the bedbugs in Russian fashion. After a while, when the woodwork started to smoke and catch fire, we dashed on water, which froze instantly. In this way we managed to kill off several thousands of our nightly tormentors.

It is easy to imagine how the bunks looked after several treatments with kerosene. They were charred and smoky, and had to be scraped with pieces of glass every time.

And of course we did not get to the source of the trouble by merely burning out the cracks. Vermin was by uncounted millions in the hemp-stuffed fissures of the logs, between the boards of the ceiling and behind the blisters of the whitewashed wallpaper.

As soon as the lights were blown out, they attacked us from all sides; we could hear them swarming behind the wallpaper, and we could feel them dropping themselves on our bodies from the ceiling. Here and there a candle was lit for the hunt, matches flashed up and, somewhere, somebody always swore subdued curses with gnashing teeth. Bunks creaked and squeaked from the violent movements of the tormented writhing bodies, and the occupants of the lower tiers of bunks protested being disturbed by the upper row. Down there it was too cold for bugs to dine comfortably; they preferred the upper regions, near the low ceiling, where the heat accumulated to such an extent that it was impossible to cover ourselves.

No human nerve can stand this longer than a few weeks. It was impossible to sleep at night, and it was also equally impossible to snatch a few hours of sleep by day, for the lucky occupants of the lower tiers were a very lively bunch after a fairly comfortable rest at night.

There were incurable morons who whistled from morning until night, and there were singers, howling at the top of their voices.

Some would drum on the tables, others would sit on their bunks and clatter untiringly by knocking the inner sides of their hobnailed boots against each other. Then there were table-leg-kickers, and bunk-post-kickers, tinbox-throwers and loud-yawning champions who would yawn with a snarl, like a lion.

Some would imitate the bark of a dog—lap dogs or big hounds equally well—and some would crow and some would grunt. From morning until night it was like a mad-house.

True enough, there were a few serious-minded young men who did not participate in this infernal din, boys who tried to study by putting their thumbs into their ears, but it was rather a hopeless enterprise.

This captivity was getting on the nerves. There was no theme that had not long ago been exhausted. One got tired of always seeing the same faces, hearing the same voices all day long, knowing exactly beforehand when and what the other fellow would do.

It was a sure bet that the lieutenant, living in the lower bunk below me, would arise in the morning always with exactly the same yawn, would crackle his toes before pulling his red socks over them and then poke a finger into his right ear, shaking his wrist with such vehemence that both bunks shook. Not once in sixteen months did it occur to him to try the performance on his totally neglected left ear, and the only welcome change was that, when his red socks finally wore out, he covered his crackling toes with green ones. After that he stuck to green as long as we were together.

There was an ensign who crossed his arms over his chest every morning and scratched with his right hand his left ribs and with the left hand the right ribs. This was as sure as the sunrise. There was another ensign who would never stand before the window without rocking to and fro, and a third one who banged with his fist on the lid of his tin tobacco-box as often as he closed it, which was quite unnecessary, as the lid was worn out and would have closed by simply dropping it. I knew exactly where a perfectly strange man's dresser stood at home, and it would have been easy for me to find his collars in the dark.

This was worse than a regular prison, because there was no privacy at all. Everybody was high-strung, annoyed by the constant presence of somebody else. There were instances where true friendship sprang up between two, of the same disposition and of similar temperament. This occurred mostly between the more dignified and settled types, who tried to live peaceably together by avoiding too many silly questions and, mainly, talking only when both felt the urge to talk. There were even small groups of three or four who formed small congenial units which held pretty well together.

But the longer the captivity lasted, the harder it was to get along with others. Friends quarreled over insignificant trivialities, and groups started to hate other groups with such fierceness that sometimes strong measures had to be applied.

Discipline was dwindling with each day. Individuals became apathetic to threatened court-martials that were promised on their return after the war. There were insubordinations and even open defiances. In the end, the only thing these hastily drilled youngsters would respect was brutal force.

Months dragged on—months that seemed like years. We felt miserable, as not belonging to anywhere, not even to this world.

We were isolated hermetically from the outside world. The uncertainty of what was happening on the fronts was nerve-wracking. We had not seen newspapers for months. Postcards from home traveled two or three months before they had passed all the censors and, when they reached us, all the news that might have been of interest was struck out by some pasty black liquid that covered the underlying script completely.

Each morning we were escorted for an hour's walk. That was the only recreation we ever had. We crossed the large marketplace, which led to the outskirts of the city, and circled it once. If the wind was not too violent, and no fresh snow obstructed the dug-out roads, it could be made in an hour exactly.

An hour in that intensive cold was quite sufficient. Everything was frozen bone hard. Peasants brought milk to the market in rough flour sacks, frozen into solid opaque cubes; there was no need to bother with bottles or containers. Bread froze to the hardness of stone, and had to be kept for hours on a warm spot before it could be sliced.

Slaughtered hogs froze to such rigidity that they would stand before the butcher sheds on their own lifeless stiff legs, and baskets were piled on their backs and moujiks would sit on them as on benches.

Beef carcasses stood on their trimmed hind feet, six or eight reclining against one another like a ghastly row of mutilated, skinned and beheaded monsters.

There was no danger in dropping eggs; they fell to the floor with the rap of a heavy pebble.

One could not look out on the street, for the window panes were covered with an ice crust, half an inch thick. And, of course, on account of the arctic cold, there could be no proper ventilation. Here, windows were solely for the purpose of letting in light, but not fresh air. There were no such things as hinges. Frames were built in, not to be opened. Each room had a small ventilating hole, not larger than an opened book, which was permitted to be opened while we were walking and also for ten minutes before the lamps were turned off at night.

During the day the air was thick with a bluish tobacco smoke, and in the morning there was a foul smell of used up air, a sour mixture of sweat and unwashed bodies.

For it was impossible to keep clean. In that part of the world there are no bathrooms and they never heard of bathtubs.

If a Russian ever decided to bathe during the seven months of winter, he went to a steam bath. But even for that we had to have a special permit from the command. We tried it once, and were convinced that this sort of cleansing was a trifle too much for Europeans of the Occident. Sixteen of us got pneumonia, and all of us got some kind of a cold.

A true Russian steam bath is nothing like those luxurious establishments, under identical names, to be found as curiosities in all large cities of the world. The real thing is a low hut with two compartments. One compartment, the dressing room, is smaller than the other and has a bench around the wall and nails driven into the logs. The dressing room is unheated. If it is 40° F. below zero in the open, it won't be more than thirty-one below in here. As often as the door to the steam chamber is opened, a thick woolly cloud of steam rolls in, which freezes before your very eyes.

From the ceiling, as in some fantastic cavern, thousands of icicle-stalactites hang, which, in the short time they are dripping, form just as many stalagmites on the floor. There is a sporadic shower of icy rain whenever the steam puffs in, which makes one shudder. One tries to undress as fast as possible, hoping that things will be different in the steam chamber, and in fact they are.

There is an immense brick stove in here, in which logs burn. Cut into the stove is a large opening, about the size of a newspaper, and before this stands the caretaker, to be seen only very dimly. There is such a steam that one cannot see one's own outstretched hand. From time to time the caretaker picks up a bucket and dashes water over the fiery embers—exactly the amount necessary to provoke a furious outburst of steam and smoke—being very careful not to extinguish the fire completely. The live steam is so scalding hot, and the accompanying smoke is so acrid that it is impossible for anyone who is unaccustomed to eruptions of this sort to stand it longer than a few minutes.

If by some luck one is fortunate enough to find the door, one may rush out from this boiling pot into the arctic dressing room, to contract on the spot a sound, double sided pneumonia.

It is unnecessary to say that there are no sheets or towels to dry oneself, and one tries to get back wet into one's clothing before the moisture freezes on the body.

One may not sit too long in such a condition on the bench, for the wet skin freezes to the ice-sheeted board, and, by now the steam-drenched uniforms that have been hanging out here are as stiff as if made of tin.

So we had to give up bathing in the winter after trying this once.

We were not allowed either to correspond with or to visit any other officer-billet, but of course we found a way to get our letters to other groups very soon. Our orderlies went to the barracks regularly to get their bread rations, and there they met the orderlies from other groups, so it was an easy matter to communicate with each other and find out what was happening at other billets. As a matter of fact we never expected any sensational news, and we just kept up the correspondence because it was a way to kill time.

Toward the end of March we succeeded now and again in getting hold of a newspaper. There were some German civilian internes in the city who tried to help us to news whenever they could.

With one of the butchers we made an agreement whereby we promised to buy our supply from him if he was willing to slip us the papers which the internes left with him. After some hesitation he accepted the offer, and in this way we were able to get a newspaper once or twice weekly. But, even so, it was hard to read them because we were so strictly watched. However, there was a way to get around this obstacle.

As the guard always sat in the large room, it was evident that the paper would have to be read in the adjoining small room, but there was no door between the two rooms and sometimes the guard would appear quite unexpectedly to see how things were in there. Thus suitable arrangements had to be made to outwit the guard, and finally we worked out a plan that functioned accurately.

Altogether, it took twelve men to read the paper. First of all there were two or three entertainers, whose task was to stay around the guard and divert his attention by talk. Anybody who had managed to master two or three hundred words of Russian was fitted for this job, and most of us already knew much more than that. These entertainers were to tell the guard how cold it was outside and ask him whether he thought that peace would be made soon; further, whether he was married and how many children he had. If he was single, what was the reason, and what did he think of women generally?

While one was asking, the other two were to think up new questions to butt in at the right time and see to it that the conversation kept going without interruption. Of course it was against the rules that a guard should talk while on duty, but the poor devils were glad not to sit there for hours without a word.

Near to this group was the first link of the communicating relay. The second was near the entrance of the small room, and the third one was in the small room itself. If the guard happened to move, in spite of all conversation, toward the small room, the relay signaled to each other in time.

In the small room were two copyists, noting the translation, and one man with a dictionary to look up the strange words for the reader. The reader himself was seated on a lower bunk, and a fair sized shipping box served as a table on which the paper lay. The paper itself was cut into separate sheets, so that a single sheet could be handled at a time; otherwise, the crumpling and folding of the paper would have attracted the attention of the guard. Left and right, close to the reader, sat two men ready to lift the case if any emergency arose. If danger was signaled, the reader simply folded his paper once, the two case-lifters lifted the box, so that nothing should fall from its top, and the reader pushed the paper under its bottom, when it was lowered again.

After the translations had been read by our group, they were sent through the orderlies to the command, whence the other billets could fetch it through their men. The official reports of the staffs, regarding the fronts, were those which received most attention, and which were translated first. After this the editorial comments were of greatest interest, and finally the political news. Now that we had been out of the trenches for so long we again became bloodthirsty and were rather disappointed with the slow progress of the Germans at Verdun.

Bets were made on when the fort of Douaumont would fall, and when the whole fortress would be taken, on the number of prisoners to be reported in the next paper, on the amount of captured machine-guns, and on everything else.

So long as news was favorable, the spirits were better and the discipline improved. Everybody was confident that the Germans would hammer on the western front until somewhere they pounded through, and then the war would come to a speedy end. We never expected a decision on the eastern front, on account of our weakness there. The eastern front in fact slipped into secondary importance as the war dragged on. Nothing of importance had happened there since the fall of 1915, when the great Russian fortresses were taken. We followed the activities in the Caucasus, where the Turks seemed to have been victorious over the British at Kut-el-Amara, but this was an episode only. The Italian front was rather lively at that time, but we regarded any action there merely as a waste of our troops, and expected nothing, even if we achieved some good results.

It was always an event when we got our paper, it meant that there would be some subject to discuss that day.

Toward the end of April, warmer weather set in and while the sun was up the snow melted. The soft dirt roads were flooded, and the outskirts of the city, where we used to walk, became impassable. For a few weeks we were not taken out, but were permitted to walk for several hours in the yard.

General Broussiloff started his gigantic drive in Galicia, and soon the battle was raging over a front of 400 kilometers. Things looked favorable for the Russians and, after some weeks of progress, while they captured a quarter million men, it was decided to break the great news to us. One day an order came whereby we were permitted to read the two official government newspapers, the *Moscow Russkoe Slovo* and the *Petrograd Novoe Vremia*.

Things looked bad for us again; the whole eastern front was shaking under the furious assaults of the Russians.

However, they did not penetrate very far, they seemed to have squandered their vast reserves before time.

There were great stories in the papers that we wouldn't have missed for anything. It was hoped by the Entente that Roumania would side with them and support the advancing Russians, but Roumania had not decided yet. In her opinion the Central Powers were still too formidable, and for the while she remained neutral.

The Roumanian prime minister stated with a baffling frankness that Roumania would finally side with that group whose victory seemed probable. Meanwhile the Entente was courting her and the Central Powers did the same. Roumania bought horses from the Russians in Bessarabia, and then sold these promptly to the Germans, whereupon the *Russkoe Slovo* printed what it thought about them, and it was about the limit that could appear in print.

It is nearly a year now since I was captured and sometimes I feel that I cannot stand this kind of life any longer. The inactivity is dreadful. One cannot do anything without one's subconscious mind working and saying that, whatever one does, it is just to kill time. We are all nervous and irritable, quarrels occur every day, for nothing at all, and we wish that differences could only be fought out immediately on the spot and be done with.

But of course there are strict rules against that, so out of every silly little thing a large complicated affair is made. The offended party sends two representatives to his antagonist and asks for explanation, or challenges immediately. The offender also assigns his representatives, and these four get together, take the evidence and put it down into vast protocols—to be submitted after the war to the various regimental courts-of-honor.

Each week there are two or three of these affairs, sometimes even more. Affairs of honor have been made of whistling, of bunk-post-kicking, of disputes over who should wash first in the morning and even out of mixing up shirts returned from the wash.

Outside of these affairs of honor, there were a few dozen official reports against insubordination and mutiny—which meant immediate arrest and court-martial at the termination of the war. However, there were many of a rebellious and sullen nature who did not care much, and who might have had a presentiment that their cases would never be tried anyhow. These were the ones who made things especially difficult for the rest.

In many instances one could not be sure of the rank of the other fellow. Since the Russians had ordered the removal or the covering up of the insignia, there was a widespread misusage of higher ranks, especially when the Russians undid this order at a later time.

Sergeant-cadets, who were noncommissioned officers, promoted themselves to cadets by simply removing a yellow collar strip, thus being recognized by the Russians as officers and entitled to receive the salary of fifty roubles a month.

As a senior lieutenant, I had the disagreeable duty of being the commander of one of the billets. Out of some trouble, which arose in connection with the mess, it was reported to me that one of the officers was no officer at all, but merely a corporal. I had to investigate, and found to my dismay that the charge was true. In order to get this mutinous crowd in hand, I ordered that a rank list be set up, and every one of them had to declare upon his word of honor his actual rank at the time of the capture. On this occasion I revealed not less than six self-promoted gentlemen out of a total of thirty, and my action had a very calming effect as long as I held the reins there.

However, being commandant, without sufficient means to exercise power, was an ungrateful and unsympathetic job, and after several months of successive unpleasantnesses, I decided to buy the benevolence of the supervisor at the command, to have me transferred to another billet, where I would be just a plain prisoner with only my own affairs to look after.

For the price of ten roubles the change was made, and I moved to a smaller billet. There were only seventeen there; we had three rooms, and the billet was in every way better than the other. We had no double bunks here; the furnishings were somewhat cleaner and better and, most of all, there was a little less noise. Otherwise, life here was just as dreary and uneventful.

Through the Agencies of the Danish Red Cross it was possible to send a limited amount of money and parcels to the prisoners of war. Sometimes packages did arrive, but there was no great joy in receiving them. They were censored and examined so often that in one instance I received only the addressed lid of the box; even the box was censored away. Another time I received a box containing three empty sardine cans and a humorous message, tucked into a coiled lid, saying that the sardines were excellent.

As a matter of fact, not once did I receive a package that was intact, nor did the others. We complained to the command, but they merely shrugged their shoulders. Of course we could not investigate. Each package passed through our own censors at home and then was examined two or three times by the Russian authorities.

When every censor was satisfied to his heart's content, the parcel was allowed to pass through the post office of the city where the prisoners were, was opened again here and kept for more days. From here the remnants were taken to the command for a final inspection. By this time everything of any value was gone, and the examiners at the command had to put up with whatever remained.

All we could do was to write home and ask them not to send us anything, but this again was misunderstood as modesty on our part, for we could not give a written explanation of the real cause for not wanting any more packages.

However, after a while, something must have leaked out, for the senders became shrewd. Thereafter they did not send a pair of breeches all at once. They ripped the pants at the seam and sent one half at a time. If the prisoner was lucky, he received one half of his pants and, if his good luck still held, he received after some weeks the second half, sent separately. Then he could have the two shipments placed together to make a pair of breeches. But sometimes only one part arrived and the second never came, so there were quite a few in possession of one-half of a pair of breeches and one perfectly good shoe.

As soon as the weather was warm enough, we asked the command for permission to bathe in the little river near the town. It was permitted, for each group, at certain days, at certain hours, at a certain place. Two posts were driven into the ground on the shore, about a hundred yards apart. We were told to remain within this space, and the guard was to see that this rule was strictly observed. Downstream, a hundred yards farther, was another space marked with two posts. Here the undrafted males of the town could bathe if they liked. And upstream, at an equal distance, was the reserved shore for the ladies and women of the town—marked with another pair of stakes.

There were some bushes on the bank, where the women could undress. They did so, and afterward walked the thirty or forty yards to the edge of the water with nothing more on than their white skins. And they never hurried. The summer is very short and very hot. One would not believe that there could be such a tropical heat in this cold country, but nature has to provide for food in little more than three months, and the sun ripens the corn in exactly as much time.

The days are tremendously long—one really does not know what to do with them. One can read the newspapers as late as eleven in the evening without any artificial light —and the sun shines bright at two in the morning. Even from eleven to two the darkness is not night-like—it is more like dusk.

While the town sleeps, the Tartar fire-watch goes on his beat, and sounds his wooden bell while he crosses the town in all directions. The sound of that wooden bell is so intense that one can hear it from a great distance. There is a high watchtower on the marketplace, from which a second Tartar controls the moves of the fire-watch and sounds the alarm if there is danger.

It is like a miracle how fast the crops grow. Whenever we walk around the city we pass the wheat fields and are amazed to see the growth from one day to the other. It is so good to be close to nature, to walk in the sunshine amidst the ripening grain. As far as the eye can see there is a vast rippling sea of wheat, of a delicate greenish hue. There seems no end to it. And at the end there is probably another huge sea of bobbing bearded ears, northward, southward, down to the Caspian Sea, from the German border to the far eastern Wladiwostok. It is stupendous, and we feel so small, so unimportant, just forgotten, discarded, miserable prisoners of war.

Once we set out to conquer these infinite plains—one hundred and eighty million people—"On to Moscow!" There are gray weather-beaten shocks of corn everywhere on the fields, crops from last year and even years before. Nature was kind, crops were good, more than needed. The sheaves are just piled into shocks and left there; nobody bothers about granaries.

The moujik waits patiently until his wife tells him that they are eating their very last loaf of bread, then shoulders his flail, goes to the nearest shock, and threshes there and then enough to fill half a sack. If he is young and ambitious, he might even thresh enough to fill the sack completely. He shoulders his sack and then drives to one of the sluggish windmills which abound here and, while his corn is ground, he sits patiently on the stairs of the creaking mill and smokes.

Then he pays, either in kind or coin, throws his sack of flour on his cart and drives home, well satisfied that he has done the work for a month in advance. No more work for him until the last shovel of flour has been scraped from the bottom of the sack!

That "poor, miserable, suppressed" moujik is as happy as a bird, lazy as a sloth, but very content with things, just as they are and ever have been. And he certainly would not want to change with anybody in the world. The Tartars thresh on other fields. They live in a different part of the town, around the mosque, and keep to themselves. The Russians hate them, and the Tartars do not like the Russians too much either.

Since the glorious days of Djengis Khan and Tamerlane much has changed. There are still the obliterated ruins of the once great Tartar bulwarks around the town, decrepit and crumbling, like the Tartars themselves. A morbid and sickly crowd they are, hunchbacked men with cheesy faces and hollow cheeks. True to Mohammedan custom, only the women work.

The women thresh in full war paint. Young and old are painted alike; their mouths a purple-crimson, their eyebrows a heavy black and their eyelids violet. They work in the blazing sun, and the greasepaint melts like wax on their faces. Silver coins jingle in their tresses and half a dozen silver bracelets clatter on their wrists. Their cheap calico gowns flutter. They wear multicolored soft high boots with upturned, pointed toes. Everything about them is so theatrical and unreal.

In the midst of the night, a patrol came from the command. We were lined up, counted and then searched. Something quite unusual must have happened, for they were very excited, but not a word was to be gotten out of them. On the following morning, we learned that from one of the billets three cadets had escaped. In consequence we were all punished; the daily walks and bathing were stopped immediately, the heavy window shutters were put up from the outside, and we were kept in the dark and stuffy rooms for a week. There were regular dog days then, and the brain sizzled in the unventilated, foul-smelling low rooms, which were hot beyond endurance. It was impossible to keep any clothes on; the heat was maddening.

Letter writing was stopped, and our mail was destroyed.

After eight days the cadets were brought back by gendarmes and locked up in the county jail. They did not get farther than eighty wersts—and there were still eight hundred more to the Caspian Sea.

They had slept by day and marched at night. Each one of them had carried two loaves of heavy black bread, forty pounds of rice, four dozen hard boiled eggs and a pair of swimming trunks for a contemplated swim in the Caspian Sea. It must have been pretty soft for the gendarmes to overtake those fools.

There was a small military lazaret in the town. One of the wards, with four beds in it, was reserved for the captive officers.

The pharmacist and chief caretaker was a Czech, who spoke fluent Russian, one of our captive privates. Before he deserted to the Russians, he belonged to one of those Czechish regiments which went over in a body. In civilian life he was a small clerk in a Pilzen brewery and did not know more about pharmacy than you or I. However, here he was Magister Stepanek, chief pharmacist, a very influential person, with whom everybody tried to be on good terms.

The lazaret was regarded by the officers as a comfortable recreation place, for half a dozen reasons preferable to the stuffy quarters. Here one could walk for two hours with the hospital guard, or, according to the tip, even longer. The place was quiet, and the beds were better than those in the billets.

The goodwill of Magister Stepanek could be purchased at the daily rate of half a rouble, and the number of half roubles one had to spare meant just so many days in the lazaret. Of course, there were certain limits as to the length of time that could be spent in there, for there was a long waiting list; but two or three weeks could be managed.

Stepanek was making money at a furious rate, in fact, nobody knew how much. From the public hospital he received each day one full pint of undiluted pure alcohol. This was intended to be used in medicaments and also to sterilize the medical instruments. Stepanek, however, did not use this precious stuff for either purpose. He added flavors and made liquor out of it. This was his chief source of revenue. He had such distinguished customers as Colonel Chebanoff, the commander of the garrison.

Also young ladies sought his advice, on how to get rid of the consequences of fervent and careless love making—and Magister Stepanek never refused to help, if the lady was sound financially. Then, well-to-do old Tartars came to see him at regular intervals, and, after each such visit, the Magister's face beamed with joy. He was to see that their soldier sons did not recover too fast from their self-inflicted wounds.

There were young Tartar soldiers under his care whose eyes had been burned by brown streaks of acid, whose scalps were destroyed by infernal caustics so that the white skull bone was visible. Some cut gaping wounds into their arms and calves and sprinkled the dust of powdered machorka tobacco into it. They preferred blindness, amputation and a slow death to taking chances at the front. They smeared their eyes with the contagious blinding discharge of venereal patients and infected their cowardly blood.

It happened more than once that young Russian rookies, about to go to the front, asked us bashfully for advice on how to surrender—but they were never so base as to degrade themselves to such horrible self-mutilations as these Tartars.

Autumn came and the war dragged on. We were entering the third year. How many more were still to come? Roumania finally picked the probable winners and declared war on us. There was a deathlike quietness in the billets. We had some Transylvanian Magyars with us. They were heartbroken, and some of them wept hysterically. When they had no more tears, they just squatted on their bunks, frowning, grinding their teeth and clenching their fists. They muttered curses and prayed in turns.

What did they care as long as the foe stood in Galicia and Tyrol? What did the Polish Galicia and the Italian Tyrol mean to them anyhow? But this blow struck home, and it hurt them, so that they bowed with grief. Those poor wild-eyed, suffering, impotent Transylvanian prisoners. Our private soldiers were in a terrible condition. They were dying from typhoid fever, scurvy and consumption at a terrific rate. They lived crowded like cattle and one infected another. We tried to intervene in their behalf at the command, but were told to keep out and mind our own business.

The plight of our soldiers brought the officers together. Differences were ironed out for a while and there was a secret understanding among the billets. Everything we did had to be done secretly, behind the back of the command. We were not allowed to go among our soldiers, not even to help them, for the command was afraid we might incite them to an uprising. However, we secretly passed circulars to the different billets and each officer pledged himself to pay two roubles a month at least into a fund for our soldiers. There were a hundred and seventy officers, and at least five times as many common soldiers. Three hundred and forty roubles are, of course, not much, if the sum must be split up into so many parts, but that was the limit we could pay out of our salary, which was worth less each month.

Prices had doubled and trebled within the last year, and we could just manage to make the two ends meet.

Out of this money the sick men received some little help. They could buy a little bread and rarely a very little tobacco. The others smoked the dried leaves of the nettle and sunflower. We bought them discarded clothes to replace their completely tattered uniforms, also rags with which to patch their clothes, and thread and needles. It broke one's heart to look at that ragged, bearded crowd that once were soldiers. They were not human anymore and if we did not help them out of sheer pity, we would do it in order that not all of them should become revolutionists and anarchists.

If we officers were often bitter and reproachful against our government, that seemed to forget us completely, so much more were these miserable common soldiers, who were the very outcasts of the fighting and war-maddened Europe.

Winter was approaching and they had good reason to dread the coming winter. The Russian government was supposed to care for them, at least in such a manner that they did not starve or freeze.

They were kept from starvation by a meal once a day of a foul-smelling fish soup and some groats, but they did not receive any adequate clothing whatever. I saw one of the shirts the soldiers got. It was made of cheesecloth and was the length of a vest. Very probably, there were regulations in which there was a reference to the clothing of prisoners, and possibly out of the army supply stores sufficient linen had been supplied to take care of the most pressing cases. Somewhere this strong, coarse linen had been sunk and exchanged for some poor quality of cheesecloth. But even this substitute went through the hands of a dozen grafting officials, and it shrank every time it was passed on. By the time the soldiers got it, it was no shirt at all, for it was too short to be tucked into the trousers.

Each night we sit on our bunks and play solitaire. We ask the cards when peace will come and we play until a favorable answer is forced. We play solitaire for hours and hours and ask a hundred questions. I have not missed my game of solitaire for one night, and I would not do it.

There is an elderly landsturm lieutenant in one corner, diligently whittling toy furniture for his little daughter. He has worked every day for a year; his only tool is his pocket knife. He works with infinite care and with very great love. Each piece is hand carved and decorated. It can be taken apart, so that it will be easy to pack away when he returns to his little village. He is all finished with the dining room; there is a little table with chairs around it and a wee little cupboard with tiny plates and dishes—even the doors can be opened. Now he is working on the bedroom for the doll-house. The miniature bed is not much larger than a matchbox.

Sometimes the old lieutenant stops work, rubs his strained eyes and sighs. Then he is thinking of his little daughter. He hopes that he will be able to finish the bedroom—before peace is concluded.

Yes—he will have time to whittle the furniture for a whole Lilliputian hotel. By the time he gets home, his little girl won't play anymore with dollhouses.

There is another lieutenant here—in civilian life a lawyer. During his captivity, his young wife died at home. We did not see the card bearing the sad news, otherwise we would have destroyed it. Months have passed since he received this card—he is losing his mind slowly. For hours he sits on his bunk, his legs crossed under him, and the tears are streaming down his cheeks. There is a void look in his reddened, swollen eyes; his hair is tousled and his shaggy beard is soaked by his tears.

"Don't cry, Paul," we try to comfort him, very half-heartedly; for really, why shouldn't he cry?

He does not answer for quite a while, just keeps on staring before him as if nobody had spoken, and then he replies very absently-mindedly: "I'm not crying, brother. It's just those damn tears I can't stop."

Then all of a sudden he jumps from his bunk, and while racing out of the room, tears his hair with wild curses: "Oh, the damned war! the God damned curse!" We leave him alone. It is best for him. He races up and down in the yard, and then leans against the fence to stand there motionless. After a while, he picks up a small whip that he keeps hidden on one of the rafters of the woodshed and keeps on cracking the whip until he tires of it.

Lieutenant Wessely shocked his quarters by his strange doings. Among those many reports that were to end in court-martial, there was one against him. However, it was destroyed later on because he was evidently unaccountable.

He used to tie his Cross of Valor with a piece of twine around his dog's neck and thus parade with the dog. He was told several times to quit this practice, but he kept on decorating his dog with great gusto.

"You don't seem to value your decoration very highly," remarked a first lieutenant.

"Don't I?" he retorted bitterly. "Do you want to know how I got this thing? Well, I'll tell you. I managed to get a calf for the brigade-mess, when there were no calves to be had in the whole sector. His Excellency, the Brigadier, valued nothing quite as much as a good Vienna-Schnitzel. For three months before that I had tried very hard to do my duty honestly. Once I brought in with my platoons forty Russians, among them a captain. I was shot twice. D'you think they recognized my feat then? Like hell they did! You can't make a Vienna-Schnitzel out of Russians, can you?"

"Hold quiet, you silly little beast," he told the dog, while he tied the cross. "How can I tie the Vienna-Schnitzel-Cross if you fidget all the time?"

Captain Mankowsky was one of those few who enjoyed his captivity thoroughly, until much later, when he was put against a wall and shot by the Red Guards. The good captain was supply-officer in the Galician fortress Przemysl. When the fortress was starved sufficiently, it was given up to the Russians, who liberated the captain from the dungeons, where he was confined for embezzling not less than the equivalent of sixty thousand roubles. However, neither the Austrians nor the Russians could ever recover the money.

When the captain, together with a few hundred other officers, was sent back into the interior of Russia, his beautiful Polish mistress followed him on the next train, bringing all the sixty thousand roubles with her.

Here, Madame lived in splendor, in a house that adjoined one of the billets, and the captain was well cared for. The paltry fifty roubles he received as a monthly salary from the Russians was divided among the guards of his billet, the supervisor of the command and the local police force.

True enough, they deserved their tips, for they never molested him or her. Besides, Colonel Chebanoff became a great admirer of the fair lady and came rather often for a friendly chat around her samovar. To make things as convenient as possible, the captain had a small door cut into the fence that separated the two yards.

After a while, when Madame grew tired of the dull little place, she plastered her way with some banknotes to a larger city, taking her captain along. Nothing remained but the grouchy guards and the unsatisfied policemen—and of course the little private entrance in the fence. This was, however, closed for good, by nailing some boards across it.

If this captivity lasts much longer, there won't be merely half a dozen madmen amongst us—all will go crazy. Most of us are young boys in the prime of age, and natural instincts cannot be suppressed too long without serious consequences. By day, the forcibly suppressed energy vents itself in nervous bursts of furious quarrels, but the long nights are becoming intolerable tortures. One tries not to think; one tries to forget everything that reminds one of the furiously burning untamed blood in one's veins—and then one gives up in sickening despair. From the bunks in the dark come deep sighs, desperate gritting of teeth, a constant fidgeting, and low whispers.

On those endless nights we cursed the infamy of the war, which seemed kindly, by comparison, so long as it demanded blood and life only, but which now, sneaking in the dead of the night, stole our youth. There is a curly haired fat boy in the billet, always in the company of a morbid looking young cadet, with hollow cheeks and sunken eyes. Their bunks are side by side and, if they believe themselves unobserved, they hold hands. They are outcasts even here; nobody speaks to them. At the table they sit at the far end, and there is a large gap between them and the rest of us. The billet-commander tried to get rid of them by asking the command for their transfer to some other billet, but the other billets protested vigorously, asserting that they also had their own outcasts and did not want more of them. So they are tolerated. However, the billet-commander told the sunken eyed cadet that if he were caught just once more taking his white bitch dog into his bed at night, he would attend to knocking out his teeth in person.

Again the furrowed mud hardened into stony scars, and over the frozen puddles swept a powdery snow that seemed to fall ceaselessly. Now we were too low-spirited even to rejoice over the crushing of the Roumanian army. It's like swatting rats, when the lions around are still full of fight. Will this bring peace nearer? Of course not. This is just another bloody episode, costing the lives of many ten of thousands—but no decision.

But then shortly before Christmas our hope ran high. The Central Powers suddenly published their peace proposals and for several days we waited in great excitement for the developments.

Protopopoff, a favorite of the Tsar, held the reins of the government—and if he only could have his way, the war would not last much longer. For there were unmistakable signs of Russian war-weariness, and behind all the sword rattling and drum beating of the jingo press, there was a profound yearning to make an end to this inglorious venture.

Of course, it never could be admitted. The militarist party knew well enough that their power would last just as long as this butchery could be carried on successfully, and right then they knocked the bottom out of every pacific movement by setting that cowardly assassin, Prince Youssupoff, to murder Rasputin.

But the war party was not those that faced the enemy. Those were grumbling soldiers, on the defensive for the last year, who put bullets into the backs of their hated officers. The glimmering spark of the revolution already burned in their hearts. They were those who had grown tired of being driven into the German and Austrian machine-guns, without any artillery support, with only every second man carrying a rifle, and practically no ammunition. A very peaceable herd—still keeping quiet in the stiffening cold of the trenches—but ready to stampede as soon as their limbs thawed up a little. There were already too many gaping blank spaces in the censored papers, and there were too many deserters already, to suppress this fact entirely.

So we waited for a few days, while the Entente looked anxiously toward Russia. Once more, but for the very last time, the Grand Duke Nicolai-Nicolaiewich's war party could spit to its heart's content into the outstretched hands of their foes; and, disregarding the rumble under their very feet, they rejected the offer with jeers.

The Entente could sigh, relieved. There were still a few millions of muddy poilus and Tommies waiting shivering in the trenches for their hearts to be ripped out by German grenades, and there were still millions of the Kaiser's pale and underfed soldiers, who were to stop the singing bullets with their skinny breastbones. But to Hell with them, with all of them, as long as the Russian jingoes sat on their ears and were too drunk with glory to feel the tremors caused by the snorting, dirty moujik soldiers. Jusque au bout!

It is again so quiet in the quarters—one would not believe it was Christmas Day—called by some men the Fete of Love. One thousand and nine hundred and sixteen years ago Christ was born to lead Humanity on the Path of Love and Truth, but His road was deserted.

Bordered by rushing streams from the tears of Russian and German mothers, French wives and British sisters—silent sufferers of all nations—Humanity elbowed its way furiously on the skull-pebbled road to Inferno. On dragged the days, incredibly long days, weeks like months and months like eternity.

The Germans grew desperate; the road of desperation was the only road left to them. The outstretched hand clenched to a fist again. They declared the merciless submarine war, and were now fighting the whole world. All our hopes faded just as fast as they flared up. When America severed its relations with Germany, we were too downcast to grieve much more. This was our death-knell, we knew well; only it would still take long before the bitter end came. And then, we prisoners of war would be the very last ones to get home anyhow.

It was February. We still had to sit back patiently and wait nicely for the spring offensive of the Entente, in which final drive Russia was expected to be the great factor. March came, and this was generally the time for the beginning of increased activities. The Entente grew impatient on the west and seemed to lose its patience waiting for the much needed Russian help.

Then for six days we were shut in and received no papers. We tried to guess the cause. Had somebody escaped again or was it that the Russian offensive had started?

All our guards were ordered to the barracks, from which they returned in great excitement, but no word was to be gotten out of them. In the evening the supervising sergeant from the command came and gave them instructions in a low tone. By that time we were tormented by such curiosity that we raised five roubles to loosen his tongue.

While he pocketed the money, we crowded around him anxiously.

"Gentlemen," he said, "there is revolution in Petrograd; the Tsar has abdicated; we are going to have a new Tsar. You will be going home pretty soon."

We seized him in exultant joy, raised him on our shoulders and carried him around the quarters, yelling frantically.

Once more the eyes flashed and the cheeks reddened. Once more our spirits returned and the glorious feeling that we were soon to return from captivity fired us with a radiant, exciting joy.

There could be no doubt, now, that Russia would conclude a separate peace with the Central Powers, and then the rest would be easy. Before America could be ready to fight, the issue would be decided for good. Furthermore, how were the Americans to bring their troops to France, while the submarines sent one steamer after the other to the bottom?

The war was as good as won; that was evident now. Never before were we so anxious for news as now. The blank, censored spaces disappeared, and the papers could write whatever they pleased. The most reactionary publications turned pink and then red in no time.

For the time we did not feel anything of the great change that took place in the capital. Life at the billets went on exactly as before. There was a sharp drop in prices for a week or so, to be followed immediately by a much higher upward swing.

Parades passed our quarters, singing the Marseillaise, carrying red banners and placards with huge inscriptions. There were Russian parades and Tartar parades—the two never mixed. Once we saw Colonel Chebanoff in the row of the paraders with a huge red sash across his shoulder, and under it he looked very meek and dejected. Formerly, he used to visit the different billets once or twice weekly, but now he never showed up.

Orders continued to come from the barracks, but they were signed by somebody else, whom we did not know. Later we found out that it was the signature of a corporal, formerly a military clerk at the barrack office. Now he had become the head of the Soldier's Council and, together with a cobbler, now heading the Workmen's Council, was master of the town. Old Colonel Chebanoff received his orders from the big-mouthed corporal until the very day when he was told to go to the devil. Poor old Chebanoff must have been grateful to the Soldier's Council for sparing his life, especially after reading that several days before the large mutinous Syzran garrison had murdered all its officers and that out of the fourteen hundred dead in Petrograd there had been also quite a few officers.

Meanwhile the newspapers were becoming more interesting each day. The lawyer Kerensky, who used to be the leader of the extreme left wing of the imperial Duma, a known pacifist, became a member of the newly formed Provisional Government and we felt sure that now he would find ample occasion to put his pacific doctrines into practice.

Gutchkoff, the Moscow merchant, became minister of war. During the two years of war the German and Austro-Hungarian armies did a lot of damage to Russia's fighting force, but no cannons and machine-guns were ever so effective in the annihilation of Russia's army as a few orders of the Moscow merchant. The iron discipline, which it took the Romanoffs hundreds of years to build up in the army, vanished with a stroke when Gutchkoff ordered that in the future the common soldiers were not to salute their superiors, except on duty, and that a common soldier had just the same rights as any general.

Desertion was quite a serious problem even before the revolution, but now it became a menace. Six weeks after Gutchkoff's attempt to make the life of the private soldier as sweet as possible, there were about two million deserters, who not only did not care to salute, but did not care to fight any longer. Those who, for the time, were not successful in fighting their way to the overcrowded trains leaving for the hinterland went to fraternize with their foes, who now sat back comfortably in their trenches and smoked their pipes with the kindest thoughts of Gutchkoff.

Whole battalions and regiments left in a body. Spring was here and they were returning firmly resolved to till their fields at last. They did not need any rifles for that. Infantrymen sold their rifles to the moujiks, and good horses could be had from the cavalry at very reasonable prices. In the town of Minsk the artillerists sold their guns, with gun carriages, horses, harness, ammunition and everything. It was a tremendous sale; goods were plentiful and customers were eager to buy, to be in an advantageous position at the much heralded coming division of the land. Sometimes not even cash was needed for these transactions; excellent French army automobiles were bartered for a fair sized cask of vodka, and a good truck brought as much as three barrels.

Railroad trains were crowded to such an extent that often the worn out rolling stock broke down under its human load, causing a series of terrible disasters.

Ammunition trains to the front were held up, the cases were thrown out and after they were loaded to capacity with revolting soldiery the trains were turned to take them home. Railroad officials and convoys that dared to put up any resistance were killed on the spot.

On the shore of the Black Sea and in the Ukraine, already civil war flared-up on a large scale. Hordes of pillaging marauders stormed the distilleries, destroyed the spirit casks with axes and, in the true sense of the word, lapped the liquor from the cellar floors. On such occasions they were joined by the ever ready rabble of the streets, and hundreds drank themselves to death. Some drunken soldier would drop a match, and then the alcohol soaked bodies, lying unconscious in dense crowds in the spilled pools of high grade spirits, were charred by roaring flames.

Troops were burning and sacking cities and villages that lay in their way. The inhabitants were praying to God to send the German troops. An army cook was elected to a divisional command, and orderlies became regimental commanders.

In the Caucasus, deserters banded together into robber bands, in the strength of divisions, supplied with cavalry, artillery and even flying machines.

Owing to the fact that the Petrograd Soviets had declared an eight-hour working day for all, there was a tendency at the still existing parts of the front to adopt this innovation. There were field hospitals where the personnel refused to care for the sick or wounded when their eight hours were completed, and stretcher-bearers simply dropped their wounded when their time was up. Scenes which once would have been considered too fantastic and impossible even for the lowest grade of penny dreadfuls now became facts that were enacted in innumerable instances by the hooligans of the demoralized Russian army. As soon as the peaceable, ignorant moujik no longer heard the crack of the whip, he turned into a bloodthirsty animal, ready to murder anybody who dared give him orders.

Thus were things at the great centers and at the front. Anarchy spread in rapid strides over the vast country. In some parts a semblance of order could be still observed—as in Siberia and the Far East—but European Russia was aflame with the fire of Revolution.

We wondered how long this nightmare could go on before the provisional government became aware of the fact that it had no power whatever, and would decide to conclude peace, confronted by the cold fact that it had no army any longer.

But what the government did was to talk, talk and then still talk. Kerensky, the fiery pacifist, became bloodthirsty as soon as he came into power. He became drunk by his own bombasts, and doped himself with drugs to be able to talk more. He was carried off in hysterical fits and faints, while he was ruining his country by talking of carrying on the war to a victorious finish. Lawyers were always known to be especially capable of bungling perfectly good revolutions, but never did one of them surpass Kerensky.

First he just became minister of justice, which was something in his line; then he added the portfolio of the minister of foreign relations, and finally he became minister of war.

While he kept to rhetorics, his very capable enemies spoke less and acted more. Right then the Soviets of the Soldiers and Workers started to grow very uncomfortably over his head.

Until now the Germans stood back and let things happen. The breaking up of the Russian army was proceeding fairly well, without the need of spilling German blood, but matters could be speeded up considerably. Now that Kerensky swore allegiance to the Entente, and frothed to whip up hatred in the demoralized troops to carry on the war, the Germans got busy.

A railroad coach was rolled over the Swiss frontier. It was then duly sealed before it was coupled behind a German locomotive, to be sent through Sweden and Finland to Russia. It carried a group of Russian emigres, among them Lenin and Trotsky. They were the trumps to be played out against too much talk of Kerensky.

Up to this time we had been just prisoners of war, never well cared for, but at least under the protection of the Russian Government. Now there was no government and no protection whatever. Russian officers were murdered in droves, and there was no reason why the revolutionary mob should consider us anything else but the hated "bourgeois" and treat us accordingly.

True enough, there were at least as many of their prisoners in our captivity as we were here, and any transgression on us would have been met promptly by reprisals; but much did they care if there were to be any reprisals against their officers in the prison camps of the Central Powers!

However, it was made quite clear to them that reprisals would not be taken against their officers, but against a tenfold of their common soldiers. In this threat there was some kind of guarantee for the moment, but, defenseless as we were, we could not feel anything but uncomfortable.

As long as the provisional government stayed in power, we were sure that the rulings of the Geneva Convention regarding prisoners of war would be somehow observed, but the government did not impress us as being able to hold its ground successfully against the devastating activity of the Bolshevist Soviets. First we tried to joke half-heartedly over our critical situation, but this mood soon gave way to a genuine uneasiness. Judging from the facts we read in the newspapers, it was not advisable to try to escape, but I was willing to take chances rather than to live in this soul racking uncertainty of constantly growing danger, against which we felt totally powerless. And so I decided to take a fling at liberty.

Chapter VIII

Shortly after the outbreak of the revolution, the provisional government issued an order, whereby all the civilian internes were allowed to apply to the local police commissioners for passports permitting them to return to their domiciles. However, the immediate war zone was excluded.

All over Russia, the internes were under constant police supervision but otherwise were permitted to move within the town freely, without any special guards until nine o'clock at night. Once or twice a week they had to report to the police, who checked them up carefully.

The order of the provisional government caused great joy among the internes, which, however, did not last long. The government could issue orders in Petrograd, but it was an entirely different question how these orders were to be put into effect. There was no provisional government here, and the local police commissioner ran things as he saw fit. He soon discovered that there was money to be made, and he was perfectly willing to sign passports for those who wished to pay for it. Unfortunately, his price was high, and most of the internes were too poor to pay it. So for a while, very few passports were issued, and when there were none who could pay the commissioner's price, the sale of passports stopped altogether.

However, by that time the commissioner's secretary had his duplicate key to the desk where the commissioner kept his blanks and rubber stamps, and he was willing to sell passports for the considerably reduced sum of forty roubles. For that amount, he was willing to sign the commissioner's name just as beautifully as the old crook himself. But it was not an easy thing to get in touch with the police commissioner's secretary, who was a very cautious fellow and never committed the mistake of dealing with his client directly. For that purpose, he had a go-between, in the person of an interne, by the name of Lippman, a shrewd little Jew with a ferret-like face. But it was even impossible to deal with this go-between directly. Lippman was very shrewd and very timid, and did not wish to be caught with one of the captive officers, though decidedly he had a foible for roubles, and each successful intervention meant a profit of ten roubles for him.

Nevertheless, there was a way to get around all these difficulties. Before I decided to go any further I wanted to speak to Juro, an ensign of my regiment, that same Juro who was with me on that memorable night raid in the Carpathians, and who was afterwards captured together with my company. Juro by now spoke Russian fluently, and I knew him as a determined fellow whom I could trust, and who would be glad to join me wherever I went. The trouble was that Juro was in another billet, and these things were too dangerous to be taken up by written messages. However, I managed to get out on a dark night and we decided to escape together.

We were to masquerade as Bukowinan civilian internes, and we were to try to get passports to a place as near to the front as possible. For the while we decided on Odessa, but soon we had to alter our plans as, in the meanwhile, the situation on the southern front changed considerably.

General Korniloff, a very capable Russian general, took over the command there, and his reputation was such that he managed somehow to brace up his demoralized troops. His front stiffened and, as there was no pressure from the Austrian side, the Austrians at that time conducting a vigorous offensive against Italy, his front was closed, with no possibility of getting through.

Kerensky, with his last efforts, managed to get some fanatics together, willing to show the impetus of the revolutionary army. He organized Women-Battalions, Death-Battalions and Battalions of the St. George-Knights, and was massing his troops for a final attack, with which he hoped to break the Austro-Hungarian army.

Aside from this, the southern part of Russia was a place from which it was advisable to keep away. Loyal troops of Kerensky fought Bolshevist regiments in bloody battles; Cossack tribes fought with each other; robber bands trespassed on each other's territories, which resulted in further battles, and, outside of these there were still two dozen armed villages and groups in a furious mix-up. So we decided that the Ukraine was not the place for us.

Things were rather quiet in the German sectors on the northern front, and we thought to try Petrograd. From there we might try the front, if it was loose enough, or otherwise go to Finland and then through Sweden to Germany. We changed our plans accordingly. I was to get the passports and make all the preparations for the escape, and Juro was to act his part with his good Russian when we were on our way.

We had an orderly on our billet, Corporal Franz, who knew Lippman fairly well. Orderlies were not kept under such strict surveillance as we, and Franz managed to get out several times without being observed. I took Franz into my confidence, and he was willing to take the matter up through Lippman with the commissioner's secretary, who, of course, was never to know that the passports were intended for captive officers.

Franz had a civilian coat and a round flat cap, of the style that was worn commonly in Russia, and got out in the evening. He returned and reported that Lippman was quite willing to take the matter up with the police clerk. Several days passed before Franz could arrange another meeting with Lippman, and when he returned he had nothing to report. This occurred several times, and I became impatient. To conduct affairs through the mediation of two men proved too slow for me. I determined to borrow Franz's civilian outfit and to talk with the police clerk myself, so I instructed Franz to tell the interne to advise the clerk accordingly. But the clerk refused flatly, whereupon I decided to see Lippman at least.

Lippman hesitated, and it took some time before Franz could persuade him to meet me one evening. Although I did not like the idea of going out myself, on account of the risk of being caught—not wishing to expose myself to unnecessary complications prematurely —I had to do it, for it was the only way to see Lippman and I succeeded in getting out of the billet one night without anybody noticing my absence.

I waited until it grew dark enough and then sneaked behind the pigsty in the yard. While some of the officers were still pacing up and down, Franz helped me into his civilian clothes, which were there in readiness. He wore a sweater and could pass in that outfit on the unlit streets.

As soon as the yard was cleared by the guards, we left our hiding place and crossed the yard to a spot where the fence was lowest. We wiggled behind the woodshed and then worked our way carefully to the top of the fence. We paused here for a while to look around, and as nothing moved we climbed over the roof of the neighboring barn and then dropped to the ground.

We picked this particular yard for our starting point because it belonged to a Tartar, and they never kept dogs. We could not use our own gate, which was guarded constantly by day and night. After we had made sure that nobody was roused by the thud of our jumping from the roof, we walked stealthily around the yard, unbolted the gate and reached the street in safety.

Franz led the way. We crossed the marketplace, proceeding carefully among the crooked lanes of the small market booths, and reached the outskirts of the town after a hurried walk.

At one of the very last houses we stopped, and Franz went in to get Lippman. Lippman was not at home and nobody knew where to find him, but now that I had taken the risk of walking out I did not want to return without having effected my purpose, and I told Franz that I would find Lippman if it took me all night.

We started for another section of the town, where we knew internes were living, and nearly met with disaster. A small boy, who kept following us, suddenly began to yell at the top of his voice, "Austrians! Austrians!"

There were some policemen quite near who were roused by the yells and started to run in our direction. We turned, shoved the little traitor into the ditch, and started to run toward the market booths, which were a few hundred yards farther. As the streets were empty and dark, we reached the booths in safety and, after zigzagging a while in the alleys, we crept under a tarpaulin with which the barrels and baskets were covered and squatted there for a time, while the policemen kept poking around, swearing fluently. After they tired of this, we crept out from under the tarpaulin, which reeked with the smell of sauerkraut and vinegar, and continued our interrupted walk, resolving not to speak anything but Russian on such excursions.

We went to two houses where we thought to find Lippman, but he was not there. In the end we found him; he ran straight into us, while on his way home. We told him to come along and we marched out to the windmills that were not far away. This was a deserted place and we could talk things over undisturbed. In a quarter of an hour, we had agreed on the details. He was to furnish two passports, made out according to my instructions, within a week, and receive ten roubles in advance. As soon as the passports were in his hands he was to hire a Tartar driver, whom we were to meet at one of the windmills at a prearranged hour of the night, to take us to the nearest railroad station—a two days' drive if he did not spare his whip.

We shook hands and the deal was closed. Franz was commissioned to keep in touch with Lippman, and we returned to our quarters much in the same way as we left. Nobody had even noticed our absence. A sentinel stood in the gate, yawning, well satisfied that the prisoners were all safe.

The escape I was planning kept my mind busy day and night. I often imagined how it would be if I were able to carry out my plan successfully. It would be a thrilling adventure and a great satisfaction after all those unsuccessful trials of my predecessors. So far there had been several breaks for liberty, but each case had ended disastrously.

The crucial point was to proceed with the preparations so imperceptibly that no one, even of my fellow officers, would get wind of the planned flight, for I knew very well that Juro and myself were not the only ones who cherished the idea of an escape. In all the billets there were feverish preparations in various stages of progress which became a race for the first jump. It was evident that those who managed to start first would deprive all the others of the possibility of starting at all. There could be no doubt about it that, if the first team got away, all of the efforts of the others would be for naught.

The absence of the first fugitives might not be remarked for several hours—or half a day maybe—but, once the escape was discovered, the Russians would make things very hot for those who stayed behind and guard them with redoubled vigor. For that reason, we had to beat everybody to the start.

But this was not the only reason which we had to keep in mind. The Majority of those who would never plan an escape felt hostile to such plans and, even if they dared not hinder one openly, they certainly gave no assistance. This could be explained readily by the fact that so far, each venture had ended ignominiously, and in each case, the Russians had unleashed their fury on the stay behinds.

In several cases in the past, the fugitives had set childishly to the task and their performance lacked any thorough planning. For that reason, it became a habit to try to talk adventurous youngsters out of their plans and in the last resort any financial aid was refused. In most cases this refusal was more efficient than the best arguments.

I had to bear all these things in mind, and these obstacles had to be taken into consideration. Selfishness had to be met with the same selfishness on our side, for in such case one had simply to disregard the comfort of the others.

It was exceedingly difficult to get civilian clothes. There were, of course, no ready-made clothes in the town. Town folks went to the larger cities to buy clothes, and the moujiks wore nothing but homemade things.

There was a small tailor in the town where I could have ordered a suit of clothes, but it would have roused the suspicions of the tailor, for captive officers were not allowed to wear civilian clothes. Furthermore, it would have cost a lot of money, and my funds were rather limited.

However, for the time, luck was with me. Franz bought two Russian caps on the market and smuggled them into the billet in his shopping basket. They were well hidden in the garret of the woodshed. One of the lieutenants in another billet happened to have a very shabby suit of clothes, which he was willing to barter for my overcoat. After the suit was hidden in the garret, my equipment was complete. But I had great difficulties in getting the required things for my partner.

Finally, an interne of Juro's stature was willing to part with his most threadbare clothes, which were then brought in, hidden in a sack, by a civilian, whom we employed as a woodchopper.

Two weeks had passed since I had been to see Lippman, and we did not have our passports yet. Franz went out as often as he could, but frequently he gave such confusing reports that I began to doubt his reliability.

Juro was pressing, and I grew tired of the long wait myself. During the preparations we did not meet each other; it would have been unwise to take unnecessary chances, but we corresponded regularly in cipher, for ordinary messages would have been too dangerous if intercepted. We cursed Lippman for the delays but were powerless to speed up things, and each day the risk became greater that somebody would be ready to start ahead of us and thus frustrate all our hopes.

Momentarily the situation was not unfavorable for the flight. For a year nobody had ventured to escape, and the vigilance was lax enough to make me feel that, with reasonable foresight, I could manage to slip out any night through the neighboring yard, as I had done before. My partner asserted that he would succeed too, although things were more complicated with him. As he spoke Russian fluently, he conversed with the guards rather regularly, and for that reason each one of them knew him well. Therefore I advised him to keep away from the guards from now on, and not to remind them constantly of his presence. It was of no advantage to be popular.

After beginning the preparations I avoided the guards as much as possible, and they would never have missed me until the checkup. And so Juro, following my advice, stayed in the background.

This whole affair started to tell on my nerves. Here it was June, and no passports yet. Waiting with such nervous expectancy proved a little too much after two years of captivity, and it took all my energy to retain self-control.

Lippman had fooled us now for three weeks, with different promises and excuses. He had postponed the delivery of the passports from one day to the other, and had then failed again to bring them.

Once the excuse was that he had not been able to meet the police clerk, then again the police commissioner would remain so long at his desk that the clerk could not get the rubber stamp, and on a different occasion the clerk had had to leave town on a special mission for a few days. And so on and so forth. Besides, Lippman demanded further advance payments, which became imperative, for we were entirely in his power and could not well refuse.

As often as I wanted to meet him in person he declined to see me under various pretexts, and it became evident that he tried to do his best to avoid an encounter. Also, Franz was becoming more difficult with each day. Although he always went out when I sent him, he could not be trusted as before. He acted queerly, as somebody who has something to conceal. All I could do was to pay him regularly for his services, but I had no means of checking up his movements while he was out. However, I was firmly determined not to give up.

In the basement of our quarters was a small grocery store owned by a young Tartar merchant, by the name of Fedkulin. For several days he had had a visitor from Petrograd, in the person of his father, who traded in wool at the capital.

Old Fedkulin was a jovial and friendly man around whom we sat for long hours, while he related the latest happenings at Petrograd. He had come to visit his son and was to take a consignment of wool on his return trip. While we sat on the flour sacks and listened to old Fedkulin, he gave away such details as were of greatest value to me in the flight I was planning. As he spent most of his time in the grocery, it was an easy matter to be in his company. The little store had a rear entrance from our yard, and we could go there any time to buy tobacco for ourselves and our guards.

One afternoon, when most of the officers rested on their bunks after the midday meal, I entered the store hoping to find the old man there. I wanted to get some information concerning the trip to Petrograd, where we intended to go. As luck would have it, even his son was out in some neighboring village, and everything seemed to favor a private talk with old Fedkulin. I bought some tobacco from him, and then sat down to roll a cigarette. Fedkulin liked to talk, and very soon I had him talking about the conditions of which I wanted to know more.

I had to be very careful with my questions, so as not to arouse his suspicions and, although I could juggle with a few thousand Russian words already, I found it rather difficult to form sentences which he would also understand. Sometimes he would slap his knees in great mirth about my gibberish Russian, but that only improved the cordial feelings.

To gain his confidence, I told him a fantastic story—that I had been to Russia several years before the war in the employ of a British shipbuilding firm at Nijni-Novgorod on the Volga, where I used to supervise the repairs on the British built Volga steamers that plied between that city and the Caspian Sea.

I knew there were British steamers on the Volga, but of course I did not know that there were any British repair shops at Novgorod. However, to my satisfaction, he did not know it either, and thus swallowed the yarn with hook and sinker.

I told him what an enjoyable journey I had had from Novgorod to Petrograd—exactly the same route I intended to take now.

He replied that travel was not so comfortable now as it was then, and now I had him exactly where I wanted. He told me everything of the present conditions. I learned that, although the lines behind the front were in complete disorganization, the lines in the hinterland were still controlled sufficiently to make the traveling risky. In spite of the huge traffic, passports were required from the civilian passengers, which were often controlled on the way. He even blurted out how many trains there were a day to Petrograd, and remarked that very soon this number would be cut down considerably.

After I had rolled my third cigarette, and had learned when the trains departed for Petrograd, I bought some bread and assured old Fedkulin how much I enjoyed this friendly talk with such a cultured gentleman as he was. Saalem alaykum!

After five weeks of painful waiting, I wrote a note to one of my friends in another billet, telling him that I would escape in the next few days and this was to say goodbye. Lippman had sent word that he would bring the passes on a certain day for sure.

I was greatly surprised by the answer I received from my friend. He wished me all luck and asked me to notify his mother of his well-being, should I be successful and get through. Furthermore, he asserted, that he had known of my preparations for several weeks, for Lippman had a similar deal with two officers in his billet, to whom he had told everything. So I reasoned that not only his billet but all the others might be wise to my plan now.

I was furious at the treachery of Lippman, for it was he himself who always stressed the need of the greatest secrecy. I informed my partner of the way things stood and that our plan was no secret any longer. There were still three more days to wait, and the situation was becoming more critical with each hour. Between ourselves and the rival groups now ensued a frantic struggle for priority that became a mad race.

Franz went out that night again. The interne denied emphatically that he ever gave us away, and he repeated that the passports would be ready as promised. He would also see to it that the Tartar driver would be at the windmill at the prearranged hour. There was nothing else possible than to take his word; one could not well battle around with him holding all the strings as he did.

After all, it was evident that we were completely in his power, and we were dependent on his good will. The fact that he was about to furnish passports to other officers, too, complicated our case considerably, and if we fell out with him now, he could easily avenge himself by giving the preference to our rivals.

All the things I had to leave behind, I entrusted to the care of Lieutenant Andy. We were great pals, and Andy took all my things for a lump sum. When I was gone, he was to sell the things to the others, in order to reimburse himself for his outlay.

I just feel that I cannot stand much more of this lurking. I have not slept for days for I lie awake at night with my thoughts constantly on the subject. I can see well enough that by now all my fellow officers know of my plans, even if nobody asks a word. It is quite impossible to make all necessary preparations, in such close proximity with others, without being observed sooner or later. Constantly they put their heads together to consider the affair in subdued conversation; it is easy to guess what their topic may be.

The senior officer of the billet, First Lieutenant Rohmer, shoots furious glances at me. I can see by the reproachful looks that he is considering all the disagreeable consequences which will result from my escape. He, as commander of the billet, will be held responsible for my escape, and I know that he will be in a bad hole. However, this cannot be taken into consideration.

The situation became desperate. I wanted to send Franz to the interne with a letter, and he refused to go.

I was taken aback when he reported that he intended to escape himself that very night. I realized that, if I lost his help now, everything would be lost. Suddenly I found an explanation for his changed attitude, which I had noticed recently, and I could not help feeling that he had not given me a square deal.

However, I had no means to detain him. After all, he had just as much right to escape as I, or anybody else. I told him that if he escaped that night he would nullify all my efforts of the last five weeks, but that did not seem to impress him at all. Then I tried to persuade him to postpone his flight for a few days, and time it together with ours. I even asked him to join us and form a group of three. But he was firm in his resolution; he was not willing to wait for anybody, not for an hour.

I threatened him with court-martial for disobedience, but he just shrugged his shoulders, fully aware of the fact that I could not do it anyhow. I gave up in despair.

That same night he escaped.

His flight was not detected until the morning roll call and thus he got a start of seven or eight hours. However, there was a great commotion at the barracks as the report was received. A large committee came to investigate, and First Lieutenant Rohmer was taken to the barracks to be questioned. Considering that it was not an officer that got away, but only an orderly, Rohmer got off this time with a severe reprimand, and returned in the evening in a murderous mood. But the Russians resented greatly this newest break for liberty. This was the first case in a year, and they intended to put a stop to similar occurrences.

Our entire guard was relieved. We received a fresh guard of line troopers. They were Lettonians, ferocious looking cutthroats, each one of them well over six feet. We knew them by reputation well enough. They came from a Syzran regiment that was one of the first to mutiny, murdering several of their officers and chasing the rest to the devil. It was not very reassuring to be entrusted to their care. Immediately they undertook a thorough search, but by this time we knew where to hide our things, and nothing was found outside of a few books, which were promptly burned.

We were not allowed to go to the market, and were not led for walks either. We were checked up every two hours, and the nightly inspections were resumed regularly. After a few days, while the wires were humming in all directions to effect the capture of the escaped prisoner, things quieted down a little. Our Lettonian guards were morose fellows, who kept to themselves and showed no inclination to talk much, but soon we found out that they felt the same veneration for the bluish-green banknotes as their Russian predecessors. It became once more possible to pay for the price of a walk or even to buy a refreshing bath in the river.

I kept up my correspondence with Juro, though we had not much to say to each other since our situation had become hopeless.

Franz was captured a few days later and, after he had been beaten up thoroughly by the infuriated militiamen, he was locked up in some kind of a prison not far away. The knowledge of this and, furthermore, that the Russians threatened very strong measures in the future, had a very soothing effect on the other plotters, and most of them dropped their plans for good.

Although our situation had changed considerably for the worse, I did not see the future so black as immediately after the escape of Franz. Even if we were guarded more strictly now, than before, I was confident that I could sneak away when it grew dark enough.

True enough, I could not possibly figure on such a start as I would have had before, but in the worst case even a few hours would be better than none at all. Possibly, it would take us a day longer to reach the railroad, for it was evident that now we had to avoid the shortest route through the numerous villages and make a big detour to be seen as little as possible.

The main thing was to find a suitable man who would resume the broken off relations with Lippman. Then, quite unexpectedly, Juro found out that their cook, Rudolf, knew the interne. This was helpful, for now Juro could direct the operations much in the same way from his billet as I used to do with the help of Franz.

I gave him detailed instructions, and he put Rudolf to work. As Juro's billet had a good reputation among the Russians, and was even regarded as a model quarter, Rudolf found no difficulty in going on his nocturnal errands. The first news he brought was not favorable.

Lippman had been scared by the unexpected escape of Franz and had become still more timid. He was not very enthusiastic about resuming the intervention and, to persuade him, it cost more money.

Once more he promised the passports for a certain day and once more he failed to deliver them. Rudolf found it increasingly difficult to get hold of him; he was slippery as an eel and evaded our man as often as he could. There remained nothing else than to go out myself to speed things up. So I sent word to Lippman, but he did not want anything of that kind. Then—as a last resort—I took to a desperate measure. Through Rudolf I sent him a letter in which I threatened to denounce him anonymously to the police commissioner if he did not deliver those overdue passports. It was a bluff, but Rudolf said that it did not fail to work, and he was of the opinion that there would be results now. However, Lippman swore never to have any business in the future with captive officers.

Juro informed me that it would be the night after tomorrow. We were to meet about eleven at the largest of the windmills. The Tartar would be waiting there with his cart to take us to the railroad. He demanded a rouble for each werst, which was exactly thirty-three times the official rate, but we had to pay without demur —half of it in advance.

Rudolf gave the money to Lippman, who promised the passports for the following evening.

Well—tonight at last! I am feverish with excitement and I am counting the hours. Rudolf will come in the evening, as soon as it is dark enough, and bring my passport. The driver has promised to be at the windmill a little before eleven and everything is set.

In the morning I decided to make a few pounds of hardtack by cutting up black bread into small bits and baking them in the oven. At noon an orderly gave me a little note of Juro's which said that he was ready and, when we received the passports that evening, we should wait until everybody had retired and the first checkup in the bunks had been made.

Toward three in the afternoon our Lettonian guards quit for good— walked out and left us unguarded until five o'clock. Things were getting very lively in their little northern country and, prisoners or no prisoners, they were going home to make order.

By five o'clock another guard was scraped together with great difficulty, and brought from the command to guard us. But these were not willing to sleep together with our orderlies atop the baking oven, and wanted the same accommodations as we officers had. This was a democratic country now and there was no preference to be shown to "bourgeois" officers.

We were crowded enough without the Russian guards; however, they picked out the room they liked best and settled down there. The inmates of the room were somehow pressed among the occupants of the other rooms, with the exception of two, for whom there was simply no more place to be found.

So two officers were to be transferred to some other billet, and they asked who would volunteer. But there was nobody who was willing to give up of his own accord the surroundings he had grown accustomed to through all these months. In consequence, two were to be ordered by command to another quarter, and First Lieutenant Rohmer was told to designate them immediately.

I was the first and the other was my friend Andy. Thus, a couple of hours before fulfillment, I was to be cheated out of the results of all the preparations I had made. I was boiling with rage, but was powerless. First Lieutenant Rohmer had a maliciously triumphant little smile over the corners of his mouth, and I had a good notion to knock him cold.

Together with Andy, I was to be escorted to the billet "Semenoff" the same night. It was a close race now with minutes. If I could get my passport from Rudolf while I was still in this quarter, I would beat it immediately to the windmill, and then they could take Andy to the "Semenoff" billet alone. When I told Andy about this we had to laugh. It would have been a great surprise to First Lieutenant Erich von Rohmer!

On the other hand, if they took me to the other billet before I could get my passport, then I would lose everything. It took much time to get acquainted with new surroundings and to know the ins and outs of a new quarter.

It is eight o'clock and there is no trace of Rudolf yet! Of course it is summer and days are long. Why should he come before the darkness, as was originally agreed upon?

I am waiting at the window, craning my neck in the direction from which I expect Rudolf to come. I can think of nothing else but the passports and Rudolf. After a while, I can't stand it any longer; my nerves are ready to snap. I go to the yard with Andy to pace up and down, but he has a hard time to keep up with me.

A little before nine one of the guards approaches and tells us to get ready to be escorted to the billet "Semenoff." I give him a rouble and a package of cigarettes and promise him two more roubles if he will let me stay until ten o'clock. He does not know exactly what to make of this peculiar wish, but he would like to have the two roubles.

Then we continue to pace up and down again. It is a little after nine now and an orderly comes.

"Sir, Rudolf wants to see you; he is in the kitchen."

I manage to stifle an outcry of joy, while I race towards the kitchen. My heart is up in my throat and I must be rather pale.

"Well, Rudolf," I say, "a damned close shave, but it's just in time!"

Rudolf bites on his lips. "Sir," he begins, "we won't get the passports before tomorrow morning."

At ten o'clock sharp I was led with Andy to the "Semenoff" billet. I felt utterly dejected. Andy—good fellow that he was—tried to cheer me up as well as he could.

We threw ourselves on bunks, that were if possible more miserable than all the other bunks I had encountered during my two years of captivity, and tried to be as civil with our new roommates as we could manage.

Around two in the morning we were roused by some soldiers from the command, who swore terribly while they checked up the billet. They had good reason to be furious, for three hours previously a cadet had escaped from First Lieutenant Rohmer's billet, and I had to chuckle over Erich von Rohmer's malicious little smile which he had worn so triumphantly that very afternoon.

Well, my flight was definitely off. So long as I was a novice here there was no way to get out of these quarters.

As a fact, Juro got the two passports the next morning— but what good were they now? We were guarded with the same stringency as convicts, and the Russians became very nasty. They immediately inflicted on us a strict prohibition of meat, milk and eggs, and for two weeks we were to receive no mail and send none. Again the window boards were nailed up, and we were kept in the steaming dark roomsuntilwe threatened to fire the building.

Then, however, the Women's Revolutionary Committee protested in our behalf and the boards were removed and we were allowed graciously to buy, per person, one full pound of meat monthly.

To all these inconveniences could be added that the billet "Semenoff" was in every respect the worst quarter that existed.

Juro had to give up his plans for escape too. Together we would have split the expenses, but it became prohibitive to him alone as he did not have sufficient funds.

By this time the Russians were determined to put an end to all escapes in the future. The local committee of the Workers' and Soldiers' Council met in a conference, where they discussed the ways to concentrate all the prisoners, soldiers and officers together, into one large concentration-camp.

There were several large barracks at the command, which were built during the Russo-Japanese war, barracks where Japanese prisoners had been kept. But these were in such a desolate and tumbledown condition that they could not be used without extensive repairs.

And repairs cost money. One of the barracks had been reconditioned lately, but there the pigs of the garrison were kept. This pigsty would have suited excellently, as some really suggested, but the idea had to be dropped, as no other suitable place could be found for those few hundred hogs.

So—for a while—we were to remain in the billets, as before, until some solution was found.

Then towards the end of June the miracle happened. It was a miracle and did not last long. War Minister Kerensky finally decided that the war should go on under the same slogans as under the Tsarist masters. The Entente sent him huge quantities of artillery ammunition, armored cars and also British and French officers who were to help to brace up that armed mob that was once the Russian Army.

General Korniloff, an excellent soldier, was put in charge over the southern sector of the front in Bukowina, where the last effort was to be staged.

In all fairness to Kerensky, it should be acknowledged that the bloody carnival that followed was rather well prepared and in the beginning had the semblance of a success and carried a promise of victory which, if it had, materialized, would have had an immense effect on the demoralized armies of revolutionary Russia. Kerensky did no less than talk a number of newly formed divisions into such a frenzy that once more they were willing to attack the Austro-Hungarian front—which in Kerensky's opinion was no front at all.

True enough the Hapsburg monarchy held its lines with very weak and inferior forces, and the Russians at that moment had exactly six times more troops there than we, and there stood nine hundred Russian guns against three hundred Austrian pieces. The good troops we had had there were needed to run down Roumania, and the best troops were waging a bloody battle on the Italian front.

General Korniloff applied some very drastic measures and, after a ruthless massacre of his most mutinous regiments by some specially formed officer-battalions, got the upper hand for a while.

After a furious drum fire, which wiped out the Austrian lines completely, he attacked with some crack divisions of infantry, Cossack regiments and newly formed Women Death-Battalions. It was a walkover, and the weak Austro-Hungarian forces were pushed back, taken by complete surprise. For a while the victorious troops of Korniloff scarcely met any resistance, and they advanced fast, taking one town after the other.

Revolutionary Russia gasped with the unexpected success of its troops, and a furious hatred flared up against Kerensky's most dangerous enemies, the destructive Bolshevist Soviets.

Suddenly everything looked excellent. The troops were pressing forward vigorously and, thanks to the general enthusiasm, Kerensky was able to put down the Bolshevist uprising at Petrograd with such ruthlessness that the communist leaders fled to Finland and, for the time, the Bolshevists were put out of commission.

Then, when the jubilation was at its height, the tide turned. The Austrians hurriedly gathered reserves and fought back. Korniloff's troops broke down in an annihilating rifle and gunfire. The Women-Death-Battalions died bravely, but the men were not to be talked into further action. While solitary officers advanced heroically and were picked off to the very last man, the ranks remained in the trenches to jeer at them in contempt. When the Austrians counter-attacked the Russians walked away, and General Korniloff ordered his artillery to fire on his retreating hordes. In response, the retreating infantry promptly stormed and bayonetted their own artillery, killing off the gunners without mercy.

To make things worse, the Germans threw in some crack Saxon divisions—and then the bloody show was over. The Russians escaped head over heels and when the pursuers passed their old lines and reached the boundary they called a stop there to dig in.

Russia passed out completely. It did not mean necessarily the formal end of the war, as the Germans did not bother much about it. Kerensky, like a parrot was still repeating the same catchwords as before his disastrous offensive, but he could not hurt with bombast, and he had shot his last bolt. The Central Powers now sat back and watched Russia fall to pieces.

While these things were happening, we were sweltering in our billet, watching the events. The successful battle in the Bukowina gave me new hopes that resulted in the planning of another venture.

I had to give up the thought of escaping with Juro. It became very difficult to communicate regularly with other billets, and this circumstance would have caused great delays, but there was a lieutenant here on the "Semenoff" billet, who proved to be a very good substitute for Juro.

Lieutenant Revay spoke very good Russian. Maybe he did not master it to quite the same extent as Juro, but after all we were to figure as internes who were not expected to speak Russian as the Russians did. Furthermore Revay was very crafty. There are men who might be dropped almost anywhere and in a few days they will know more about that place than those who have spent the greater part of their lives there. Revay was one of these. And so we teamed up.

It would have been comparatively easy for me to get Juro's passport for Revay but, after careful deliberation, we decided not to use Lippman's passports at all, for there were flaws in them. In view of the advance in the Bukowina, we decided to take our way there. It was also much nearer, and that fact alone favored it. Furthermore, we did not want any passports that were issued in this town. If we were captured, we had no desire to be brought back here, for we knew that we would receive a very memorable reception.

Our plan was to get the blanks here, where we knew how to get them, and when we had our blanks to escape to the next district town, where we would hide for some days. We were to fill out the blanks ourselves, and I undertook to manufacture a stamp. Those that were used were everywhere much the same; in most cases the only difference being the name of the town. Thus I could cut out the seal while we were here, leaving out the name of the city, and then finish the task by cutting the name of the place wherever we hid. In the same manner the signature of the police prefect could be inserted, after we had seen some examples of his handmark.

With things thus simplified we actually got down to work. It took me well over five weeks to get my first passport from Lippman, but Lieutenant Revay never thought of going to him.

In exactly three days he had secured two passport blanks from Magister Stepanek, the all-powerful "apothecary" of the lazaret, for which he paid ten roubles apiece. Now all there was to be done for the moment was to start the preliminaries on the seal. This, however, proved not so simple as I thought.

Never in my life before had I thought of counterfeiting, and I must admit that even now I abhorred the thought. Once, as a young schoolboy I did sign an abominably poor half-yearly school report in the name of my father, and for this I came very close to being barred from every high school of the country. This was duly followed by a sound thrashing and was such a moral lesson that I resolved never to do it again. However, this was war.

Not far from our billet was Prigunoff's little store. I would be inclined to call it a department store, were it not for its diminutive size, for the whole thing was not quite as large as a small town trolley car. Here could be found brass watch chains, fishhooks, velour bound albums and German lamp glasses, German pens, German pencils and German ink. In the third year of the war, Russia was importing just as many German goods through Sweden as in the pre-war days.

A part of Prigunoff's merchandise was constantly hidden by sleeping furry cats of tremendous size, of whom old Madame Prigunowa seemed to be especially fond. She had seven cats of her own and, when the cats had visitors from the neighborhood, there were considerably more. As they were really good-looking, well fed, stout pussies, there were always visitors. It was like going to a pet shop.

If a customer came and asked for some article on which at that moment some big whiskered puss was asleep, Prigunoff either said that he had no such thing or suggested coming at some other time. He really had no competition there, and could run his little business just as it pleased him. He never would have thought to awaken one of his feline friends merely to make a sale.

So to Prigunoff I went to look around for some suitable material. I was lucky, for the cats slept on merchandise I wasn't interested in. Between two huge tomcats, napping on red velour albums, I found some rubber heels and I picked out the largest.

Then I went home and sharpened my knife on a flint, with which operation I managed to kill several hours.

After that I made a careful tracing of the stamp on Lippman's passport and tried to place it on the rubber heel.

But I was out of luck, for a nail hole in the center always interfered with a part of the design, no matter how I tried; and so the rubber heel had to be discarded. I cut a rubber ball, boiled it soft, and then stretched it over a wooden block; but even so it bulged. Furthermore it was too thin to be of any use.

From rubber I switched to linoleum, with even less luck. True enough, here I had an uninterrupted smooth surface, but the linoleum was of such a poor quality that the letters I managed to cut out chipped off constantly. Then I tried some hardwood, and encountered the same trouble. I would have succeeded with a proper instrument, but it could not be done with a penknife with a very bad blade.

Again I had to try some other material. I got some heavy tin foil, such as is used for the lining of tea boxes, melted it in the oven and then hammered it flat with the back of an ax. After I had polished it smooth with sand I tried to work it. This had to be given up, too. True enough, I got sharp outlines, but the proof did not look at all like the one made by a rubber stamp. Then I tried pasteboard, and got no better results. But still I did not give up. I knew there would be a way around all these difficulties if I only had the patience to try and try again.

Any prisoner who has been confined for a long time becomes a sort of inventor. After all these unsuccessful experiments I arrived at the conclusion that it would be advisable to try a different method. Lacking suitable materials and tools, I gave up the idea of making a raised relief and suddenly hit on the idea of a stencil. I took some drawing paper, traced the design once more, and then cut the letters with infinite care. It was a tedious job exacting great patience, but it could be done. There was a double-headed Russian eagle in the center of the stamp, which proved to be especially difficult. In order to keep the cut-out center piece in its proper place, I had to leave special radiating connection strips around it, to hold it to the borders. In two days I cut the stencil, the size of a half-dollar piece. I dissolved a copying pencil and soaked a piece of blotting paper with the solution. This was to be the stamping pad, as there were no stamping pads to be bought. With this blotter I tapped the stencil gently, and when I lifted it to examine the results I found a perfect proof. It was perfect; nobody could have told it from an imprint of a regular rubber stamp. There were some white streaks, caused by the connection strips, but these were easily corrected with a brush.

Now the last obstacle was removed, and there was no more time to be lost. Lieutenant Revay went to Magister Stepanek and told him to look for a driver with whom we could cover the first lap of our journey.

To be sure it was not an easy thing to get out of this billet Semenoff, but so far there was no quarter yet in Russia from which I had not managed to get out for a couple of hours if I really tried.

The only thing that remained was to get my civilian outfit from the previous billet, where it was still hidden, and I instructed an orderly to have the clothes conveyed. He was to get them at the barracks from one of Rohmer's orderlies when they met there to get their daily bread rations.

However, the orderly did not bring my outfit. The Russians had found it a few days before, when they made a thorough search of all billets.

This was the last link in the series of misfortunes during the long time of preparations, and I felt it to be sufficient for a time. I couldn't think how to get a new outfit now, as I did not have enough money. Lieutenant Revay advised waitinguntilwe received our next salary, which, if it arrived in time, would be a week hence. Then he was willing to get me a new outfit with the help of Magister Stepanek. But this was a very faint hope. So far we had never got our pay when it was due, and since the outbreak of the disorders it was worse than ever. We received long overdue payments now and then, quite irregularly, often split up into insignificant little advances, so that we could not rely on this in any way. But as there was nothing else to be done we settled down to wait.

The surveillance became very strict, and there were nights when we were visited as often as four times. Things grew worse each day and we were starving with the insufficient food we were able to buy. Our new masters succeeded in rousing such hatred against us among the civilian population that we could not go for walks any longer.

Finally it was charged that our mess-officer boosted the market prices and, as a result, thereafter no prisoners were allowed to go to the market. We could get our supplies—the quantity allotted to us—through our guards, and these were the most unscrupulous scoundrels we ever had. They brought rotten vegetables and musty groats at double the prices we knew they were for sale, and we had to accept it with thanks and pay extra for their services.

Those of our cadaverous looking unfortunate soldiers that were still alive begged and whined for bread. What could our scanty two roubles help now with prices shooting up like rockets!

Ever since we had been prisoners we had felt as forgotten men—but now we were not only forgotten but doomed. Our government could not or would not care about us, and the Russians cared still less.

Democracy certainly is a great thing, but it is dreadful in the making.

And then one morning a Russian soldier came from the barracks. He told us to pack our things, as we would be transported the next day. The local council of Workers and Soldiers were not willing to tolerate our presence in this town any longer. We asked him where we were to be taken. He was not sure, but thought it might be to the north, into the Vyatka Government somewhere.

Chapter IX

We were split into three groups; two of these were sent south and sixty others, including myself, were taken north.

Little did we care where we were taken as long as we could leave this hated place, for we were convinced that it could not be worse anywhere. We were loaded on peasant carts and in a day reached the Volga. After spending a night on the planks of the landing stage, we boarded a steamer going upstream and followed the course of the Volga for a day.

We were herded into the steerage and told to remain there if we did not want to be thrown into the river. So we decided for the steerage, for all our pride was gone by now.

Then for two days, we steamed eastward on the river Kama, sweating on the sacks and barrels on which we sat.

We did not get any food, with the exception of a little bread, and hot tea which was very appropriate at the hottest time of the summer. There was such a heat in the hold that we stripped ourselves to the waist. On the fourth day of the journey, we transferred to a small steamboat that took us in a northern direction upon the river Vyatka, a tributary of the Kama. For half a day we were locked in a suffocating hold, in comparison with which the journey on the Kama steamer was a luxury. However, we were driven out of the steaming hole, as the Soldier Delegates, traveling first class, objected to our presence.

A flat barge was taken in tow, and we were ordered on its deck. The tar melted in the fissures between the deck-boards, under a blazing sun, and there was no roof whatever under which to take shelter. The barge was loaded with large bales of fish, the stench of which rose to Heaven, and while we got the fish smell from below, we received all the smoke that could come out of the funnel, which swept our deck in black clouds.

It wasn't anything of a journey that could be rated as comfortable, but nevertheless, we could not keep a straight face. We were blackened by smoke in no time to such a degree that we could not recognize one another, and again we were forced to strip ourselves, partly on account of the heat and also to save our only blouses from the soot.

We started to pull pails of water overboard and dash it over each other. Thus we managed to keep cool and also to some extent clean. Over on the steamer's railing stood a dense pack of Russians, comfortably shaded, enjoying immensely our splashing, calling encouragements to our party on the far end of the tow-rope.

For two days we proceeded in this manner, and much preferred it to the infernal hold of the steamer. On the third day, the steamer slowed down considerably. The river bed grew very shallow. Here and there long poles were stuck in the bottom, indicating sandbanks, and many of the buoys lay on their sides in the low water. The steamer zigzagged carefully, stopped suddenly, then floated back to try another course. On the bow of the steamer stood a sailor with a long pole, poking at intervals into the bottom and calling out the depth.

Twice the steamer ran aground on sandbanks and got stuck. All the passengers were moved to the stern and pulled our barge within a few yards of the boat. Then our barge was released and as it drifted back it pulled the rope tight and jerked the boat off the bank. It was a very crude but effective method, which knocked us all off our feet. But we made port somehow, the barge was made fast; we were taken off and put once more on peasant carts.

In half a day we reached our place of destination. The command took us over from the transport commander and we were marched off to a school that lay on a hillock near the city. We were to remain there for a day or twountilthe command found suitable quarters.

For a few days we waited at the school for billeting orders, but none came. We were marched now and then to the barracks to be inspected and looked over.

While our previous garrison in the Symbirsk Government was decidedly Bolshevist, these Northerners adhered to the provisional government of Kerensky. There seemed to be rather good order here.

The garrison was run—I would not say commanded—by a mixed commission of the newly formed Soldiers Council, who, however, kept the Colonel of the old regime as an expert advisor for the time. Thus Corporal Cheremisoff was considered as the real head of the garrison, and the Colonel—as long as he behaved nicely—was permitted to be the adjutant of the corporal.

Cheremisoff had formerly worked in a tannery, three years previously, and his nails were still mahogany brown, though in all probability he had not gone near a tanning vat since.

In the barrack yards we met some of the officers who were here long before us. They said—considering all other places—this was not a bad place as long as we kept on good terms with Cheremisoff. They were strictly guarded, but lived in private quarters, and there were no double bunks in the whole garrison. There weren't any troubles so far—as nobody had escaped and the Russian population was not hostile to the prisoners.

This news was rather comforting, as we pondered over it for two more days on the floor of the school. After sleeping so long on landing stages, barges and school floors, we hoped dearly that Cheremisoff would come soon to put us into one of those mythical quarters. But it took three more days before Cheremisoff announced his arrival by kicking in the door and picking forty-eight officers to follow him to a newly requisitioned quarter.

The lucky group marched off proudly, leaving twelve of us guessing our future.

Next day Cheremisoff again opened the door with his heels. He seemed to stick to his habits. He said that we were too small for an independent group and that we would be divided among the established billets. He was tired of looking for billets; there were none. But we were also tired of being split up among foreign groups. A ten-rouble bill flashed out. Cheremisoff pocketed it and said that there might be a possibility. Another ten-rouble bill was produced, whereupon Cheremisoff did not say a word, but went out.

In the evening we were in our private billet. It was just right for twelve officers, three orderlies and our convoys.

We spent another night on the floor of our new billet, but Cheremisoff said it would be positively for the last time. On the next day he sent us a dozen rough boards, some nails, and a saw which was to be returned to the barracks. He thanked us for the five roubles and did not kick the door.

Once more we were established. These quarters were decidedly the best we had had so far. There were three rooms, and we were not overcrowded. This was a small house, and we lived on the first floor.

In the basement lived the landlady, a kindly old woman. She would milk her mottled little cow in the evening and sell us the fresh milk, still warm. She also had a large garden in the rear. Half of it was a kitchen garden, from which we could get our supply, and in the other half there were some flower beds, which may have been well kept once, but now were unweeded and rather bushy.

But the whole place had an unspoilt and cheerful look, like some ungroomed, tousled country lad. There were some fruit trees in the garden and raspberry bushes and, among the high grass, and like so many rubies, plenty of strawberries.

After all those barren, dusty and muddy yards we had grown accustomed to, during our prolonged captivity, this primeval little green spot was truly a charming place of succor, which soothed our jumpy nerves. All around there was such an appeasing quietness. The broad streets were bordered by shady trees; even the carts rolled with a muffled rattle over the soft road which seemed to be neither dusty nor muddy.

Our house stood on a gently declining slope, rather on the outskirts of the town. A straight road led to the forests which surrounded the little town in the broad valley.

After sunset a wonderfully scented breeze swept from those deep glades, the mingling sweetness of lime trees and fir. Sometimes I felt an urge to bolt to those blue-green giants, to inhale their invigorating perfume, to hug their trunks and thank them for their delicate fragrance. One could not get enough of it...

Our guards were good-natured, silent fellows, elder landsturm men, who drank their tea peaceably, smoked their machorka cigarettes and didn't bother us as long as we remained quiet and made no trouble. They thanked us for small tips, and were always ready to take us for a walk if we asked them. We were anxious to be on good terms with them, and they were easy to handle. We remembered things in our previous garrison, and we could appreciate our present state of affairs. In a few weeks we felt rejuvenated here. There were no quarrels to speak of; our nerves calmed down and we lived as good comrades. Old differences were ironed out, and in several instances malignant protocols of an earlier date were torn up.

The peaceful surroundings contributed to the good feeling. The town was a pretty little place with very wide, straight streets and well-kept houses. It wasn't much larger than our last garrison, but a hundred times better looking. There were several high schools here, and the population belonged more to the wealthy middle class.

Many houses were built of stone, and there were even some two and three-story buildings.

On the center part of the main street were some decent little shops and, outside of the high prices, one would never have noticed the war. Here again one could see ladies, well dressed, not only bulky peasant women in sheepskin coats and clumsy stiff skirts.

Often I used to sit with Andy in the garden. We got on so well together because we never pestered each other with superfluous talk if we did not feel like it. There was no bench, and not even a box on which to sit, but we never felt the need of it.

We sat in the hay-like, long grass among the beds, sucking at a grass stalk or slitting them into fine strands with our fingernails. The summer was nearing its end, and the sun shone balmy with an agreeable tingle on the skin. We just enjoyed the pleasure of being alive, and, strange as it may sound, it was the first good rest we had had while in captivity.

We made glossy little ladybugs walk on the smooth stalks, and intersected their climb with another stalk, to which they changed their courseuntilthey grew tired of the endless promenade, loosened their lacquered wings and flew off into the sunshine.

Striped bumblebees landed carefully on some delicate stem, that rebounded elastically with a gentle swing, and dragonflies vibrated in the air as if suspended by an invisibly fine thread, to shoot like a flash to some other place and hang there glittering. Furry little bees hummed above the flowers and rummaged between the flowery crowns. They backed out carefully, alighted on some other flower and then returned again as if carrying a secret message that was to be delivered promptly.

Here we could buy newspapers regularly. By now I could manage to read them without much use of the dictionary. There was no very important news since Kerensky's offensive, which was settled definitely, and, though it ended in a complete disaster, Kerensky was still very popular. Here and there the Germans made some little push, not so much for tactical, gains but more to test the strength of the Russian front, which, kept breaking up as before. But we were seasoned observers by this time and knew that we would spend our third winter in Russia.

I did not feel any urge to try to escape now. Things were tolerable here. There must be special reasons to warrant an escape. It is not done out of patriotic motives, for prisoners of war cease to be patriotic after a while, just the same as the firing lines, if they have faced each other long enough.

Fighting men, with soaked uniforms, lice on their bodies and aching trench feet or rheumatism, are too miserable to hate the other fellow in a similar plight. They will do the duty their countries expect of them, silently and honestly, but without the patriotic zeal that is to be found together with hatred in the hinterland only. Hate starts at the comfortable bombproof artillery dugouts and increases with the size of the gun calibers and the distance of the trenches. Patriots do very little of the dirty work themselves, being too busy in spreading lies, fostering hatred and sending others to do the fighting.

Out there, among the shell holes in No Man's land and in the crumbling trenches, there is a human understanding, a silent sympathy toward the fellow wearing another uniform—and a chivalrous feeling, inborn to every fighting man.

True enough, hundreds of infantrymen escaped, among those eight million who were captured in the great war, who cut the wire with the determination to fight once more, but this was not the case generally. Men escaped because of cruel treatment, because of the tedium of captivity, and for the sake of thrill and adventure of the flight itself. Men got away with the sole desire to get away, not caring what would happen thereafter. By the time they reached their countries, they had generally forgotten their original impulse, and the reception committee took it for granted that they had returned to fight.

As this was the natural thing to do; they went back to the firing line once more without demur.

After a time prisoners get afflicted with symptoms that are known as "barbed wire disease," even if they are not kept actually behind barbed wire fences. They feel like outcasts, sneered at by their captors and forgotten by their government.

For a time they may revolt inwardly and feel unjustifiably treated as convicts for doing their duty toward their country, but after their spirit is broken once—nothing counts. For a while they rage, but not long. The interest in the outside world wears off, and they become indifferent toward everything, and most of all, to their own fate. We were cheated out of the hope of peace so often that we finally gave up our hopes and became fatalistic.

We felt that our youth was stolen irrevocably, and this made us hard and bitter. Whoever was to repay us?

If the war was won, our ignominious silent sufferings would never count; and if the war was lost, whoever would care about us? An estrangement crept up against everything and everybody.

But this was a good place here. There were bees and we could watch them creep into the flowers; there was juicy grass that could be chewed without being pestered, and there were ladybugs with red wings, and trees—beautiful big trees. I had not seen green trees for two years.

Good smelling trees too—they made us feel like human beings again...

We were allowed to walk with our guards outside the city. Our small group banded together, and we had brisk walks, but here was the garden, where we could get all the fresh air and exercise too. For this reason we gradually discontinued those official airings.

Sometimes, together with Andy, I went out. We gave the sentry a tip to accompany us and he led us to those beautiful forests. There were deep ravines and clear little brooks, bordered by tall ferns. We would pick out a sunny glade and sit silently on the thick carpet of reddish-brown needles. It was so good to sit here under those whispering trees, and so soothing.

Bright specks of light flashed on the dark carpet among the trees, and woodpeckers glided up the stems, hammering rhythmically. Now and then a bird called or some little animal pattered across the sunny glade and stopped for a while to be kissed by the sun. We picked up green fir cones just to smell them, or picked the bristling scales of dried cones in a happy absent-mindedness.

Sometimes we gathered mushrooms. There were plenty of them in the shady nooks, among the moss and springy turf. The guard showed us the good ones, which he could tell with the unerring eye of men who live close to nature. We filled our caps and handkerchiefs to overflowing and even cut vines on which we threaded them into wreaths.

Chapter X

Summer passed and autumn died slowly and gracefully, fading into a beautiful Indian summer. There was a stilly radiance in the clear sunlit air, and long silvery threads floated, glimmering like pure metal, caressed by the chaste and mellow rays. They bent gently to the shape of delicately chiseled long silver bows, then straightened out again in the drift with a gentle ripple like a lash in an unseen hand.

A faint breeze swept them over the roofs and, as their lower ends got caught in the gables, they flickered and writhed like slim tongues of flame.

The tall grass that had been cut was parched to a silvery gray, emitting a sweet fragrance mingling with the scent of the ripe sunflowers, which bowed on their long stems, twisting their black mosaic plates toward the sun.

Now I went out with Andy each afternoon to our favorite haunts in the forests, just to enjoy the calm. The guard came along, following us good-naturedly. He liked to sit around and smoke in those glades himself. A few miles away, we found a sunny little birchwood and a clearing, where there was a rifle range that evidently had not been used for a long time.

Leaves were falling in a steady litter, descending in a zigzag or twirling around their stems, and some shiny leaflet would plunge faster, describing spirals like a corkscrew.

The sun was declining as we started home from our pine-scented glades, and the rays fell obliquely on the furrowed stems glowing in a reddish hue. We reached the border of the wood and before us lay the grassy long road winding in the direction of the city.

Toward the forest strolled a slim woman. She stopped for a moment to take off her wide-brimmed summer hat; then, after she had hung it on her arm, she proceeded.

She would have to pass us if she kept on the road—and after a while we moved over to the left to offer her the better passage. She noted our courteous gesture, but made no sign of acceptance.

The sinking sun was at her back, and her face was in shadow, with a bluish halo around her jet black glossy hair. She cast a glance at me—and I felt it burn. I had to stop; I don't know why—it never occurred to me then that it was rude—but I felt such a strange sensation, never felt before ... breaking down in the presence of another being.

The guard nudged me in a friendly way to move on. She was a long way off now and I was still turned in her direction. Slowly I turned, lost in thought and then I marched beside Andy for a while without so much as a word. I did not quite know how to begin, but I knew he was expecting me to say something and so I said: "A beautiful woman ... Andy... I never saw such a beautiful woman before."

"Yes," he replied deliberately, "a strange beauty. Perfect features she had, and her eyes—I really couldn't say whether they were proud or languishing—but they were certainly beautiful and dark."

"And what long lashes," I said. "They are so rarely to be found."

There was a long silence again. I did not want to reveal my feelings just then and it was Andy who spoke finally.

"I wonder who she is," he remarked. "She certainly gave you a good look—you lucky dog!"

We had reached our billet by this time, and I did not wish to say how unlucky I felt and how much that encounter had upset the calm happiness of the last weeks that could be soothed with sunshine, little red ladybugs and the fragrance of the forest.

Thereafter we went regularly to the forest each afternoon. I did not go deep into those glades as before, but sat on the edge of the wood, overlooking the gently ascending road, hoping that she would come once more.

But in vain was my patient wait.

Sometimes sweethearts came up the road, and once a solitary woman came that made my heart leap with joy—for I thought it was she. So I kept up the torturing watch amidst hope and sinking heart, faithfully for days.

A week passed—and then two weeks, but she came not. While I was in the billet, I stood at the gate, trusting and hoping that I might be lucky enough to see her pass—just once.

Then the rains came, long, stubborn autumn rains, and there was no more sunshine. The sky was overcast and out of a gray mist fell a fine drizzle that made everything so much more dreary. Rain pattered softly against the window panes, while I sat motionless for hours on my bunk in the small cabinet in which I slept with Andy.

"Cheer up old boy!" Andy used to repeat, without much conviction. "You'll get over that. Forget it. Probably she was just visiting the town—I tell you—that's why we don't see her."

Dear old Andy, faithful good chap that he was. She was not to be forgotten; she was not the type that could be forgotten in those circumstances, where my only occupation was to think of her beautiful pale face with those deep and dark eyes she had once cast upon me. I wished that I did not see them constantly, for they burned me up and made me miserable; they made me feel again—and I just wished that my heart could remain quiet and dead as for those last dreary two years.

It was hopeless. It was like showing bread to a starving man and then hiding it again and letting him perish with hunger. It was just a torturing reminder of this miserable captivity.

Who was that ravishing woman? Who was she? Did the devil send her to rob me of my senses, to whip me out of the tranquility which had finally come after these accursed two years?

And suppose I knew who she was, and suppose I knew where she was! What would it have helped? I was just a wretched prisoner, locked up together with his rebellious young heart and bursting feelings; so really what could it matter?

"Now don't be a damned fool," said Andy. "What's the use of acting the way you do? Look at yourself, damn it all. See how you look! I don't recognize you—by God!"

He tousled my hair in his kindly rough way.

"Now cheer up, old boy, I'm telling you! Look here," he said, "it's clearing up a bit. If the rain stops, we'll go to the forest tomorrow, and we'll wait there. Maybe she will come along and ..."

He stopped short, bit his lip and went out. He was too good a fellow to go on cheating, for he was such an abominably poor cheat.

A group of invalids was to be exchanged and sent to Sweden. There were a few dozen of our privates, hopelessly crippled and sick, and also fourteen officers in different stages of consumption and stiff with rheumatism, who were to go.

On a gray day in October the transport went off, and in consequence two of the billets were to be discontinued.

This meant fewer guards and also a simplification of the control. Our group was divided between two billets. Together with eight I was put in the billet Nogovikoff, on the upper end of the main street.

Nogovikoff was a wealthy merchant whose property extended well over half a block on the wide main street. It occupied a corner plot and faced on two streets with a solitary entrance from Main Street. Right on the corner stood his residence, a good-looking, sturdy, two-story brick building, and right beside that, with its front on Main Street, stood a long low edifice housing his store and supplies. Between these two buildings was a brick pillar that separated the door and the wide gate. The plot was bordered on both sides by sturdy low storehouses and an immense shed with an open front.

The heavy slanting roof of the shed was supported by several stout stone pillars, and served as a shelter for the carts and sleighs which drove up to the weekly market from the surrounding villages.

Still farther back, at a right angle to this shed, stood a long granary with a projecting visor-like roof, likewise braced with pillars. Composing the fourth corner of the enclosed yard, stood another two-story brick building, where we lived. There was a wide passage between the granary and our house. This led to a second large yard in the rear, part of which was Nogovikoff's garden, and here stood some very tall trees. Some more sheds surrounded this backyard and garden, and a very high and solid stone wall encircled the whole property.

Everything was spacious and solid here; the houses might have been built a century ago, for they had very thick walls with small windows and heavy oak doors.

The front yard was very large, built to hold several dozen carts without crowding. Occupying a part of the ground floor in Nogovikoff's residence, right beside the entrance, was a small barbershop—a luxury which I had not enjoyed for the last twenty-eight months. Two of its side windows opened on the passage leading to the yard, throwing at night a warm glow on the opposite wall of the store building.

There were no policemen and gendarmes at that time. The hated Tsarist organization was the first to be disbanded and its members chased to the four winds. There was a militia instead, and these had their guard room in the large basement of our very building. They had their bunks there and benches and tables, and there were always a dozen or so sitting around, sipping their tea and smoking. Furthermore, our own guards, when they were off duty, stayed here, and they had constant visitors from the barracks and the other officer billets.

This guard room was quite a lively place, and soldiers came and went rather frequently. One guard was posted at the front gate, right at the barbershop, and two militiamen stood on duty farther away, at the street intersection—doing police work.

Where there are too many guards, the surveillance is lax, as we found out pretty soon to our satisfaction.

Our rooms were rather comfortable—at least spacy enough, well-kept and clean. It was the first and only place without vermin.

The furniture was largely of the homemade kind, but there were several decent chairs and tables which Nogovikoff left there, as unfit for his sumptuous apartment. We even had a cracked mirror, pockmarked with plenty of blind spots.

There were eighteen of us living here and I shared a room with only Lieutenant Revay and Andy. Once more I became the commander of the billet, but, as the boys were decent here, it meant no trouble and it wasn't much more than a title.

It was cold again; the breath of winter and snow hung in the air. Crows came to the city in huge flocks from the surrounding fields, scrabby black crows and gray-bellied crows, also large stately ravens. They circled high up, like so many dense black clouds, croaking and cawing. In swarms they descended upon the trees in our yard, giving the bare branches an appearance of scanty black foliage.

The ravens kept more to themselves and perched on the topmost branches, cawing and laughing with that characteristic choking, coughing chuckle of their sinister kind.

The road was streaked with the white lines of icy ruts and one morning the snow came that had hung for days above in the gray Heavens. It fell softly, in very fine grains, as if sifted through a vast sieve.

It filled up the ruts and smoothed the roads. Once more the runners were greased. Now for the third time.

There was good comradeship in this billet, mainly because every room kept to itself. This could easily be done, as each room had a door and no one adjoined another. They opened on a fair sized hall which was bounded by the railing of the staircase that led downstairs to the entrance.

We had a common mess at regular hours, but outside of this each room could do whatever it liked. We agreed not to disturb each other at an undue time in the morning or at night.

Our own room changed its method of living, in a thorough way. We changed hours. We hired a samovar from the barber and, with the help of this, we stayed upuntilthree and four in the morning, smoking as long as our tobacco lasted and drinking tea.

It was very hard to get tobacco now. Speculators were cornering it and we simply could not afford to pay their prices out of our pay, which was scarcely enough for the simplest kind of food.

Now we were all smoking machorka-tobacco—a cheap sort of weed—which formerly made us cough and caused the tears to flow. However, we were glad if we could get a package now and then of this acrid stuff, and always divided it faithfully into three parts.

But there was no way to get sugar, outside of the rations which were allotted. A year ago each officer could buy two pounds of lump sugar, which was to last for a full month, but this had been reduced lately to one pound. So now we were drinking tea in the Russian fashion and, with sufficient practice, one could sweeten as much as sixteen cups of tea with a single lump of sugar. We bit off small pieces, held it between the teeth, and then sipped the tea through it—as through some sweet filter.

Toward four in the morning the samovar was empty and cold; then we turned in and sleptuntilten or eleven.

There were no outside walks in this billet—one could walk all one wanted in the wide yard. Sometimes our room had company. There was a boyish-looking young cadet, Cornelius, whom we called for short Cornel. He had been in this quarter before we came here and he could come as often as he liked—provided he brought his own sugar and tobacco. Fire and hot water were to be had for the asking.

Often I thought of her. I still could not forget her lithe figure, with the bluish halo over her head. But by now I had given up the hope of seeing her again. Andy, I think, must have been right when he said that probably she did not belong here, but merely came to visit.

It was November and we had a deep blanket of snow now. It was snowing that evening too, but only gently.

The cold was not too intense, so I took my peaked regulation cap, turned up my overcoat collar, and went down to the yard for a walk. It was about eighty steps from the front door to our steps and, as the snow had been shoveled away that afternoon, one could walk unhindered. The yard was empty except for the sentinel, who stood outside, in front of the building, guarding the entrance.

I had been walking for scarcely ten minutes when Cornel joined me. He asked if I permitted him to join me and I told him I would be glad to have company.

It was about nine o'clock and outside the street seemed to be deserted. Once and again I heard the faint creak of a passing wooden sleigh, or the squeaking of the raw-hide harness, but otherwise no sound came from without.

Sometimes the iron door latch rattled as some soldier entered the yard, and while he stood at the door his figure was silhouetted black against the white road of Main Street, faintly lit by oil lamps. In fact I always turned when I heard the latch move, because it was the only distraction these passing soldiers offered.

We were just turning and retracing our steps toward the door when the latch moved again and the silhouette of a lady in a fur coat appeared in the dark frame. She closed the door and started toward the entrance of Nogovikoff's residence. As she passed the window of the barbershop I thought I was dreaming. It was she—and there was no mistake about it!

She reached the corner of the house by Nogovikoff's entrance before we were halfway, and disappeared. She must have seen us coming, for we were facing her all the time. My heart stood still; then it began to thump furiously and joyously. We had made a complete round before I made up my mind to ask Cornel. He had been in this town for two years, and he might know something about her.

"Do you happen to know who that lady was?" I asked with an effort to be very casual.

"Why, of course," he replied, "she is the wife of the Commissar, some big gun with the local government."

"And what is she doing here?" I inquired.

"Madame Nogovikowa is some kind of a relative of hers," he replied. "She comes here quite often. Haven't you seen her before?"

I said I had not, whereupon we made another round.

"Listen, Cornel," I said to him, "do you want to be a good boy and do me a big favor?"

"Why, I'll be glad. What can I do for you?"

"Will you do me the favor of going in? I want to wait for the lady here and speak to her alone."

"All right, sir," said Cornel, and then he hesitated as if reflecting whether he should still say something.

"I want to tell you, sir, if you permit," he continued, "that some have tried it already—but she isn't that kind. She won't even answer."

He saluted and went. I paced up and down for another half hour and was trying to steady myself a little.

I did not know what I was going to tell her, should she open the door and come out that very minute. I shortened my beat in order to be near the door when she came.

Two soldiers entered and stopped to talk right there, where she was to appear. I was boiling with rage. If she came now, it would be impossible to speak a word to her. Then they moved away to the guard room, and once more I was alone. Outside the sentinel paced up and down; I could hear the snow crunch under his feet.

Then I heard voices inside. "Good night," said a clear voice, and I felt a tightening in the throat.

She appeared at the door, closed it and started down the stoop. I was standing quite near. She threw a rapid glance in my direction, just to see why somebody should be around, and then slipped on the icy stoop. She did not fall but just lost her balance a little. I jumped and caught her arm.

"Merci, Monsieur," she said with a little fright.

I saluted. "I hope, Madame, you did not hurt yourself?"

"Mais non, Monsieur."

I still held her arm and assisted her down the stoop. As she reached the ground, she freed her arm gently. Now she stood in the light of the window, and I had to think fast before she was gone. I started in the best Russian I could manage.

"Madame," I reeled off rapidly, "I had the pleasure of seeing you once in the summer." I stood in the light and she looked at me.

"Oh, I recall," she said with a smile. And then I blurted out without restraint—"And I have been thinking of you ever since—I could never forget you—you were so beautiful."

She raised her muff to her chin, and I saw her eyes smiling.

"Madame," I went on, "won't you let me see you once, just once, please?"

"Mais non, Monsieur!" she said with a little surprise, but still smiling. "You certainly don't mean it? Why—it's impossible!" and then she added, "Eh bien. Bon nuit."

I still wanted to say something, but she slipped her gloved right hand from her muff and held it gracefully at a height with her shoulder. It meant the end of the conversation, and it also meant the end of six weeks' dreaming.

I saluted and bent to kiss her hand. Then, after conforming to courtesy, I turned her hand gently but firmly and kissed her palm three times rapidly at the opening of the glove.

She started towards the street, but before she reached the door she turned rapidly and whispered, so that the sentry on the other side of the door should not hear: "Be at the gate tomorrow at eight. Perhaps I might pass here. Bon nuit!"

Cornel sat on the topmost stair in the hall, waiting for my return, and jumped up when he saw me.

"Well sir," he commenced, with all his boyish eagerness, "did you speak to her?"

"You bet your life I did!"

"And did she speak to you?" he went on hesitatingly.

"Yes—just enough to get acquainted."

Cornel raised his eyebrows and then said smiling, "Well, sir—I—I think you have broken the ice."

Poor Andy was surprised when I slapped him with force on the back, and looked up askance. Now for a change I was tussling with him, and he made a silly face.

"Andy—old boy, I've found her!"

And that night we sat up even longer, heating the samovar for a second round. Somehow the following day seemed to me like a week. Shortly after seven I went to the gate to do a little scouting. It was Ivan's turn to guard the gate, I found to my great satisfaction. I was on good terms with Ivan. In the summer it was always he who accompanied us to the forest, and more than one package of machorka had I bought from him when he was in need of money.

Ivan sat on a small bench between the barbershop and the small door adjoining the gate, beating the soles of his boots together, for it was very cold. The snow had stopped and the sky was clear.

"It's cold tonight, Ivan," I said.

"Yes, the devil take it!" he replied promptly and naturally. "Especially if you have to sit here outside."

"I wonder why there weren't any newspapers today," I went on.

Ivan shrugged his shoulders. "How should I know?" he replied. "The trains may have been delayed by the snow, or something like that."

By now I was leaning against the stone pillar that separated the gate from the door. I was trying to find out whether he would have any objection to my standing in front of the billet, right on Main Street. He did not protest with a word, but to make sure, I went to the yard, made a few rounds there and then returned this time straight to the pillar, outside the billet. Again he let it be. Men and women were promenading up and down amidst cheerful conversation. Peasant sleighs were returning to their villages, and some troykas [1] with splendid horses shot past.

It was nearly eight o'clock, and the street was clearing. Eight o'clock is late in a small town, and besides it was too snappy to walk long. The snow crunched under the feet and the stars shone without a sparkle. Opposite our billet, the dark building of the high school loomed big and black, and on the bare trees that bordered the street clung slim pads of glittering snow, like icing.

A little after eight she came. She was not alone, but was accompanied by a fair lady with an impertinent little pug nose—extremely pretty. I could not salute as they passed, for the guard sat quite close. She was more ravishing than ever, in her trim fur coat and high patent leather knee boots. Her cheeks were colored by the crisp air, and her eyes flashed dark and mischievously and made my heart leap. As they passed the gate, arm in arm, she whispered something to her friend and then they laughed in sheer joy.

After a while, they returned and passed our billet in an opposite direction. Her friend looked me over carefully, and there was some rapid talk and more laughter as they went on. It was evident now that they were promenading with the sole purpose of passing our billet as often as possible.

While they were gone, Cornel appeared and remained standing in the opened door.

"Good evening, sir," he said, "am I intruding?"

"No, you're not," I said. I was rather piqued that he had butted in, but then I reflected that so far there was nothing on which he could possibly have intruded.

"Any news outside?" he inquired.

"Yes, she is walking with a friend up and down. Keep back in that door, will you? They're coming back."

Again they passed; then returned and passed again. Ivan got up, flung his arms several times across his chest to promote circulation, stamped with his feet and then sauntered over to the corner to talk to a militiaman.

Never such a chance again!

"Have you got a piece of paper, Cornel?" I asked rapidly. He dug into his blouse and tore a sheet out of his notebook.

"All right, boy. Now you stand here and watch. I'll be back immediately."

At the light of the window, I hastily scribbled: "Madame, I would like to kiss your left hand three times. I missed it yesterday. F."

Hurriedly I folded the paper and pressed some snow around it to make it look like a snowball.

"They are returning," warned Cornel.

"Good, stand back again."

As they approached, I gently flipped the snowball to the center of the sidewalk, and she picked it up very nonchalantly.

Now it took somewhat longer before they returned, and I hoped Ivan would still find some topic to discuss with the militiaman and not come back to his bench at an undue moment.

Finally they came with rapid strides and she dropped a small note, crushed to the size of a marble. I picked it up and read at the window:

"Tomorrow at ten at the cloister church. Au revoir."

"Fast work," commented Cornel. "I'll try it myself on the other lady. She's pretty enough to risk it."

It was not quite ten o'clock when I arrived at the church. I wondered if she would recognize me in the kit I wore. It was not much like a uniform, and not very pretty. I wore heavy felt hip-boots, which covered my blue-gray breeches completely, and a rawhide sheepskin coat over my blouse. Furthermore, a large fur cap of white lambskin adorned my head. Cornel had got me the coat and boots from one of our orderlies and had smuggled them under the dark shed where I dressed. At nine thirty we started to maneuver, for I had to get out somehow, if I had to blast my way out.

Cornel suggested that we take a ladder from the shed and set it against the wall where it was dark enough, and I drop into the neighboring yard from which I could reach the street in safety. But there were many good reasons against this. For one thing, it would have involved too many preparations and, furthermore, there were dogs in the other yard.

Then as the time was nearing, it occurred to me to try the simplest way, and that was to walk right past the sentinel at the gate. Not all of the militiamen wore uniforms, and I was quite willing to take the risk, trying to pass as one of them. So I told Cornel to keep the sentinel busy and, if everything appeared to be reasonably safe, to strike a match as a signal.

Meanwhile I stood under the shed and kept an eye on Cornel. Suddenly the match flared up. At the same time three militiamen came out of the guard room and started towards the gate. However, Cornel could not have seen them.

But for me they came at a very appropriate moment. I ducked behind a pillar and let them pass, then I emerged from the shed and followed at a little distance. They marched out of the gate and turned to the left in the direction of the marketplace, and I marched out right behind them and turned to the right, to reach the cloister church in good time. It had proved so easy that I had to chuckle.

I had my doubts whether it would be quite so easy to return, but there was still time to worry about that. I was out to meet her and that was the only thing that mattered.

I waited for a quarter of an hour. Now and then some pedestrian passed, without paying any attention to me. This was very reassuring after it had happened several times.

Then a woman, dressed in a long, thick, felt coat, like those worn by the peasants, her head covered by a kerchief, passed me and said, "Bonsoir, Monsieur."

We must have walked well over an hour, for we reached the top of those little hillocks above the town and meanwhile I had had a chance to kiss her left hand, then the right and the left again more than three times.

For a time we mixed French with Russian, but only until she saw that I could get along in Russian pretty well.

At first we joked and talked of silly little things, but mainly we asked questions of each other. Then, as the hour progressed, I felt a strange change creep over me. This woman was not to be taken lightly; she was not of that charming, flippant, easy going type with a taste for fleeting adventures. Deep in her heart I felt there burned a suppressed passion, which, if once loosened, could be destructive to any man.

I linked my arm in hers and pressed it gently, and she did not object in the conventional manner. For a long while we stood silently on the hill, while down in the valley slept the little town, under its peaked white roofs. It was so peaceful and lifeless; nothing around seemed to live, only our hearts. The inky black of the sky was studded with golden jewels, too stupendous and too beautiful for humans to comprehend. Many things can be told best without words, in the silent speech of love, and I told her of all that rapture and desire that could not be expressed with words. I felt my eyes burn, and in my veins raced young, rebelling blood, consuming with a mad storm the shackles of suppression. Then I found her lips. She swayed in my arms in a daze of delirious happiness as she closed her eyes—and threw back her head—Days passed. If I could not see her—it was torture. The unleashed fury of this torturous captivity was whipped to a new frenzy with each kiss of hers. That singeing hot breath that came so short from between her pearly teeth—I felt would drive me crazy.

Bullets spattered on the ancient walls of the Winter Palace in Petrograd. Bolshevist bullets whizzed through the cold from across the frozen river Neva. Women soldiers of Kerensky's Death-Battalions died in the snow and sank behind the high iron fence of the palace, for their dope-crazed master— they, and pink-faced cadets of the Military Academy. Against them—the fanatics of Lenin.

Once more the long naval guns roared fire and destruction, but now on their own kind. Amidst the howls of ragged hooligans, and lit by scarlet flashes of their guns, Red Prince Carnival arrived triumphantly to shake humanity, to mottle the white plains with crimson roses of blood.

Things moved fast now, at a breathtaking pace. Rifles cracked all over Russia, as the victorious Bolshevists fought their way across the vast country. Moscow fell as they battled eastward. There was no more talk of war to the victorious end; the trenches were empty; the army was going home. For the soldiers had decided to become moujiks again, and one could not plow well in those coarse long military mantles. They were cumbersome; they went cheap, for there were many of them. I bought one from a deserter—a good one—for ten roubles.

From that time, I went out at nights masquerading as a Russian soldier. It had many advantages. First of all, no militiaman ever dared to challenge a soldier and then, under the long cloak, which came down to my ankles, I could wear my own uniform and soft leather knee boots. Those heavy felt hip boots were rather awkward and clumsy and that rawhide sheepskin coat did not smell too sweet, either. One of our orderlies used to be a theatrical wigmaker, and he made me, out of fleece, a regular slouching moustache, such as was worn by all good Russians. It was cleverly fastened to an arched piece of wire, which I held between my teeth while I was on the streets.

Getting out was simple enough, and it never caused me any worry, especially now in that soldier outfit; but the return was rather difficult. True enough, there were plenty of soldiers in the garrison, but any solitary, silent soldier would have been suspected after a while, never speaking to the sentinel who had to be passed. When reentering the billet, often I had to linger for a long time in order to out-maneuver the guard. I kept to the dark wall of the school, across the road, until he reached a favorable spot on his beat when I could time my dash so as to get in while his back was turned. But this was always dangerous, in case he shortened his beat and turned around sooner than I expected. So far I had had luck—but this would not hold forever. When it grew dark I stood at the door. I had to see

Sasha, no matter whether I saw her later that same evening or not. She always came with her friend and, if it could be managed despite the sentinel, she gave me a reassuring smile.

I was acquainted with her blonde friend too. We had met her once as we were walking, out on our favorite spot. It was so deserted that it could not have been a chance meeting, and Sasha told me later that Yelena arranged it so herself. She was a vivid little creature, always very talkative. I told her that Cornel admired her greatly, and she wanted to know whether it was that handsome young boy who always hung around me. Then I said that I might bring him along and introduce him, if she really thought he was so handsome. And so once, on a prearranged occasion, I brought Cornel along and, while she thought him handsome, he thought her beautiful.

But these fourfold walks were not frequent, for Sasha preferred to be alone with me. Furthermore, Yelena was under a rather strict surveillance by her husband. Sasha was very unhappy with her husband. She rarely spoke of him, and now she rarely saw him. Our particular county was still loyal to Kerensky. To be exact, the Bolshevists had not yet fought their way quite so far. However, they were progressing daily and, if they kept up, it could not well be more than a few weeks before they would sweep over our heads in their cross-country march.

But so long as they were not here, the local government was busily preparing to retain power and Sasha's husband, the Commissar, was sent on errands that kept him out of town for weeks.

While he was on such a mission, Sasha arranged a little party one night. Yelena and Cornel were invited to join, and the party was to be held at Sasha's own apartment. It was a dangerous venture, but Sasha liked thrills, and this certainly was as good as any other she could think up.

Each with a box of candy under his arm, we marched out from the billet, very nonchalantly, as Russian soldiers, and arrived in Sasha's garden at the fixed hour.

We waited there behind a garden house, where we could keep an eye on her windows.

The shades were drawn, and now and then I saw her lithe figure silhouetted against it. After a while I flung a small snowball against the window pane, as we had arranged previously. Like a shadow I saw her come toward the shade and then close the inner shutters. Soon the house gate opened softly and, wrapped in her fur, Sasha fleeted out and started toward us. While she held the coat wrapped with one hand, she stuck out a warm little paw that was good to touch on that frosty night.

She told us to wait for her, and then ran to the garden gate and bolted it securely.

"All right," she said smiling. "All set. Entrez Messieurs."

Yelena greeted us cordially on the top of the staircase, and then they both helped us out of our tight-fitting Russian coats, which we hung in the dark hall. Sasha had sent her servants away for the evening, so there was nobody around.

We stepped into a well-furnished large apartment, cozy and warm, and it felt good to be in such a place after all those trenches, barracks and billets to which we had grown accustomed.

One had to be careful on that highly polished parquet floor, for it was slippery compared to the rough boards in our billet and the stamped mud floors of the peasant cottages.

It was good to stand on a thick rug again; it felt so soft and springy. One had quite forgotten there were such things—and also fluffy white curtains, upholstered furniture, pictures, statuettes, a real grand piano and, in an alcove, a gilded samovar on a set table. By God, a real white tablecloth, pure and sweet—probably just taken out of a linen chest!

Why! Everything looked unreal—the glossy parquet, regular china dishes and no tin cups and battered aluminum plates, white curtains and white tablecloth, and beautiful Sasha and Yelena with her golden hair! Not even the fork ends were crooked and crossed here.

We had some drinks, good drinks—rather stiff. Everything seemed to appear as behind a gauze curtain, and the walls seemed to tilt and sway a little. It was getting hot, and one could not well unhook blouse-collars in the presence of ladies. We had still another round, and then Sasha told me to put my head back and she unhooked my collar herself.

"I'll put your collar on my dresser," she said, "so you'll know where to find it."

She ran with the collar to her boudoir, flung it on the dresser, picked up a perfume bottle and touched her ears with the glass rod of the stopper.

I stopped at the door and she turned around.

"Now I am going to kiss you, Sasha, just for relieving me of my collar."

"Go easy," she said. "You'll break the stopper. Stop now," she said, flushed. "You're choking me!"

I took the bottle from her hand and set it somewhere on the dresser.

"Sasha," I said, "isn't it wonderful, just too wonderful?"

"I love you," she breathed, "and it's going to be my ruin." Again she swayed, as that time under the stars on the hilltop, and passed her chin gently over my burning cheek in a submissive ecstasy. We did not speak.

I was drunk with her presence, with the fragrance of her black hair, with the whiteness of her soft skin...

Then she played on the piano, parts of "Sniegourotchka," and sang some of the opera "Oniegin." She played well, with a fleeting soft touch, never too loud—just as good players are wont to play; and she sang in a clear subdued voice, so agreeable to hear.

She would sing some beautiful folk song, with just a trace of accompaniment—touching the keys now and then. She conjured up a hidden, enchanted world of transcendental presages and perceptions, beautifully unreal and ethereal. Never before had I felt the power of such wonderful simplicity as that with which she could touch the heart and carry the feelings wherever she pleased.

Yelena got some records out and we danced. Sasha dimmed the lights, and I could hold her close again.

What else mattered then? She clung to me and snuggled close—how marvelously smoothly she could glide! She stopped suddenly and listened with a startled look.

"Stop the music!" She turned to Yelena in excitement; then ran to the window. Somebody was banging on the garden gate; the latch rattled with an ominous clatter, and there were some furious kicks on the door.

"My God!" exclaimed Sasha getting pale. "Quick—it's my husband— if he finds you here—"

"Yelena," she said hurriedly, while she slipped on her fur coat, "take the boys quickly through the kitchen, while I run down to open the door."

She raced down the stairs and was gone. We grabbed our cloaks and Yelena shoved us into the dark kitchen, from which another stairway led to the garden. She closed the door and we were outside. We were to wait there until Sasha and her husband entered the house from the front and then make away as quietly as we could. Yelena ran back to put into order whatever she could manage.

Sasha unbolted the gate before which her husband stood raging. We pressed flat against the kitchen door, out on a platform, partially covered by a protruding roof, and could hear every word in that crisp, icy air.

"Why in the devil do you bolt the door?" he flew at Sasha when he was inside.

"Don't swear. Is that the welcome I get? And why shouldn't I bolt the door?" we heard her snap back very promptly and efficiently. "I always bolt the door if you are not at home. What other protection would I have, if I may ask?"

He grumbled something we could not hear, which Sasha ignored entirely. Then we heard him fumbling with the bolt, trying to close the door from the inside. I nudged Cornel.

"How are we going to get out, I wonder?"

Then Sasha spoke: "You need not bolt the door now. I am not afraid if you are at home."

They started toward the house entrance without another word, but before he opened the door for Sasha he said very despondently: "The Bolshevists took Rybinsk two days ago, and they will be here before the year is over."

We slid down the bannister, ran to the garden house and waited for a while. Some talk filtered through the windows, but it did not sound like a quarrel.

We reached the garden gate, opened it carefully, and, when closing it again, I held the blade of my knife under the latch, that it might not clatter when falling down.

Walking briskly we reached our billet, rather out of breath. There was no sentinel outside and we entered the yard. He stood inside, for an icy wind swept the street.

It was so dark that we just saw him dimly and, as he muttered something, we replied in a similar unintelligible mutter, passing him rapidly. We reached our house, hid the coats and ran up the stairs. Andy was sitting before the samovar, glaring into the lamp, blinking sleepily.

He turned slowly.

"Well—at last," he said deliberately. "I thought they'd got you this time. It's half past two, if you want to know."

"Is there still some tea left?" I asked.

He tilted the samovar. I heard a welcome splash inside and he just nodded.

"What about the evening checkup?" I asked.

"There was none," he said frowning, "but let me tell you that what you're doing is sheer madness, and they'll get you someday. I'll bet you a hundred roubles they will."

I drank a cup of tea and another one. The samovar was empty. Then I answered.

"All right, Andy, I'll take the bet. Have you a match?"

I did not sleep much that night, for I was worried for Sasha. Would she be able to explain? What if her husband suspected something? And what if we could not meet in the future? I tried not to think of that.

Next evening I stood at the gate waiting for her appearance, and she came later than usual. Yelena was again with her, and they seemed to be carefree, for they were chatting and laughing. I noticed it with relief. She must have found a way out of this difficulty after all.

I held a written note in readiness, in which I begged her to tell me whether she was in any trouble, and I also asked when I could see her again.

Very cautiously I gave her to understand that I had a note, and she took notice of it in a careful manner. But no matter how I tried, there was no way that evening to throw snowballs. The sentinel watched sharply as often as they passed the gate; the sidewalk was crowded, and, to make things worse, two militiamen were near all the time. The time was nearing when Sasha generally left, and I began to feel uneasy. They shortened their beat, so as to pass more often, but we were always out of luck. I saw well that she, too, had something to say.

Then, when it seemed that all efforts would be in vain, they returned once more and stopped right before our gate, nearly brushing the guard on the sidewalk.

"So long, Yelena," she said, acting as if they were going to part now. "Then we will meet tomorrow at nine at the church."

They parted there and then. The message was delivered.

I met her at the church at the stroke of nine on the following evening, and, as we walked up through the suburbs to the hills, she assured me that the incident had had no consequences.

There was a hospital outside the town, surrounded by a large garden. There were some benches at the garden entrance, where we could sit and talk undisturbed. Nobody ever came or went at that late hour.

"I am so sorry it happened," she said. "Wasn't it a pity to break up that party? He arrived three days sooner than he said he would. It never happened before."

"Be careful, Sasha," I said. "I'd hate to see you in trouble. How did you get away today?"

"He left this afternoon," she replied with bitterness in her voice. "He will be gone for another week."

"Didn't he ask questions?" I inquired. "How did you account for the party? There was no time to clear anything away."

"Lady friends of mine," she said, "and I told him they had left just before he came. Plain enough! Yelena was there to make the story believable. By the way, I brought the collar you left on the dresser."

She snuggled close. It was cold, and I slipped my warm, pointed, felt hood over her head and shoulders. For a long time, we sat silent. Nothing stirred around, everything seemed to be lifeless, as if murdered by the cold. Now and then a small snow pad fell from the trees, and a faint whiff of wind carried a powdery snow over the thick winter blanket. It jingled and hissed faintly, scarcely audible. The tiny crystals glittered like emeralds in the moonlit night. Everything was asleep under the bright, glimmering moon which was sprinkling every object with its silvery radiance.

"I can feel your heartbeat," she said in a whisper.

December came, and with it severe cold. Icy blasts howled through the streets, fiercely rattling the lamp windows, and the flames of the oil lamps leaped and bobbed to battle the wind.

It was impossible to remain outdoors for any time. The cold was stiffening, and the sharp wind whirled the snow into dense driving clouds that swept madly over the deserted streets.

Nevertheless, we met, just as before, but we had to look for shelter. We were on the hilltop, near the hospital, when the storm broke loose. It came with terrific force and we had to find someplace to go.

There stood a large, uncompleted building, quite alone in a field. Its windows yawned darkly; many of them gaped empty, and the roof was only half finished. We had passed it quite often on our nocturnal walks, and I never knew what it was. It loomed gray and ghostly, but it did look like a shelter in that howling storm. Sasha said it was the epidemic hospital, under construction, and we tried to make it. I thought we would have to give up, for the going was terrible. There was no road yet to the building. We had to climb a low fence, and then wade through the snow that came up in places waist deep. We also had the wind against us, and it blinded me to such an extent that sometimes I lost the outlines of the building. But we made it somehow. She held my hand and proceeded bravely.

I found the door. It was unlocked, just pegged temporarily with a piece of lath. We entered, and I struck a match. There was a door at the bottom of the staircase, but this was locked. But soon I found another door, hidden by some boards that leaned against the wall, which was unlocked. It led to the cellar, and we went down. We stepped into a brick vault. Scattered all around lay scraps of boards, bricks, wheelbarrows and some crowbars.

While Sasha lit matches, I split some boards with a crowbar and soon we had a small fire going. Sitting on an upturned wheelbarrow we gazed into the flames. We held our hands close to the gleaming embers and the flesh became translucent; one could see the dark, hazy outline of the bones.

"See what small bones I have in my little finger," she would say. And then I made some shadow pictures on the wall, forming the shapes with my fingers. I made a long-eared rabbit which could open its mouth, then a devil, with two horns and a long nose. But Sasha wanted the rabbit again and she wanted me to make it laugh.

One evening when I met her it was blowing hard and very cold. We were standing under a low roof that protruded over the church gate, over-arching the sidewalk.

The gate lay deep between its heavy pillars, and formed a small niche where the force of the wind was somewhat broken. Here we discussed where to go. It was quite evident that we could not stay on the street, and equally manifest that we did not have a place to go to. Sasha's home was out of the question, and the cellar of the hospital was an abominable place. It was cold, dark and barren. If we did build a fire, it filled the small vault soon with an acrid smoke. And then, that waist deep snow alone would have been enough reason to drop it.

So we kept on deliberating but we could not think up anything worth-while.

Suddenly, Sasha seized my hand.

"I have it!" she said. "How silly that I did not think of that before! We will go to Stefan. You probably know him; he is one of your soldiers."

I did not know Stefan, nor did I know where he lived, but that did not matter, for I was to find out immediately.

A little distance from the church, on the outskirts of the city, lay a huge monastery, on an immense site, surrounded by a tall iron fence. It had a spacious yard, where stood, in a rather secluded spot, a humble little cabin.

We entered the yard through a side door, which was unlocked, and crossed the yard. No soul was around; there was no reason to hurry. The L-shaped large building was dark and gloomy; only a few of the upper story windows were lit. Very faintly one could hear the sounds of a choir singing somewhere.

The little cabin had probably belonged formerly to some gatekeeper, or caretaker, but now it was occupied by that mysterious Stefan, whom I did not know. Sasha said that he was a cobbler, who worked for the monks. They did not pay him much for his work, but he was allowed to live there and get his food from their kitchen. In exchange, he kept their boots in good condition and also did odd jobs around the yard. Once he had done some work for Sasha's husband, and that was how she knew of his existence.

The hut was dark, with all its shutters closed, but through a tiny crack I saw a light inside. While Sasha kept waiting, pressed to the darkest side of the hut, I rapped gently on a shutter, close to the light. Soon I heard movement inside, and somebody shuffled to the door.

"Who is it and what do you want?" came the grumpy question in bad Russian from inside.

"I am one of your officers; please open the door and let me come in," I answered in German.

"Immediately," he replied in German. "I'll just bring the lamp and open."

After some shuffling, he opened the door wide enough to let me in, and when he saw a Russian soldier enter his place he was not a little surprised. I unhooked the Russian mantle and, as he saw my uniform and the golden stars of a lieutenant, he stiffened to attention and rapped out in an excellent military bearing: "At your service, sir!"

"What is your name?" I inquired.

"Corporal Stefan Riedl, sir."

"All right, Corporal—or still better, Stefan—stand at ease." He relaxed somewhat and stood there very attentive.

"Now, Stefan, do you want to make three roubles right now?" I queried.

"I will be glad, sir. What will I have to do?"

"You'll rent me your cabin." I glanced at my watch. "It's a little after nine now. Let me have it until midnight or, better still, until one o'clock."

He grinned a little, but with enough decency not to become offensive.

"Here—take the three roubles," I told him, "and make it snappy with your getting out. The lady is waiting outside, and it's cold."

Stefan dressed in a hurry but I had to keep him from sweeping the floor and tidying up the place. I told him he could do the sweeping next time but I wanted him to hurry now.

We agreed that I could have the cabin any evening I liked. I was to tell him half an hour before, and the key would be left hidden on a rafter, right above the door.

I would always find it there, could unlock the door myself and then, when leaving his place, I could replace it for him. He was to sweep the cabin each time; look after the fire, and leave some drinking water in readiness to make tea. He would always find his three roubles on a prearranged place, under his wooden peg bowl.

Contrary to all army regulations, I gave Stefan a hearty handshake, which made him very proud. In gratitude, he never disappointed me. He went out and disappeared into the stormy night.

Poor Sasha was numb with cold when she finally came in.

"Good boy, that Stefan, that soldier of yours," she said. "I'll see that he gets work from all my friends."

The wind could blow now all it wanted. It was nice and cozy in Stefan's little cobbler's hut. I used to go a little earlier than she was to come, and wait for her there. She did not even bother anymore to muffle herself in the coarse peasant coat that she had worn before. She said she wanted me to remember her looking her best. She fleeted through the wide yard, wrapped in some fluffy fur, and the hard frozen snow creaked lightly under her small, knee-booted feet.

She used to sit with cheeks aglow before the large brick oven, but sometimes a fleeting sadness passed over her features and she closed her eyes with tears quivering on her long lashes.

"Calm yourself, Sasha," I soothed her, "my only Sashenyka. Why think of the future, if we have the beautiful present?"

But my words must have sounded hollow and unconvincing. I knew very well how she felt, for those same feelings, those very same forebodings made my own heartache. We were living in a dream, in a rapturous trance that only a few were allowed to relish—in a spiritualizing, devastating love that made us happy and unhappy at the same time. The cold reality loomed monstrous, too dangerously near to be faced calmly.

Men cover their eyes before they sink in a whirlpool or throw themselves into an abyss, the spiritual ego battling in a powerless, desperate revolt to free itself from its inextricable, ruinous, carnal casing.

Yes, it was a dream—too unreal, too good to be true, too beautiful to endure—from which a painful awakening would come.

And when would it come? Could I delay the end? No, I could not, but verily I could hasten it. I do not believe in a painfully slow destruction. I prefer a glorious, swift, crashing finish. Let it come, if it has to, not sneaking and lurking, but in a mad career, riding down like thunder.

This was no light matter, no sentimental little romance, such as soldiers have, wherever they are, which ends in a sigh and maybe a few tears. This was deadly earnest, too overwhelming to regard it as a mere pastime.

At nights, when all was quiet, in the small hours of the morning, when I sat with Andy before the samovar, I pondered until I could not think anymore coherently.

While I propped my forehead with both fists, and gazed into the glossy side of the softly purring samovar, he used to watch me stealthily, now and then shaking his head in a silent despair.

"You are ruining yourself," he said softly, laying his hand on my arm, "and, furthermore, you are ruining her, too."

I did not answer—for I could not answer—it was only too true.

"Brace up, old fellow," he said after a long pause. "Try to make a gentlemanlike and honorable end to this thing, as long as it is in your power. It may not be long before you won't be able to control things, and then it will be so much the worse for both of you."

I looked at him absent-mindedly, and there was a long pause.

"Andy, you were always a faithful, good pal to me, but—please, I beg you, keep out of this. I don't know what I am doing, and I don't want to know. Leave me alone!"

"Now, now," he said—"are you going to kick up your old friendship all for her? I don't want to hurt you, so help me God, but I hate to see you go to the devil, and that's what you're doing right now."

Again he tousled my hair, with his gently rough cordiality. I jerked my head back, not out of hate, but it was the last resistance I could offer. And then my nerves, taut from battles, captivity, and that deliriously, hectic finish, suddenly snapped, and I broke down in bitterness, overpowered by a hopeless futility.

Chapter XI

Yes—it was painful, but I had to face the facts once more. If our love had to die—if it was predestined to doom—then it must die with one clean, murderous stroke, and not totter dejectedly to its death.

What were we heading for? I stopped to think in a grim despair. Where was this to lead? I might still see her a dozen times; maybe only half a dozen times. It might just as well be not once—never any more. Who could tell? It was tempting fate every time I left the billet, and every time I returned. It was a miracle that I had not been caught so far—but miracles do not last forever. Eventually, it was bound to happen, and those guards, getting more lawless and Bolshevistic with each day, would have little sympathy if they caught one red-handed.

But what—even if these trysts were to continue undisturbed hereafter? She was a married woman—true a very unhappy woman—but there was her husband, in a powerful position, to reckon with. Already he had returned unexpectedly a second time.

And then—I had to weigh the immediate future that stood before me. There could be no doubt about it that the Bolshevists were breaking up Russia at a furious rate. Much did they care about their former allies; much did they care whether France was to get Alsace-Lorraine and England the African colonies. They wanted peace, and they said so. They wanted to get out of the fray—and the sooner, the better. At the rate things were proceeding, the formal end could be expected by spring.

We would go home—with Russia settled and out; but that did not mean the end of the war to us. It simply meant a beginning on some other front—for there were many. What a tremendous drive could be made anywhere with all those prisoners that were to come!

I still stood an excellent chance of being shot either in Italy or in the Balkans. What plans could I make here; what right had I to make plans here, with the issue yet undecided? And furthermore what was I? Now I was a second lieutenant—by this time probably promoted to a first lieutenancy—but if the war ended, no matter how, I would be reduced to nothing again. In the very best case I should have to start somewhere at the bottom, to cope with all those for whom we had battled.

It was a dreary perspective, but too true to be disregarded. It was a very good reason to pound the table with hopeless despair. Soldiers were expected to have knapsacks, rifles, grenades and ammunition, and hearts to fight bravely for "God, Emperor and Fatherland," or for whatever the slogan might be—hearts to fight, but not to love. They were not supposed to love the women of their enemies, no matter how beautiful they were and no matter how their heartbeats would synchronize.

And so I struck out for the only road left, for the one and only road that I could go. If I was to fade out of the picture, I preferred to do it gracefully, voluntarily, of my own free will, and not be knocked into submission by the rifle butts of Red Guards. For I would not sit among thieves and criminals, behind bars in some filthy county jail. Sasha might not understand, and might hate me for it, but she certainly would have no cause for pity or contempt.

I did not see Sasha for three days. Then Christmas Day came, and we were to have our own little Christmas party in Stefan's log cabin. After a time Yelena and Cornel were to come too; there were to be just four of us. I went first to prepare everything for the evening. Stefan had got a tiny Christmas tree, and we fixed some candles and silver tinsel to the fragrant branches. Soon after he left Sasha arrived, with a small basket, carried by a little maid whom she sent back from the yard gate; and not much later Yelena came, followed by Cornel, carrying another basket.

They set the table—and it was again a pure white cloth —it reminded me of the party at Sasha's. We blew out the oil lamp, for we lit the candles on the tree. Christmas candles have always something fairylike about them, and never have they impressed me quite so much as on that evening. Why— the low little workshop looked exactly like a suitable setting for one of Andersen's fairy tales!

The mellow lights flickered and danced, quivering restlessly on the silver tinsel, brightening everything, even the toes of the clumsy boots that were lined in military order under Stefan's benches. The refreshing smell of tanned leather mingled with the sweetness of the crisp confections and the fragrant green twigs of the Christmas tree.

There is something about Christmas trees—something not to be explained in terms—which grips the heart and makes everything else seem unimportant, a childish and quiet peacefulness, wonderful in its purity and simplicity; the spirit of Christmas itself. It may be the reminiscence of the birth of the Savior; it may be just a wish to be once again unartificial, natural and content with things just as they are. And so it did impress those Russian women with its magic spell, for their own Christmas was not this day, but was to come thirteen days hence.

While I watched Sasha around the tree, with cheeks aglow and eyes sparkling, once again happy, I felt myself a deserter, a cheat, trying to cover my true feelings behind a mask of indifference.

"What's the trouble?" she exclaimed. "Are you not happy? See how bright those little candles burn. Look at all those good things over there! Come now, all of you, let's have a drink."

We drank. It was good to drink, for it made you forget so many things. And we drank more. They had two bottles of genuine champagne and it certainly was cold enough without a special cooler.

Just once more I wanted to hold her close, to inhale the fragrance of her hair, to feel her smooth skin, to see her eyes sparkle and her teeth glitter so brilliantly, to feel the radiant healthy beauty of her youth. I just wanted to be once more dizzy, so very dizzy that I could forget the past and the future to come—at least on that Christmas night.

It was late when we left the cabin. A beautiful, cold, starry night was outside, and the streets were deserted. We all left together. We were to accompany Sasha first —as far as it was reasonably safe—and, before we parted, I made her promise to see me the following evening. Then I proceeded with Cornel to take Yelena home. We reached a street where the passage on the sidewalk was too narrow for three of us to walk abreast. High mounds of snow bordered the walk on both sides, reaching shoulder high, forming veritable walls right and left. We walked in single file here. Yelena led, I followed, and then came Cornel. Where the space between the walls broadened somewhat, I caught up with Yelena and I walked beside her.

"Charming evening we had," she commented, and I agreed. Cornel had dropped back a little and was now trying to catch up.

"Yelena," I said rapidly, in a subdued voice, "will you please come tomorrow with Sasha to the cabin? She promised to be there for sure."

"I might," she said. "Is Cornel coming too?"

"No," I replied, "it would be better if only you two came alone. I'll have something very important to tell to Sasha."

"You surprise me," she went on. "What have I to do with it, if it is important to Sasha? Why have I to be there?"

"I can't well explain it to you, Yelena, right now and here, but if you are a good friend to Sasha, and love her, you'll come. Please do me the favor. There is some trouble in our billet."

She was rather startled as she replied, "Very well then, I'll be there as you say."

It was the twenty-sixth of December of the year 1917, and in the morning the Bolshevists took the government capital, the city of Vyatka.

After nine in the evening I marched out of the gate of the billet—but this time for good. Once more I looked back on the lighted, frosty windows, behind which Andy and all the others were sitting. This time I wore again that peasant sheepskin coat, underneath which was a combination of clothes that might have been classed as a civilian outfit.

Rapidly I walked through the streets, reached the monastery, and crossed the yard. Gently I rapped on the door, and Yelena opened.

Sasha sat on a bench in a dark corner. She stood up when I entered and looked at my outfit with a startled expression.

"What does this mean?" she asked, hardly able to speak.

"I am going, Sasha, and I—I came to say goodbye to you." There was a pause for a while. Sasha stared at me with round open eyes, which expressed fright, despair and incredulity; then she flew at me, together with Yelena. They both spoke at once, and they tugged at my coat frantically.

"No!" she screamed while she hammered my chest with her fists in a hysterical fit. "Say it isn't true! Do say it's not true! Do you hear me?"

She sank to her knees with wild terror in her eyes, and then huddled into a limp desperate heap, sobbing bitterly. I bit on my lips until it hurt; my eyes were burning, and my fingers opened and contracted spasmodically.

It was cruelly terrible, but there was no way to evade things. Gently I picked her up and put her on the bench. Yelena gave her some water. I tried to soothe her with all the endearments I knew, but she did not seem to hear them.

Suddenly she sat up and thrust me back. Her eyes flamed with an unholy fire and her lips trembled above her teeth.

"I hate you!" she exclaimed, quite beside herself. "And don't think that you can run away from me just because you are tired of me! By God you won't! I swear—I promise you! I'll scream for help, if you take another step toward that door. Try it!"

She broke down again, choking with spasmodic sobs. I knelt beside her. She threw her arms around my neck. "No," she said, "please forgive what I have just said. You know I love you so much—more than anything else—"

She kissed me with a venomous ferocity, and gritted her teeth in a fitful frenzy. Then she would stroke me kindly and rub her cheek, with closed eyes, against my face.

"You are not going—are you? Don't you love me anymore?" she asked a dozen times. But I felt it was no question anymore. She just wanted to hear and torture herself with my affirmation.

How could I explain to her what I felt then? Would she ever understand that I had to desert her because I loved her too much?

After a time her hysterical fits passed, and she lay on the broad bench, sobbing softly, too exhausted to do anything else than knead my hand with her nervously twitching fingers. I sat beside her and stroked her hot forehead and spoke to her gently. An hour passed so.

Yelena sat somewhat apart, visibly upset, and did not speak much. I looked at my watch stealthily, but she noticed it with desperation. She clung to me with all her force.

"God help us, Sasha," I said. Then I had to swallow, for it became very hard to speak without breaking down myself. "Goodbye... I will never forget you... Forgive me for what I am doing—"

That was about all I could say. With a last desperate clasp she drew my head down to her breast and seized my hand; then passed out in a deathlike faint.

Gently I pulled my hand out of her fingers and, for the last time, I kissed her forehead and her eyes. I seized my coat and fur cap. Yelena was up, standing at Sasha's head. She dabbed her eyes with a handkerchief, and stretched out her hand. "Goodbye then," she said. "Perhaps it's best so. And God help you to get home in safety."

Somehow I stumbled out of the hut and was in the yard. I was dizzy, but the cold air brought me to my senses. Rapidly I slipped on the coat and crossed the yard toward the gate. Once more I looked back—I had to stop, just to see that little cabin once more, for the last time—then I started with long strides toward the opposite end of the town.

1 - A typical Russian team, with three horses abreast.

Chapter XII

It was eleven o'clock when I reached a low building. Through the shutters filtered a little light, and I tapped gently. Soon the door opened and a tall, broad-shouldered man appeared. I stepped in and we shook hands.

"I am glad you came," he said. "The sleigh is waiting in the yard. We'll start in twenty minutes. Let's have a drink first. It's going to be very cold tonight."

I did not object, for I needed something to brace me up a little.

The preparations for this flight had not taken six weeks. In exactly four days I had made ready. Evenings, when I went out, I met Kuehne, a German civil engineer—one of the internes living in the town. He was very anxious to get home, after his internment of forty-two months, to see his young wife again.

This time I did not bother with any passports. The Bolshevists were advancing and, where they settled down on their eastward march, they had other things to do than to examine the validity of papers. Furthermore, what good were papers, made out by their adversaries?

The whole wide country was in a bloody, frenzied turmoil—fighting everywhere. Civil war was raging wherever the Red Guards of Lenin set foot. It was an ideal time for an escape—provided one did not value one's safety too much, and did not care what happened.

However, our little place was 140 wersts from the nearest railroad station—a three days' drive in that arctic weather and bottomless snow. But that could be arranged. Kuehne knew Pavel, who used to be a gendarme under the Tsarist regime and to whom he had to report at regular intervals. Pavel was out of a job since the revolution, for the free and democratic country that Russia was now did not need any boyar henchmen.

For that reason Pavel was not enthusiastic for either Kerensky or Lenin. As soon as he was divested of his uniform, he became a drayman, and he was quite willing to take us, for one hundred roubles, to Vyatka. His sleigh was waiting, ready to start, in the backyard. There is nothing quite so reliable as an old regular—even an old ex-regular.

We crept into the flat bottom of the peasant sleigh and poked our feet under the hay; Pavel squatted on the raised bow, and out we drove.

Sometimes I turned back in the direction where I had left her, utterly broken-hearted and unhappy, and with each yard we glided on, my heart became heavier. We left the very last houses of the town, turned north and were on a white, glistening, wide road—the mail route to Vyatka. Before the road curved into the forest I had a last glimpse of the little town, frozen and white, with a faint glow of warm lights filtering through tiny windows. It became blurred and hazy, fading into the placid valley, radiated by the lurid moonshine.

It was very, very cold on that crisp, clear winter night. A queer sensation coupled with my absent-minded dejection, while we sat there without much talk. It grew steadily, by leaps and bounds and overwhelmed me finally with a strangeness hitherto never felt. Suddenly I felt free of all shackles—shackles that had bound me for so long with invisibly strong fine fibers. Was I not on the road to freedom, free from the depressing tedium of captivity, free, by a forcible lunge, from a hopeless love? I felt my heart burn, but I also felt it tingle with the joy of excitement.

Deep in the heart of every male is an indomitable, primordial instinct to rove and adventure—a desire that may be suppressed or dormant, a desire that will finally flame into action.

Yes, there was danger all around, but that made it all the more worth-while! Somehow the air seemed purer and sweeter out here, in these boundless forests, among these endless plains. I had a desire to jump from the sleigh and run for a while—fast—as fast as I could, just to assure myself of my fitness, just to feel the joy of contact with a free road once more. It was that strange fascination that roads always have for foot soldiers, rovers, tramps and wayfarers—and every open road will have that strange attraction for me as long as I am able to creep on it.

We wiggled still deeper into the hay, but it did not seem to help much. The cold was cutting right to the marrow. I felt my face become stiff and immovable; the nostrils clogged after each breath and the inhaled air felt like liquid ice. My hands were numb, and after a while I did not feel my feet at all.

I pulled out a knitted woolen cap, of that tight-fitting kind that can be pulled over the head and neck with just a small opening for the face. I slipped it on reversed, so that the opening lay on the back of my head, and there was no opening in the front whatever. This helped a little—at least it filtered the cold somewhat—but after a while a thick ice crust formed, which made it worse than ever. I slid down so far that I was able to dig my chin and nose under the sheepskin coat and breathe into the clothing. This gave a feeling of a little warmth.

The runners bumped gently, with a muffled sound, over the smooth icy road, and a faint creaking of the joints was scarcely audible. I felt that strange feeling of being awake and yet dozing. The blood ran sluggish in my veins, and quite unnoticeably a deadly drowsiness came over me. Once or twice I tried to blink, just to find out whether I was still awake, and my lashes brushed against the close-fitting woolen cap. In front of me towered, blurred and indistinct, a bundle of sheepskin and felt. It looked altogether too big for a human being, yet I thought it must be Pavel driving. My head became so heavy that I simply could not hold it, and then I tried to move my feet and was not sure whether they did move or not. But it was good to lie in the soft hay—so very drowsy—and it did not even feel so cold now...

Very far off I heard dull thuds coming quite fast. Why certainly! Now I even heard the metallic clink of horseshoes, clashing in mid-air, as of galloping horses, phantom riders. How they raced, scarcely touching the ground; and a woman on a black steed, with flashing eyes, pointing—yes, pointing straight at me! I must creep deeper into the hay or she will see me. She said I would not get away... But now—it's so hard to move. Everything is so heavy. I have no fingers—and no legs ... I won't move, but just stay where I am. Only, if she would not look with those flashing black eyes! They burn so terribly...

Somebody shook me violently. Through the cap I saw dimly a huge, bearded head and a big bulk of something right over me, and I heard words spoken, but I was not sure what was said. I could feel heavy mitts on my shoulder, and then they even slid under my shoulder and shook me so forcibly that my head wobbled.

"Pan!" he said. "Pan, Pan, awake! You shouldn't sleep on a night like this. You'll freeze to death! I have been shaking you for a full minute now. Try to get up!"

It must have been Pavel, the driver. Somehow I came to. I asked him to pull off my cap and replace my large sheepskin headgear. I could not move a finger, arm or leg. Pavel lifted me out of the sleigh with his huge arms and put me down, as though he were setting a skittle-pin.

We stood in a village before a small house. An immense, pale moon touched the chimney—just as if it were standing on it. It was four o'clock in the morning. Light came through the frosty panes of the house in front of us. All the other cottages were dark and silent.

Two men in heavy fur coats approached and told me in German to come in. Kuehne was inside already. I tried to move, but could not; so they caught me under the arms and carried me with some difficulty inside. They were German internes—some friends of Kuehne's. Somehow they unhooked and unbuttoned my clothes and then Pavel brought a dishful of snow and I got such a rubbing that I shall never forget it. After ten minutes I could manage to move my fingers and my limbs to some extent, at least enough so that I could shake a limp hand with those Germans, and that good hairy fellow Pavel, for their kindness. Kuehne was not in quite such a bad shape, for his traveling outfit was much warmer, but he too sat there stiff and numb. I scratched the thick crust of ice from the window to look at the thermometer outside, and I began to understand when I read 62° F. below zero.

We got tea and brandy and then they offered us some bacon and tasty black bread. For an hour we talked, as long as the samovar lasted, then we turned in for a three hours' sleep, right on those benches on which we sat, for we had to be on our way not later than eight o'clock —before it grew light.

For we were escaping—not merely traveling.

We drove a day, spent another night in a peasant cottage, this time with some kinsmen of Pavel, and on the third day we saw the faraway church steeples of Vyatka.

We began to run into traffic. Sleighs came, sleighs, and more sleighs—all packed with soldiers—deserters from the front and from garrisons. Many were armed; some were not. At least they had no rifles in their hands; they may have lain on the straw beside them. On one of the sleighs was a machine-gun, turned upside down, the thick clumsy wheels sticking up in the air—a familiar sight to me.

We crossed the railroad tracks. I had not seen steel tracks for years, and if Kuehne hadn't been around I think I should have got out, knelt down beside them and patted those shiny, glossy steel rails running westward—toward home.

A little after noon we drove into Vyatka. There was still a little desultory rifle fire in some suburb, and there were huge masses of slovenly soldiery everywhere. But nobody bothered about us.

Pavel stopped before a roadhouse. We paid him off and said goodbye to him. Thus far we were safe from all pursuit. There could be no communication between our deserted garrison, which stood for the provisional government, and that sailor who ran the government business for the Reds here.

But this was as far as I could go with Kuehne. He intended to go to Moscow—to decide there what to do next—and I wanted to go to Petrograd and then dope out everything there.

It was still a nice little walk of two thousand miles to the Swedish border from here. However, if Kuehne insisted on going to Moscow, we would part right here and now, and that's exactly what we did in the friendliest manner. We had some tea and a bite together, and then we parted, wishing each other lots of good luck.

Things looked rather reassuring from my standpoint. There was a topsy-turvy condition everywhere that made my heart leap with joy, and after a short deliberation I decided to take the risk and try to travel to Petrograd without further ado. I went and hung around the station to find out whether there were any trains, and, if there were any, when? Chalked upon a blackboard was a temporary schedule. There was a train for Petrograd at nine that same evening. Then I hung around the ticket window and pointed my ears to learn the correct way to ask for tickets. I also wanted to know if civilian passengers were asked for passports. To my great comfort, Bolshevism had done away with these things. People paid, got their tickets, and that was all. I stood in a long line and in about half an hour I proceeded far enough to shove my banknotes into the ticket window. I received a ticket and some stamps, which at that time were in use for small change.

Much relieved, I left the station and went for a stroll in the city, which was quite a good-looking place. I could not well understand the reason for rifle fire, which I could hear quite distinctly; for though there were thousands of soldiers, moujiks and burghers everywhere, all seemed to smile and go around peaceably, with seemingly no work to be done, like a holiday.

I passed a little place with a big glass of coffee painted on a sign. By God! hadn't I quite forgotten how coffee tasted during all this time? I went in and asked for a glass, then for a second, and then a third. I was simply rolling in luxury that day.

In the morning the first signs of civilization—those shiny tracks—then a regular ticket to Petrograd, and now three glasses of coffee—not very good coffee to be sure, but you are not so particular if you have not seen coffee for three years.

It was seven o'clock—still two more hours, provided the train really started on schedule. It was getting very cold as I lingered before the shop windows. There was a confectioner's shop with some boxes of candy displayed.

Yes! Why not? I would not sign my name anyhow, only a simple F., and she would know, and nobody else. I bought a box of candy and had it wrapped, good and strong, to be shipped out of town.

"We will send it," said the merchant, "if you'll give us the address."

"Much obliged," I replied—"but I will attend to this myself."

A little before nine the doors were thrown open, and a horde of several hundred civilians and soldiers rushed the train. It was full when that surging mob pressed and twirled me nearly under the wheels. I tried to get out somehow, but there were too many feet, so I tried on the opposite side with far better results. So far, nobody had thought of storming the train from that side. But already they were coming, bobbing up from under the cars, through the buffers, everywhere. With a desperate lunge I reached the tread and grasped the rail. From then on it was easy, for I was lifted off my feet by those behind me, and I only had to press down the door-latch.

Inside the coach, on the other side of the latch, stood humanity pressed and packed, swearing furiously, as generally happens when democracy is born. Another combined thrust and the door opened just wide enough for me to squeeze in, with all my ribs cracking. So I was in, finally, and after me still a dozen others.

As often as somebody was strong enough to squeeze in, I was brushed, pushed and rolled farther inside. Finally, I was crushed against a small door. When the next crush came, the door gave way with an ominous crack and, together with four soldiers, I was hurled into a small place, not much larger than an oversize family icebox, only somewhat higher. For the sake of decency I will refer to it as a washroom, though to be sure there was nothing there to wash with.

Often since, getting on the subway at Times Square, at the rush-hour, I think of this place. We were mummified into some kind of a position, some with arms crossed over their chests, others with arms pinned to their sides; and there was no fidgeting to be done until seven o'clock next morning, when a bearish corporal wanted to exchange places with us. However, it was impossible to move, and he had to wait until we came to a station where some of the passengers got off.

After that I traveled for three days in the corridor, and if I got, all together, five hours of sleep, I make a pretty close guess. The journey was uneventful, and I was sorry that I had been foolish enough to pay for my ticket. Nobody ever inquired about tickets, since it had happened a few times that soldiers and civilians had thrown the conductors through the window. The state railway belonged to the people—and the people were to use it. Remarkable regulations those were! I felt a profound admiration for them.

On the day before we had been delayed somewhat. I don't recall where, but we met a transport coming from the front, and they held up our train a little more than two hours. Their own locomotive had broken down, and, as our machine was puffing vigorously, they wanted that.

It came to arguments, disputes and finally, as was then customary, delegations were appointed and the matter was duly taken up by the delegations of the two trains.

They won, having more rifles, coming from the front. We were voted down and our locomotive was promptly uncoupled.

For two hours they rode up and down in a vain effort to find a suitable switch, then they gave up and we received our locomotive back on condition that we would have another one dispatched for them from the next big station.

160

After that nothing remarkable happened. It is true that I had to serve the soldiers, all the time I was on the train, in any fashion they deemed fit; and at each station I returned from the hot water tanks with a dozen tea kettles, which I had to fill to the brim. I also helped them with their boots, but that was only fair, for in exchange they gave me bread and some tea, too, and, being their orderly, I was under their most benevolent protection.

It was the last day of the year when our train pulled into Petrograd.

Across the station, in a rather disreputable looking side street, I found a public house where they took me in and gave me shelter without asking any questions. All they wanted was to be paid in advance. I had just enough strength to creep up the stairs and drop in utter exhaustion on a shaky bed in a dingy cold room. There I lay for three days shaking with fever—that sleigh ride of course, and traveling in that draughty corridor without sleep. I lay on my back with all my clothes on, in sheepskin and high felt boots. I never knew whether it was day or night, for the room had no window. Sometimes I became delirious and had weird visions. Always I saw Sasha—very pale with a silent reproach, even hate, in her dark eyes.

There was a pitcher in the washbasin on a tin washstand. I put it on a chair, near the bed, so that I could reach it while lying there. On the second day there was not a drop left, and on the third I had to do without water, though I thought my throat was shriveling for sheer thirst.

Somehow I propped myself into a sitting position, but my head turned—or rather everything around seemed to turn. I fell back again, but I was so thirsty that soon I tried again. This time I succeeded. There was a faucet with running water at the end of the hall, and there I drank until I could drink no more. I also let the water run over my head, and that steadied me somewhat. I did not want to die in Petrograd, if they hadn't succeeded in shooting me at the front, and after I had come all that way now from Vyatka. I was still wobbly, but after a while I could walk about slowly, without holding the wall or the table.

There was something corrugated on the wall, right above the washstand—framed too. In it I could see that the way I looked was no way to go out. I still had some long discarded safety blades—much too dull to shave a decent visage—but this was no decent visage, and that ten-day old stubble had to come off somehow. Well—somehow it did come off, and I decided not to shave for another two weeks.

Then I felt terribly hungry. There was a sharp pain on top of both my shoulders, but I felt starved all the same. I had three or four pounds of hardtack—the very same hardtack I had made six months before—and I ate until all my teeth hurt. Then I went out and had a hot tea in a "chaynaya." [1]

Feeling warm again I went on a stroll on the Nevsky Prospect, world-famous, even before the war. At a stationer's I bought a plan of Petrograd, and also a railroad map of Finland, quite up to the Swedish border.

After that I followed, at a safe distance, two men who spoke German. When I had overheard that the Danish Consulate was at number ten Sergeyevskaya I followed them no longer, but went to number ten Sergeyevskaya to see what could be done there. Around the building and in the plaza-like yard I heard a lot of German. The Danish delegation was supposed to care for the German and Austro-Hungarian civilian internes. As there loomed no danger, I went up after a while. There were a few dozen men, women and children waiting there. I sat down and waited for three hours. It was nice and warm, and I was in no special hurry. Finally I was allowed to go in. An official asked very formally what I wanted and who I was. I said I wanted to go home, and that I was an Austrian officer. Whereupon he became still more formal, and said that, to his greatest regret, the Royal Danish Delegation wished not to violate its neutrality, that it could not assist military persons—but civilians only. Upon which the next case was considered.

However, my visit was not quite fruitless, for I learned from an interne that there was some kind of a secret German organization at the Hotel Riga. He did not know where it was, but for such emergencies I had a plan of the city. I went straight there, but nobody was about. The whole place looked shady enough.

I started again for the Hotel Riga, the next morning. There was immense traffic everywhere, plenty of autos and Red Guard patrols with machine-guns before each bank and public building. Dazzling women strolled on the sidewalk, and splendid troykas whizzed by.

True, some of the windows had been shot, and some of the walls showed signs of the recent fights, but otherwise life went on without any noticeable change. At the Nicolaewsky Terminal I saw some ex-officers carrying sacks and unloading wagons in their well-cut, tight-fitting uniforms, very unshaved and without shoulder-straps, and some were selling papers and cigarettes on the Nevsky.

I arrived at the Hotel Riga and now this was rather a busy place, but I could not well ask the concierge where the Germans were. I kept in the hall for a while reading the Pravda and watching for something to turn up. I had not quite finished the paper, when I saw the German enter who had told me the day before at the Danish Consulate that he did not know where this place was. He saw me and came over.

For a time we scrutinized each other, and then he had become possessed of the knowledge that I was from the First Kaiserjaegers and I knew that he was a Saxon Uhlan.

Together we went up to the second story, to a room marked in no special way.

A very fast speaking, rasping little German was there. Yes—we could go through Finland with special reindeer sleighs that would drop us on the Swedish border somewhere. They had special Finnish scouts, who kept their drivers posted of the whereabouts of the roving Russian border patrols.

The journey lasted from twelve to fourteen days, and of course he would not guarantee a successful crossing. Anyhow it would cost twelve hundred Finnish marks, payable in advance. There and then the deal fell through. How far was I from twelve hundred Finnish marks, and where was the Uhlan from it?

For two days I pondered. The Uhlan said he would come to see me and maybe we could team up somehow, and he really came. I suggested that we buy skis and ski over the solidly frozen Gulf of Finland and the Gulf of Bothnia to Sweden.

The Bothnian Gulf was not more than thirty-five wersts at the most, and halfway lay the Aland island and a dozen lesser isles. It was nothing extraordinary for good skiers.

To this he had a dozen of objections. The ice was very rough; it was not solidly frozen, and there were broad stretches of open water; it was terribly windy; and where were we to get skis and regular ski-shoes? You could not ski for four days in felt hip-boots, the straps would have worn them out after a few hours. We debated for a long time and he said he would think it over and then we could resume the talk tomorrow. That was, however, the last I saw of the Uhlan, for he never came again.

I pondered more about that ski tour to Sweden. There was so much for it. On the other hand I was in too run-down a condition to undertake such a strenuous dash all alone. No, that was no good. I might break down on the very first day, with my shoulders aching as they did. It was too risky and too crazy, after those three deliriously feverish days.

And the other prospects were cheerless too. There was good order in Finland, not chaos as in Russia. Furthermore, Finland was anything but Red; you couldn't travel there without proper passports.

Here I was sitting now on the seventh day, feeding on salt fish and tea, begging for bread at the barracks, and I had not the slightest idea what I would do.

It was so cold in that gloomy room that I shivered. Once more I went out to the Nevsky for an evening stroll.

There were plenty of lamps on the Nevsky, but only a few burned. There was no coal, and therefore there was not to be any extravagant illumination. In the houses the current was cut off at midnight sharp, and on the streets somewhat later. After that it was pitch dark until eight o'clock in the morning, and the Red patrols went around with small oil lanterns.

However, there was gay life on the scantily lit Nevsky.

The sidewalks were thronged with people and the merry laughter of dense crowds came through the heat dimmed glass windows of the restaurants.

Prices were atrocious, but there always seemed people who could afford to pay. The advertising bulletin boards were pasted with gaudy posters, invitations to meetings, dances and even to masquerades.

Why—this was certainly not the Petrograd I had expected to find! The Winter Palace, true, was badly battered by shells and rifle fire; most of the large cathedrals were closed, also the museums and picture galleries, but life was going on gaily, with plenty of dash and vigor. In the suburbs there was dire poverty, and hungry men were begging, stealing and robbing, but of that you saw nothing here.

I was just about to move from the advertising bulletin, when a piece of colored paper—like a theatre ticket—caught my eye. It was half covered by snow. For no special reason I picked it up. It proved to be a whole ticket, not a stub, probably from some previous day; otherwise, it would not be here. I examined it closely.

Sure enough it was a perfectly good ticket for tonight's performance at the Mariynsky Theatre—the Petrograd grand opera. Somebody must have dropped it. I looked at the advertising bulletin: Carmen. All right. I had seen half a dozen times at different places, but I had never seen it in Russian. And then there might be the famous Russian ballet. Furthermore it would be nice and warm at the top of that second gallery. I looked at my watch. If I stepped out, I could just make it on time.

I crossed the Fontanka Canal and reached the Theatre Square. Assuredly, those autocratic Tsars were not stingy when it came to building. I bought a program—to keep it for a souvenir—having had no other expenses, and then peeled off my coat and stuffed it under the seat. The opera was crowded, but most of the second gallery was not much better dressed than I, so that I did not feel out of place.

I glanced at the program and then folded it.

"Comrade, will you please lend me your program," said a huge, disheveled fellow on my right.

I handed it to him and he went over it rather carefully.

He gave it back with a smile and thanked me. I hoped that there the matter would end, but it did not come out so.

There are men who will always find something to talk about and there was no way to evade this fellow. So I answered as courteously as I could, but was mighty glad when the lights dimmed and the curtain went up. It wasn't bad at all. But, as I had guessed, all the heat came up to the second gallery to such an extent that after the first act I went out to cool off a bit and also to smoke a cigarette.

I had scarcely drawn half a dozen puffs when the tousled one detected me. He took out a cigarette, tapped it and asked for a light.

Again he made some preludes—in a very friendly fashion—and then, after the third question, he came out point blank: "You're not Russian, eh?"

By this time I had got used to rapid thinking.

"No," said I, "I am a Dalmatian—half Slavish and half Austrian."

"Oh!" he said, "interesting! How long have you been in this country?"

"About five years," I replied. "A beautiful country, yours. I came to study different types. I am a painter."

"Great times these," he continued. "We're shaking the whole world, don't you think? We'll make one big country out of the whole world."

I agreed. Then he burst forth into a fanatic paean of praise of Bolshevism.

When we returned to our seats I reflected. Here was that fellow on my right, some kind of a reporter with a Bolshevist paper, fanatic and careless, as all newly-born Bolshevists were at that time, eager to convert everybody to their doctrines. And there I was in Petrograd, stranded, a total stranger. It would not be wise to snub this fellow; he might be of some help to me yet. And so I changed my attitude toward him. We chatted after the second act, and after the performance we went to a "chaynaya" together for a friendly cup of tea.

When we parted, he invited me to come the next evening to a meeting and discussion they were going to have in some large tea house on the Mochowaya. And I promised, for now I had high hopes in him.

To him I was an Austrian subject, a civil interne, once a corporal in the Austrian army. The Balkans were at that time well under Austria's heel, but the whole situation had the aspect of a man balancing a pyramid with its point down. It could remain in that unnatural position as long as there was somebody to hold it with a desperate grip, but if he relaxed for a moment, the whole thing would come down with a crash.

Right then there was a lot of talk of a new state to be formed from Servia, Montenegro, the Slavic parts of Austria, Croatia and Hungary. It was to be under Russia's protection—this newly formed South-Slav-State, to be called Yougoslavia.

While the Tsar was in power, of course it was to be a tsardom or kingdom or something like that. Thus the Yougoslavs worked towards this end. Meanwhile things changed considerably in Russia. Here were the Bolshevists now, and they did not want Tsars at home or anywhere else. True, they wanted to see Austria broken up as thoroughly as possible, but if there was to be a country known as Yougoslavia, then it was to be the Yougoslavian Soviet Republic. And any man who seemed to be a good prospect to help to break up Austria was welcome.

I went to the meeting the next night. There were a lot of unwashed fellows, smoke and noise, short-haired girls and long-haired males.

On a platform, Baranoff, the reporter, raged and roared about the coming World Revolution that would unite all proletarians of this world, and would make life beautiful, by murdering all the bourgeois and then hanging the last priest by the entrails of the last nobleman. It was a great idea, very original.

The mob howled, girls shrieked; Baranoff was kissed by a very pretty murderess with flying hair, and then somebody else mounted the platform.

Good Lord! I thought, when I went home after the meeting, those Germans certainly did start something with their load in that sealed car!

However, things moved rapidly now. The next time I saw Baranoff we agreed on the details. He asked whether I had 150-200 roubles with which to pay for my ticket.

I said I would find it somehow. In that case he would use his influence and help me to a passport, through Finland and Sweden. As a corporal of the Austrian army I was to make propaganda, and I was also to break up the Austrian army. That was easy.

He would watch my activities through their agents there, and, if they reported favorably, I was to get all the moral and financial support I wanted. But as yet, of course, it would be impossible to advance money to a stranger, of whom, although he seemed to be trustworthy, he yet knew too little. But the passport would be all right. I could rely upon that, as sure as his name was Baranoff. And after all, that was the only thing that really mattered.

Two days later I had my passport—a photo on it, signatures, half a dozen seals—square seals, triangular seals—everything. It was six o'clock when he gave it to me in the "chaynaya."

There was a train from the Finnish Terminal on the next evening. He would come tomorrow afternoon and then he would help me to secure the ticket and see me off.

166

Then I went home and got my plan out. As far as I was concerned—I did not need Baranoff any longer; he could do all the hanging on entrails himself in the future.

It did not take me long to find the Finnish Terminal. I knew it led to the North, so it was reasonable enough to look for it on the top end of the map. There it was in the Wyborgskaya borough, right across the Big Neva. I took a good look at the map and made a rapid sketch of the streets I would have to use.

Up to the Nevsky, branch off right to the Znamenskaya, then turn to the left on the Kyrochnaya until I hit the Lyteiniy Prospect. Then straight ahead, across the bridge, turn right again—and there was the big station.

I followed my sketch and found the station beautifully. All I had to do was to check the street signs, high upon the walls.

I examined the schedule. There was a train that same evening, but I had missed that already. However, there was another train leaving for the border very early the next morning.

I went to the ticket window.

"A ticket to Torneo, please."

"Your passport!" said the man behind the cage.

I gave it to him. Now, I thought, this is the crucial point. Is it good or bad? He looked at it very carefully, turned it over, held it to the light, and then finally stamped it with a huge stamp and shoved it through the window.

"Hundred and five roubles," he said.

A small greenish piece of cardboard lay under the brass opening. I wanted to grab it—but lifted it very gently, without any hurry. Then the window fell with a little thud.

There at the station I sat down for a little while, for I was tremendously excited. I thought about how I could find this place early next morning, in that pitch dark city. There was not a lamp burning after two o'clock. Furthermore, such a dense fog used to come from the sea, rivers and numerous canals, that you could hardly see your outstretched hand.

This I knew well. And according to this I made my preparations. What good were street signs if you could not see them?

On the return I noted carefully how many steps there were from turn to turn and, to be sure, I put it down on my sketch. In this way I could grope my way in the dark; there was no possibility of missing my objective.

Well—then this was to be my last night in Petrograd, and Russia. I lay on my bed, fully dressed, smoking and gazing at the ceiling. It was gray, dirty and cracked. I pictured how my return would be—provided I really succeeded on this last lap. It would be great! I was not going to notify my father, no telegram, nothing, just walk in. Some surprise!

At twelve the lights went out, and I lit a candle which I had for this emergency. It was cold. I put on my big fur cap and buttoned the sheepskin, but even so it was cold. I continued to stare at the ceiling, looking into nothing. I was in no mood to sleep. At my right stood the guttering candle, and, as it flickered, all the shadows leaped and bobbed on the wall. For a while I watched the candle burn. The wick curved into the shape of a crosier. How queer! I poked it straight with a burnt match. A charred piece of the match broke off and clung to the wick. Suddenly the flame leaped up, and a veritable little stream of molten stearine cascaded down. A big fat bug marched across the grayish pillow, a new plaything! First it puffed up in the flame, then it shriveled into a tiny charred dot and floated in the liquid stearine. Now some more of that auto-da-fé.

There were just enough of them. For a while I waited, but none came, and I was certainly not going to hunt for them now. How gray that ceiling was! It probably hadn't been whitewashed for years. Comes from much smoking. Why—I shouldn't smoke so much with all that cough ... Then I lit another cigarette. I must have, been dozing off, for when I cast a glance at the candle it was burned off and the wick was just about to tumble over. I lit another candle. For whom, in the devil, should I save it?

It was four o'clock—plenty of time yet. I'll stay until five—and I won't have to hurry even then.

Again I caught myself napping. It was nearly a quarter to five. Well—I'll start and walk slowly. The sooner I see no more of this miserable place, the better.

There was a deathlike quietness all around. I opened the door, lifting it carefully, so that it should not creak. All was silent as I listened. There was no special reason to be so careful, but you get accustomed to it and it becomes a habit. I tiptoed through a long hall to the bannister. Sounds of snoring came from behind a door to my right. The vestibule—if I may call it so—looked deserted. Leaning heavily on the bannister I went down. Right at the exit, stretched on a bench and covered with some shaggy fur, slept a half-grown boy. A long candle burned at his head, set on the floor, so as not to disturb him. Some night porter, I thought. The clumsy key was in the lock. As I turned it carefully it creaked a little. The boy turned, rolled over to his other side and slept on.

So—now I was outside and I closed the door. It was so dark that I had never known before that there could be such an absolute lack of any light. A thick fog blanketed the streets and, as I kept on feeling my way along the walls, I counted the steps carefully. Now—there should be a right turn here. Where was the corner? There it was —ten steps farther. I lit a match and consulted my sketch.

Well—that'll be a long count on the Znamenskaya now. Halfway I nearly lost my count. There was a light on the corner. Under a huge cauldron fire was burning, and men with shovels were filling it with big chunks of icy snow. They don't haul the snow away here; they melt it on the spot, if it becomes too cumbersome. While watching them —as I said—I nearly forgot about my count. Then I went on. It really did not matter much in this instance. I would just go right on until I ran into a wall; then that would be the north side of the Kyrochnaya and there I would turn to the left. Soon I ran into a Red patrol. They came along the center of the street, with a little oil lamp. I sat down on a stoop and let them pass; then I went on.

Half an hour before train time I sat in one of the train compartments. And now, for the last paltry thousand miles to the Swedish border, to the border city, Torneo. After two hours we stopped in Beylo-Ostroff on the Russian Finnish border. We all got out of the train. The passports were to be examined by a mixed Russian-Finnish commission.

There were plenty of distinguished looking foreigners on that train. Americans, English, French and Belgians were leaving Russia—this was no safe place anymore.

There were also many haughty Russian emigres who did not seem to agree with the Dictature of the Proletarians. On such occasions, I always make it a point to stand as far back in the line as possible. Those who come first are always examined very rigorously. By the time they reach the queue's end, the examiners become more human.

An hour passed and they were scarcely through with the half. A conductor came and told the commission to speed up a little. People were grumbling. The French talked rapidly; the British said that it was a shame, and the Americans said nothing, for there were ladies about, but probably thought much.

After half an hour the conductor came again, and then the stamping went a little faster, but there were still about twenty of us at the end of the line.

Once more he came—this time furious. He said he had never seen such a sleepy commission in all his life. All right, all right—what's the big hurry! But then a furious bang-stamping began, without much further ado. They just glanced at my passport, turned it fast; bang! Went the stamp, and I just had time enough to grab the rail of the moving train.

That was a mighty step forward, I reflected, as I sat again in the compartment. The coach where I had sat before was pretty well filled, and where there are many people, there is always the danger of being involved in some kind of a conversation sooner or later. So I went to the last coach—this was not half so full—especially the rear compartment.

For some reason or other, people do not like to travel in the last coach; and it's always the best place if you want to avoid company. It is said that a Balkan minister once suggested at a railroad conference that in the future the last coaches should be abolished altogether. Of course this may have been a joke, you never know with these

Balkan folks when they are serious. However, they furnished good plots for comic operas, until the movies overdid it.

I was well satisfied with my new location. True, it shook and rattled vigorously, but that did not matter. There was a clean bench to sit on—nothing like the floors and shelves of the Russian box-cars—and though it was not warm enough to take off the fur coat, it was quite agreeable while you kept it on.

There was a broad fellow sitting just opposite me, with a large red tassel on his cap. He wore soft, furry, high reindeer boots, and he slept all the time. Then there was a couple, with flaxen hair, dressed much in the same way, with very pale blue eyes—rather fishy. Sometimes they talked to each other, but most of the time they ate and did not speak so much as a word. I liked those Finns, clean cut, solid—and not inquisitive.

Outside, there was nothing but snow and telegraph poles and more snow. Now and then some little farmhouse bobbed up and, after a while, we clattered among forests that seemed to be endless. On the first day the conductor came and asked for the tickets. That was the greatest event. I started to feel very cocksure. Why—this whole thing seemed to be much less complicated than I ever dared to think!

The train was racing like a regular flyer—so different from the Russian trains. And there was order in this country, I could see that. The stations were clean and well-kept and, with the exception of bread, food could be had anywhere.

In the night I was violently shaken. Two gendarmes, with brassards on their arms, stood before me.

"Your passport!" said the taller one.

I handed it over and pretended not to be interested in the whole thing. They looked at it from all sides, very carefully, and then they discussed something in Russian, which I could not hear, and finally in Finnish, which I did not understand. After a while they returned it to me and left. After that, I could not sleep a wink.

What on earth could they have talked about so long? True, they wore Russian uniforms, but they spoke Finnish. And there were two dozen of different parties in Russia and Finland right then.

General Youdenitch was in Finland—not very friendly to the Soviet across the border. And what kind of brassards did they wear?

Very late, somehow, the dawn crept on, gray and gloomy. It began to snow and from then kept on. The train did not speed as on the previous day. We were nearing the Arctic Circle, and it became terribly cold.

Locomotives do not burn coal here, but are heated with logs, and the boilers cool off considerably in this temperature. But on it crept in the blizzard. Now it was gray outside—not white.

At a small station the sleepy red-tasseled man got off, and another couple entered the compartment. I could not tell the difference between them and the first couple.

For a while they sat in silence, then they started to talk with the first couple in Finnish.

Sometimes the train stopped on the open track—as if it had lost steam and stopped to gather more—then it proceeded slowly, jerkily. What on earth could those two gendarmes have talked of last night?

I took out my railroad map. We had just passed Uleaborg. If the train kept up its pace, and didn't slow down or stop too often, we might reach Torneo on the border by evening. Now it grew so cold that you had to hook your sheepskin tightly. For a while I looked out of the window. Again the train was making better speed.

One of the women offered me some kind of a salty tasting cake. She still had plenty, and they were getting out soon.

It grew dark; a fine icy snow beat against the window panes like sifted sand. We could not be very far now.

Just as I was beginning to feel a little more comfortable again, the gendarmes came.

"Your passport!" said again the tall one. I gave it, and I felt very shaky about it. Once more they looked at it from all sides, but this time they talked Finnish only. I became very uneasy.

"Where did you get your passport?" asked the other gendarme.

"In Petrograd," I replied. "You can see it for yourself."

Again there was a discussion in a language that seemed to be composed entirely of vowels.

"Where are you going to?" asked the tall man.

"Home," I said, very uncomfortable and also very much disgusted.

"Have you other papers of legitimation to show?" he inquired.

"That's all I have."

"That's not enough," he came back. He took a clumsy pocketbook from between the two top buttons of his coat, folded my passport and put it in there.

With sudden desperation I felt that I was losing the game—right at the finish.

"Why don't you give me my passport?" I demanded.

"It is authentic, and it has been verified by your authorities at Byelo-Ostroff."

He unfolded it once more and he and his companion examined it again. All I understood was the word Byelo-Ostroff. However, he folded the paper and slipped it, together with his pocketbook, between his buttons.

"It may be right," he said, "and it may not. We'll have it examined at Torneo. If it's all right, we will let you pass."

Then they left. There I was, right on the border and no passport! For a time I was dumbfounded. But I was not going to give up after coming all that way! I had left well over nineteen hundred miles behind me—there couldn't be much more than twenty or thirty now.

Why, in fact, we could not be much farther from Torneo now, than an hour's run. But I could not sit any longer glued to the bench there. And those four were getting on my nerves with their continuous chatter. I got up and went out.

For a while I stood in the corridor. Outside it was snowing, a regular blizzard. We must be very near now, I thought. Suddenly I grew very firm and very desperate.

After all, they had my passport—but not me. And I'd much rather break my neck than fail now.

There was the door, right at the end of the corridor. If it was not locked I was safe! I pushed the latch down, and an icy breeze struck me. Then I grabbed the rail outside and closed the door, while squatting on the top stair. Why, this train was making better speed than I had thought. The wind came in violent gusts—a regular arctic storm. Through my heavy mitts I could feel how cold the iron rail was. It was not snowing much; it was more the wind that whirled up the snow from the fields.

Between two gusts of wind—as between two opened curtains—I saw some faint lights in the direction in which we were going. It must be Torneo—only a few miles away. But this was no time for reflection; those gendarmes might come back any minute now. I let go the rail and jumped.

I rolled over in the deep snow and was dazed a little, but otherwise unhurt. The train was far away, with its red tail-lights gleaming faintly. Then it vanished altogether.

I shook the snow out of my clothes and got up. I had no compass, no map, but I did not need one. These tracks ran right to Sweden, in a straight east to west direction.

Over there, a few miles away, were a few dim lights. There was Torneo, on the Finnish side, and across lay Haparanda, in Sweden. Between lay the frozen river Tornea. So all I had to do was to take a northwestern course, make a wide bow above the city of Torneo, and then cross the border at any place, just where I happened to hit it. Of course there would be Russian border patrols watching.

I must look out for them. But this weather was just ideal for my purpose. A strong wind kept the snow shifting in dense clouds, and I had to throw all my weight in front to proceed.

For a while I followed the tracks, and then I branched off to the north. There was no living soul around. After an hour of weary plodding in the snow I thought I had reached the limit of my endurance. I puffed heavily, and I felt the sweat freeze on my forehead. I had to sit down, and I sunk into the snow to gather some breath.

Then, a little rested, I proceeded again. On, always on—it could not be far now. Once more I had to rest, just a bit.

Under the ragged fringe of a drifting snow-veil I saw a faint light to the north. There sat one of the Russian border patrols, around a small fire in its snow hut. Farther, a little bit to the south, there was another one. There must have been quite a few along this line. I was right between them. The river should be quite near...

Now I proceeded creeping and crawling, using every mound for cover. Again I stopped to breathe. My arm was full of frozen snow; it burned like live coal.

Then on again. Suddenly I stopped. Not far away lay a longish object—looking like an upturned boat. Then—I was right on the bank! I got up again. That crawling was much too slow. I wanted to fly, the tiredness was gone.

Something carried me—some mysterious force. I was running. I did not feel tired. I did not worry. Let them shoot!

What chance have they got to hit me? I slid on the ice and fell, then up again. Run! Run! ... Still faster!

... Already I saw some hazy dark objects, like bushes. God! It's land ... neutral land! Another upturned boat!

Now up a little, must be the bank. Deep snow, I sink over my knees.

Then somebody shouts; others shout too. I do not understand them. Here they come; two—three ... soldiers with rifles, in flat white fur caps.

Swedish soldiers! Sweden! ...

1 - A cheap tea room.

Chapter XIII

I was surrounded by half a dozen of them. They talked something, seemed to ask questions, but I did not understand a word. I leaned on one of them, for I thought I would drop with sheer exhaustion. I felt my heart pound furiously, and I made a sign that I wanted a drink.

One gave me a felt-covered canteen, and I took a good deep draught. It tingled with a burning sensation—tasted like brandy.

Between two bayonets I was taken to Haparanda. It took us less than an hour. We marched to a building that looked from the outside like a barrack. Here I sat on a bench and waited with a guard. All around were Swedish soldiers. After a while I was led into a room. There were some officers here. One got up and asked me in Russian who I was. I answered, in Russian, that I was an Austro-Hungarian officer, escaped from Russia.

Hereafter he spoke in German, but still he was frigid and cautious. After a while he called up somebody on the 'phone and told him to hurry over. Meanwhile I was told to sit down again.

Within ten minutes a German civilian came, carrying a heavy book under his arm. I was asked to write down my name, rank, and regiment—further, the name of the regimental commander and half a dozen other regular officers of my regiment. Then my data were compared with those in the book the civilian had brought.

It was a "K.u.K. Schematism," with precise data of all Austro-Hungarian troops. Whatever I said was correct; it could be checked right then and there.

Only now did the attitude of the Swedish officers change. After this there was plenty of handshaking, lots of good Swedish punch and afterwards a good dinner with them in their mess.

But I had to hurry to make the night train to Stockholm.

Later on the German civilian fetched me with a sleigh. He was very friendly now. Haparanda, as he explained while we were driving towards a Red Cross depot, was the spot where the transports of invalid soldiers, from and to Russia, passed through. Here they were taken and given over.

They had a large outfitting station here. My "march-route" was ready. He handed it to me. I was to go through Sweden and then take the steamer to Sassnitz on the isle of Rügen in Prussia. There I would have to report to the Germans, and they would direct me farther.

He opened the depot, switched on the light, and from those huge stocks I was given a complete civilian outfit, from shoes to cap—even stiff collars and a neck-tie.

Around eleven I rolled out of Haparanda, standing in the window of a sleeping car. For four days I rode south-ward, on that spotless Swedish train, among charming people, meeting some of those foreigners with whom I stood in line at Byelo-Ostroff.

At Trelleborg I was invited to visit our consul, who advanced me some money for immediate expenses, and who on the next day saw me off on the steamer to Sassnitz.

Four hours later I landed in Germany. A military surgeon examined me and shook his head. He told me to take care not to catch a cold. There was an Austrian captain here to look after Austro-Hungarians who came that way. He directed me to Berlin, from there to Vienna, to report immediately to the Ministry of War.

Together with freshly procured documents, I went to the Ministry of War. I had to walk, for there was no transportation; the Vienna workmen were waging a general strike for the conclusion of peace. For an hour I was directed from one section of the Ministry to the other, and a hundred questions regarding our prisoners and conditions in Russia were asked. When I thought I must be through, a captain told me that I was to be received by no one less than His Excellency, the Minister of War, himself. Great Guns!

For ten minutes I stood there, waiting and guessing. Rather unusual for the Minister of War to see a lieutenant, I thought. Of course, an escape was still regarded as a very unusual thing.

The high double door swung open, and His Excellency appeared with some folded documents under his arm. He stopped six paces away and, standing at the very stiffest attention, I rapped out:

"Your Excellency, Lieutenant F. H. begs to present himself and reports his return from Russian captivity."

His Excellency moved somewhat closer: "Sehr brav, sehr brav," he said, and then: "How long have you been a captive?"

"For two and a half years, Your Excellency."

"How is the spirit of our soldiers?" went on the Big Mogul.

I was not quite prepared for this question, so I reflected for a while.

"They long to come home, Your Excellency."

A fleeting smile lingered on the lips of the War Lord over four million men. What a drive that would be, with those million and a half still returning! Out of those, a square million were Bolshevists and Anarchists by now—ragged, hungry and too sick to resemble human beings, but that, of course, he could not know.

"Where is your regiment?" he asked.

"On the Italian front, your Excellency."

"Three days' leave," said the omnipotent, "and then report to your regimental base depot."

The audience was over. Three days leave—after going through all that hell at the front, after thirty months of captivity. Never!

"Your Excellency!" I took a terrible chance in delaying his Lordship. "It takes me two days to come and go; that leaves me one day only."

"Five days!" he said to the captain. The audience was now definitely over.

Five hectic days followed, with practically no sleep. The toughest part of it was to dodge the reporters. Then for two weeks I drilled rookies at the cadre. Shooting, bayonet fencing, hand grenade practice, extended order, digging, advancing, creeping, application of first aid bandages—good old war stuff, practiced behind a dozen fronts.

Again I stood at attention, this time before a committee of high officers of the regiment, for each officer that had not been shot to a cripple at the time of his capture had to give a detailed account of the circumstances that led to his capture. A lieutenant-colonel read aloud my report of the destruction of my company while covering the retreat of the regiment, and then he read some details of my escape. I was careful not to use the word "Bolshevik" anywhere, for it would have been worse than swearing.

While the matter was discussed I was sent to another room and, after a while, I stood once more before the assembly of gold collars. The lieutenant-colonel rose, and so did everybody else.

"Lieutenant," he said, "your case has been carefully considered and you are herewith unanimously exonerated. Congratulations."

Plenty of handshaking hereafter—exclusively with Big Dogs!

A week later I bought myself a second set of gold stars, for a first lieutenant had to have two. Now we wore steel helmets—heavy solid things. At least not every silly shrapnel would be as deadly as before.

On the city pavements you heard the constant tap-tap-tap, blind soldiers feeling their way with their sticks. Tap-tap-tap. There were dozens of them, scores of them here, alone. There were thousands of them, many thousands all over the monarchy, with that ghastly tap-tap.

Certainly, those small caliber Italian bullets could kill, but how they could splinter the rocks, right into the eyes! No steel helmets were made to guard against rock splinters.

And yet—men were still anxious to get their own share of splinters, for here they were starving—they and us officers too. The civilian population had long ago ceased to count.

Out at the front, at least one could eat once a day; but here everything was substitutes: "Kaffe-Ersatz," "Zucker-Ersatz," "Milch-Ersatz," and even these for tickets only.

There were demonstrations by "Ersatz" men—or not even those, but just sickly cripples, who were not even good for substitutes. Very pale rookies I used to drill then. We were told not to drive them too much.

"Take your shirt off," said the military surgeon, "and stand on this platform. Put both hands down."

There was a sharp crackling as he switched on the powerful X-ray lamp. For a while he slid an opaque glass in a frame up and down and pressed it against my chest.

"Now turn around," he said, and pressed the plate against my shoulders. He switched the lamp off and then turned on the light.

"Young man," he said, frowning with his bushy white brows. "No smoking, and no dancing, and no lovemaking—otherwise..." He turned to a military scribe: "Four weeks' sick-leave. Next case."

First it was four weeks, then eight, and then still more. I did smoke when nobody saw, but I did not dance, and the white-browed doctor could rest assured that I did not want to make love to anybody.

It would have been easy enough, for soldiers were always favored by women—and now especially. Everything was going to the devil; husbands and lovers were dead or at the front or in captivity, and time did not stop. Youth was passing fast; women were generous. Officers were much in demand—even in the fourth year of the war.

Somehow—I felt out of place. I could not fit once more into that changed world. Everything was so different. Why, people even talked differently now. And I felt especially uncomfortable with women. What was one to say to them, how to say it?

For, what did we talk about in captivity? Crude jokes, and swearing, swearing a lot at anything. Or, still more often, we did not talk at all. Was this the so-much-desired liberty?

We had forgotten to live, way back there, forgotten so completely that if we ever wanted to go on we would have to learn afresh. Was this the "barbed wire disease"? Probably.

Or was it something else? I felt empty. I felt split. My better half was not here. I felt divided. No. I was not here at all.

Yes—I lay here all right—I was on the list. Sure—I was not to smoke. I'll put out the cigarette. To go to the front next time I was caught smoking? Yes! Of course!

Much did I care.

I'd much prefer a good stiff fight once more—anywhere. What's the difference for whom or for what? This, here, is just like captivity, worse than captivity. There is no Sasha here ...

Sometimes I felt like getting up and going back all the long way I had come. What was she doing? If I just could see her once more, just once more, on the hilltop, or in the little cobbler's hut, or anywhere—just to ask her forgiveness because I ran away. She might have suffered, and also have been offended, for she had pride—very proud she was. She could turn down anybody. She might never—never forgive me ... Also, in Petrograd, on that last night when I gazed at that dirty ceiling. How if I turned back now? Passport—ticket? What about it? Sneak back to her; let her sway and stagger once more. Yes! ... Just bite, my savage black beauty, all you can! I can stand lots more of it...

Let's run away together! Austria is winning the war—not your dirty Bolshevists. We're going to have a much larger army than ever, and it will be swell to be an officer ... so much more with you...

Tough, lean Yankee boys stood on the Oise and the Somme, at Toul and Verdun. Marines, regulars, ten thousand of them—keen-eyed, hard-fisted, tough fighters, eager to burst forth, nothing like those tottering five-foot-two Frenchmen. Another million American soldiers waited across the ocean to be shipped over. The British were all in, fighting desperately with their backs to the wall. France was yelping for help.

There was no time to lose, for Germany. There were still many divisions on the eastern front, watching the Bolshevists straggle home, but the war here was over. On the second of March, 1918, General von Hoffman banged his fist on a conference table at Brest-Litovsk.

Opposite him sat Commissioner of War Trotsky and other Russian delegates. Sign on the dotted line—or we'll march on right to Wladivostok!

And Russia ceased to be a formal enemy.

By June the first prisoners were trickling home, and then later regular transports began to arrive—ten thousand, hundreds of thousands. Just hordes of ragged, sick beggars, tottering in rags, bare-footed or in bast sandals. Good for nothing in the world.

On the Austrian frontier, they were herded into vast "Reception Camps" to be deloused and de-Bolshevized before they were to go to the front again. But these were no soldiers any longer, and they never would be. It was a mutinous horde, sullen, hate-filled. Just one wish they had—to go home and lie down.

In summer the dirty gray flood from the east kept rolling back. Dark clouds gathered on the horizon, in Italy, on the Balkans, from Asia Minor. In the west, the remnants of the Kaiser's army were crumbling before the onslaught of fresh American troops. Back to the Hindenburg line, to the Wotan line, to the Siegfried line—or whatever they were called—were bayoneted, shot, and driven skinny, underfed school boys, thin-necked, hollow-cheeked creatures and gray-bearded men, worrying about their families, wondering whether they had eaten that day.

In the hinterland babies were dying, and old feeble folks. No life could be sustained on boiled beets and turnips any longer.

High up—well over six thousand feet—His Apostolic Majesty's soldiers were shivering in the rock caverns of the Tyrolean Alps, in thin worthless tunics made out of paper and nettle-cloth.

They were to be kept warm by huddling closer with those beggars back from Russia ...

Chapter XIV

It was dusk. The sun was sinking behind the mountains, and the snowy peaks glowed pink. Black fir trees and pines stood dark and silent. The firmament grew purple and then faded into a misty violet. Very faintly the stars lit up, one by one.

"A letter for you, sir," said an orderly. It was Andy's handwriting. There was no stamp on the envelope, just the round seal of a reception-camp. I tore it open hastily.

"... and for three days I have been here," wrote Andy. "A bunch of the boys are with me. We all wept a little when we crossed the border. I do not know how long we shall stay here; it is quite uncertain—but for another week at least. However, don't write me here; write to my regimental base, for I'll be going there from here.

"I got your card from Petrograd and also the one you sent from Sweden. We were all so glad that you succeeded in your escape.

"And now I'll tell you what happened after you left. Your flight was not noticed until the next morning, and even then not by our guards.

"The Colonel came, together with Cheremisoff. They were furious, and wanted to know who was the one that escaped. We were checked up and, from the list, they found out soon that it was you they were looking for.

"They immediately telegraphed all around, and even sent some horsemen towards Vyatka—just in the right direction. At that time, of course, you already had a good start of ten hours at least.

"Well—we were locked up for two weeks and pestered in the usual way. You know how. When things quieted down after a while, the Bolshevists came, and that was the last we saw of the Colonel and Cheremisoff. Things were more rotten under the Bolshevists than ever before, I assure you. Nobody dared to walk out of the billets after that.

"And now concerning your lady. I don't want to comment, because I know how you feel. Just let me tell you how lucky you were to break off right then and there, before it was too late.

"Her husband must have suspected something for, shortly after you left, he wanted to shoot her. As soon as the Bolshevists came, he disappeared. It was not very safe for a Kerensky Commissar to face Bolshevists. She did not follow him, however. Cornel heard from her blonde friend that most of the time Sasha lay in hysterical fits.

"Let me tell you, old boy, that you wounded her pride. Nobody probably ever left her so flat as you did; and that hurt her most. I have not seen her once; she never came our way again.

"After peace was signed, we of course thought that now we would be promptly transported home. However, all we got was promises—Tomorrow. You know what a Russian tomorrow means. For more than three months they always said: tomorrow. Well—one day the first transport really went off.

"There were regular transports after that but, outside of these, everybody could go home and travel just as he pleased. The idea was to get rid of the prisoners somehow.

"Small groups banded together. Others went alone—quite unmolested. Then, one day, our transport came to Nijni-Novgorod.

"We were there for a couple of days, before proceeding to Moscow, then Minsk, to be taken from there to home, over the old battle lines. While we waited there I met Kerny—you remember—that young artillery lieutenant.

"He looked very sad and downcast. Sasha ran away with him and after two weeks left him flat. One morning, when he looked around—she was gone. He was like a madman—raving all the time."

Now the moon was up. The sky was infinitely deep, black-blue above the snowy caps. All was quiet. Far away the black conical pine trees stood in the moonlight, all silver topped.

Myriads of stars glittered, cold and bright, those very same stars that shone on the wintry sky above the hilltop—way back there. And exactly the same moon, with its kindly rotund face, with a frozen smile, very unconcerned for milliards of years past and as many yet to come. Just as if nothing happened. Looking down smiling upon Earth, upon Humanity...

Nothing of importance happened, nothing that had not happened many times before. Men loved, and men fought each other, just as before. Little, unimportant things, that they were, with those vast starry worlds above them.

It was a generous, indifferent and impartial moon that spread its silvery radiance over the world. It glittered on bayonets and placid forest pools alike; it showed men the path of murder and it guided the doe from the depth of the forest to a cool drink. Yes, it even lit the faces of lovers, just to see how raptured their features were. Little worms in the dust—Masters of the Earth! ...

Far above the placid moon, far above those twinkling stars, above other burning and flaming worlds—too far and too staggering to grasp—may have been the Almighty Master of the Heavens. In this infinite wisdom He kept aloft in ethereal heights, as if watching ... waiting.

How long still would Man fare without Him ... ?

THE END